From isolation to integration:
the post-apartheid South African economy

Jean-Pierre Cling is currently director of DIAL (Développement et Insertion Internationale), a centre of economic research specialising in developing countries, based in Paris. He held posts in southern Africa (South Africa and Zimbabwe) on behalf of the French Ministry of Economy, Finance and Industry from 1994 to 1999.

BY THE SAME AUTHOR
- *L'analyse de la conjoncture,*
  Éditions la Découverte, Collection Repères, Paris, 1990.
- *Exporter au Japon; atouts et défis,*
  Report to the Prime Minister, La Documentation Française, Paris, 1991 (in conjunction with Jean-Christophe Donnellier and Joël Toujas-Bernatte).
- *L'économie sud-africaine au sortir de l'apartheid,*
  Éditions Karthala, Paris, 2000.

Jean-Pierre CLING

From isolation to integration:
the post-apartheid
South African economy

PROTEA BOOK HOUSE & IFAS
PRETORIA
2001

**From isolation to integration:
the post-Apartheid South African economy**
Jean-Pierre Cling

Originally published as *L'économie sud-africaine au sortir de l'apartheid*, Paris: Éditions Karthala, 2000.

First English edition, 2001, published by:
Protea Book House
PO Box 35110, Menlopark, 0102
protea@intekom.co.za

and

Institute français d'Afrique du Sud (IFAS)
PO Box 542 Newtown, 2113
www.ifas.org.za

Translated by Kato Lambrechts
Typography & design by HOND BK
Cover design by HOND BK
Reproduction by PrePress Images, Pretoria
Printed & bound by ABC Press, 21 Kinghall Avenue, Epping Industria II

ISBN 1-919825-34-7

© Jean-Pierre Cling
© All rights reserved.
No part of this book may be reproduced in any form, without prior permission in writing from the publisher.

ACKNOWLEDGEMENTS

The author wishes to thank all those who assisted in realising this book, be it through their criticism, or their bibliographical advice. Besides Pierre Berthelier, Michaela Bohn, Maud and Maurice Cling, Denis Cogneau, Florence Dobelle, Roger Hamon and François Roubaud in France, many South African economists have provided assistance of equal value. The expertise of Dr. Evert van Dijk in updating the original French edition of this book is also acknowledged. Furthermore, a special thank you goes to Susan. The author alone is responsible for any errors that might remain in the text.

Institut Français
d'Afrique du Sud

TABLE OF CONTENTS

Introduction – *page 11*

PART ONE
THE SOUTH AFRICAN TRANSITION

Chapter 1 What is good for Anglo American … – *page 16*
           2 Economic freeze – *page 34*
           3 Two South African nations – *page 55*
           4 An orthodox economic policy – *page 78*

PART TWO
SEARCHING FOR A NEW INTERNATIONAL ECONOMIC INTEGRATION

Chapter 5 Economic opening and globalisation – *page 102*
           6 South Africa and the "African Renaissance" – *page 122*
           7 A regional power – *page 141*
           8 South Africa's "anchoring" to the European Union – *page 161*

Conclusion – *page 180*
Bibliography – *page 189*
Statistical sources – *page 197*
Index – *page 198*

LIST OF TABLES AND GRAPHS

Tables PART ONE
Chapter 1
Table 1: Geographical distribution of Anglo's turnover – *page 28*
Table 2: The structure of Anglo American – *page 33*

Chapter 2
Table 3: Analysis of growth factors – *page 44*
Table 4: South Africa's share in global production and reserves of some minerals – *page 53*

Chapter 3
Table 5: Regional inequalities in South Africa – *page 64*
Table 6: Labour distribution by employment category according to gender and race – *page 70*

PART TWO
Chapter 5
Table 7: Sectoral structure of exports – *page 106*
Table 8: Geographical structure of external trade (%) – *page 107*

Chapter 6
Table 9: The weight of South Africa in sub-Saharan Africa (%) – *page 135*

Chapter 8
Table 10: Main products traded between the European Union and South Africa – *page 168*
Table 11: European market share held by ACP countries, southern Africa and South Africa – *page 173*

Graphs and map PART ONE
Chapter 1
Graph 1: Annual turnover of the CSO – *page 21*
Graph 2: Weight of Anglo's stock market capitalisation on the Johannesburg Stock Exchange (%) – *page 26*

Chapter 2
Graph 3: GDP and GDP per capita at constant prices – *page 36*
Graph 4: Development of non-agricultural employment – *page 44*

Chapter 3
- Graph 5: Development of the per capita income gap since the beginning of the century – *page 60*

Chapter 4
- Graph 6: GEAR forecasts and performance – *page 89-90*
- Graph 7: Savings and investment rate – *page 94*

PART TWO
Chapter 5
- Graph 8: Direct Foreign Investment flows – *page 117*
- Graph 9: GDP per capita and ratio between outward and inward Foreign Direct Investment (FDI) stock – *page 120*

Chapter 6
- Graph 10: GDP growth in sub-Sahara Africa and raw material prices – *page 126*
- Graph 11: Development of trade between South Africa and Africa – *page 139*

Chapter 7
- Graph 12: Complementarity index between South Africa and other southern African countries – *page 153*

Map of main corridors: Spatial Development Initiatives in southern Africa – *page 159*

INTRODUCTION

I have cherished the ideal of a democratic and free society in which all persons live together in harmony and with equal opportunities. It is an ideal which I hope to live for and to achieve. But if need be, it is an ideal for which I am prepared to die.

— Nelson Mandela, Rivonia Trial[1]

Nelson Mandela's election to the presidency of the South African Republic in 1994 signalled the end of a regime fought by the majority of the population and held in contempt by the international community.

Since this date, developments in South Africa have contradicted the prophets of doom who anticipated civil war and economic disintegration following the take-over of power by the coalition bringing together the African National Congress, the COSATU affiliated trade unions, and the South African Communist Party. To the contrary, recent years have seen a general improvement in the political and economic situation, such that some observers have gone so far as to speak of the existence of a South African 'miracle'.

Whereas the rise in political violence at the beginning of the 1980s might have led to fears that the country would generally flare up, this never took place. The peaceful atmosphere in which the 1999 general elections took place thus represented a striking contrast to the serious tensions and numerous massacres which preceded the first democratic elections.

Turning its back on apartheid, which had established the golden rule of inequality before the law, the new constitution has restored the dignity of each South African and is listed among the most liberal in the world. The considerable reduction in the number of conflicts in the workplace bears witness to the improvement in social relations. In the economic sphere, the general quality of life of the population has to some extent ceased to deteriorate.

---

1   Mandela, 1994.

At the same time the end of apartheid has not suddenly resolved the serious economic and social problems experienced by the country. On the contrary, numerous indicators show that these problems are experiencing renewed intensity.

The continuation of rising unemployment and the increase in social inequalities are glaring, judged by the proliferation of squatter camps in the areas around large cities and the rise in crime, which makes South Africa one of the most violent countries in the world.

In fact, the growth model followed by the South African economy since the beginning of the century has experienced a systemic crisis for several decades. Its entire foundation has been called into question, be it mining income, the overexploitation of black labour in the framework of apartheid, or the interventionist policies of the state in the framework of an import substitution industrialisation strategy. South Africa's level of development, which was higher than that of Greece at the beginning of the 1960s, has not made any progress since this era, while a "Rostowian" development approach led to the belief that the economy had already reached the "take-off" stage at that time. An extrapolation made in the context of this theory even estimated that the latter would reach fully-fledged development during the 1980s![2] This "take-off" did not happen: the per capita income of the population today is the same as thirty years ago and the economy is creating no more jobs than during the 1980s. In fact the South African economy shed nearly 500 000 formal jobs between 1994 and 2000.

What are the explanatory factors behind this crisis and why has economic development come to a halt all of a sudden? Beyond the general problems encountered by all developing countries, what are the problems specific to South Africa, a country deeply scarred by the mad utopia of apartheid, led by "social architects" often close to the Nazi ideology?[3] What chance of success does any policy aiming to reduce inequality have? What perspectives exist on how to resolve the crisis and put into place a new model of economic growth at the beginning of the new century? What shape will South Africa's reintegration into the world economy take, and how will this process influence the future of the country and its region? These are some of the main questions posed in this book.

---

2   Houghton, 1964.
3   John Vorster, South African Prime Minister from 1970 to 1979, was imprisoned for the greater part of the Second World War, in the company of several post-war leaders, because of his pro-Nazi sympathies.

INTRODUCTION

The initial assessment made here of the changes that have taken place since 1994 and the outline of the challenges faced show that the "new" South Africa is still at a crossroad.

The first five years following the elections had an imminently transitional character – the establishment of a so-called "Government of National Unity", joining together all the main political parties (until the departure of the National Party from the government in 1996), aimed at ensuring good conditions for the transfer of power and the development of a new constitution. Under the aegis of President Nelson Mandela, also presiding over the transition, the new government took pains to put into place and operate the new administrative structures that were established in the wake of the country's reunification and the removal of the homelands, where a quarter of the population had been grouped together and separate administrations operated.

A modernisation and opening up of the ossified economy inherited from apartheid days was also embarked upon. In the social sphere, transformation has taken place very slowly, even though the government has launched many programmes to improve the living conditions of the disadvantaged population and a body of new laws has been adopted to try to redress workplace inequalities.

To some extent this transition period, during which the dominant theme was national reconciliation and which was marked by attempts to heal the trauma of long years of civil war, came to an end in 1999 with the election of President Thabo Mbeki, confirming the strengthening and consolidation of democracy in South Africa.

Nevertheless, the main restructuring has barely got off to a start, considering not only the brevity of the period that has elapsed, but also the constraints weighing on the new government. In this sense, the transition is continuing and remains as necessary as before. The new president is confronted with a considerable challenge which consists of transforming a dual society, inherited from the apartheid era, into a veritable "rainbow nation", that is to say a multiracial society where economic power and national income would be shared more equitably among the different population categories. This is a crucial stake, for only the satisfaction of the population's immense needs in terms of employment, income, and basic services can eventually guarantee political and social stability in this country. A return to economic growth, and therefore the continuation of economic restructuring is imperative for ensuring the success of the development strategy followed by the government.

The book relies on the substantial bibliography on this country, both local and foreign. The wealth of available economic and statistical information, which distinguishes South Africa from most developing countries, and in particular African countries, has greatly facilitated the writing of this study. The population census carried out in 1996 (the first in the history of the country that covered the entire population more intensively), which has been used here abundantly, also gives a remarkable instant picture of the characteristics and living conditions of the South African population as apartheid was drawing to an end. Obviously, this wealth of information does not rule out the existence of some grey areas around key areas where, for this reason, analysis cannot go beyond speculation. This is the case particularly on the subject of clandestine immigration, a politically very sensitive matter, where the numbers submitted, although very whimsical, are giving rise to serious worries without the possibility of verification.

The first part focuses on what is at stake economically and socially in post-apartheid South Africa and on the first years of the democratic transition in this area. The outline of Anglo American, South Africa's leading company and the world's leading mining group, given in Chapter 1, tries to answer the key question: "Who has economic power?"[4] Chapter 2 broadens the perspective and is concerned with the development of the South African economy over the past decades, as well as the problems it is presently experiencing. Chapter 3 shows the considerable extent of social inequality still prevailing in the country and evaluates the actions taken to reduce these. Chapter 4 gives a review of the macroeconomic policy followed by the government.

Whereas general opposition to the apartheid regime resulted in the international isolation of the country, the democratic transition is enabling the reintegration of South Africa into the global economy. This is studied in the second part. Chapter 5 brings to the fore the difficulties of the process of opening the economy, a strategy which has been pursued since 1996. Chapter 6 analyses the role played by South Africa in the "African Renaissance". Chapter 7 describes the particular design of the relations maintained by South Africa with its neighbours in southern Africa. Finally, Chapter 8 shows that South Africa, in signing a bilateral free trade agreement with the European Union in 1999, has chosen to "anchor" itself to the EU.

---

4 Based on the question asked by Fine and Rustomjee, 1996.

PART ONE

THE SOUTH AFRICAN TRANSITION

CHAPTER 1

What is good for Anglo American ...

My philosophy has always been that people buy diamonds out of vanity and gold out of stupidity, because man has proved incapable of coming up with a monetary system based on anything else.
— Harry Oppenheimer, as Chairman of Anglo American[1]

Harry Oppenheimer, son of the founder of Anglo American (abbreviated to "Anglo"), was (he passed away in 2000) one of the richest people in the world. In South Africa Oppenheimer is the equivalent of Rothschild or Rockefeller in the popular imagination. He liked to scoff at the vanity and human futility on which his fortune was based. Jewellers and investors in fact are the best clients of gold and diamonds, of which Anglo is the world's leading producer.

Although these two minerals have been the basis of Anglo's prosperity, the Group has invested its profits in many other mining, industrial, commercial and financial activities over the past few decades. It is an extremely diversified conglomerate, which dominated the South African economy for decades. The world's leading mining group, Anglo American is also the only true South African multinational, with almost half its turnover being produced internationally, be it through the export of products from South Africa or through the activities of its foreign subsidiaries.

The Group recently went through serious changes that will radically modify its structure and its way of functioning, transforming an impenetrable and ageing conglomerate into a modern and globally competitive business. The transformation of the Central Selling Organisation in the global marketing of diamonds is one example thereof.

For a start, the end of apartheid has allowed the Group to accelerate its internationalisation process, in that this provided it, for the first time,

---
1 Cited in Pallister *et al.*, 1987.

with the means of realising its international ambitions. Anglo has thus embarked on a frenzy of mining projects and acquisitions throughout the world over the past few years. This international expansion strategy was all the more necessary since Anglo's domination in its home country was increasingly being called into question. This was due, in the first place, to the saturation of its local expansion potential, but also, in a more cyclical way, to the fall in prices of raw materials towards the end of the 1980s, which accelerated the decline of the Group's stock market capitalisation.

At the same time as developing its activities abroad, Anglo also strategically centralised its activities around those sectors in which it was a leader – or at least counted among the premier ranks – globally. Even though Anglo's organisation chart has been simplified, particularly to make it more transparent in the eyes of the financial markets, its conglomerate structure was not to be questioned. In fact, the diversification of its activities was a way of smoothing the impact of fluctuations in prices of raw materials on its turnover and profits.

Considering the preponderance of Anglo in the domestic economy, its transformation would contribute in a determining way to shape the new South Africa. For this reason an analysis of this company's functioning and strategic objectives is an indispensable prerequisite for any study of the South African economy.

World's leading mining group

Anglo American was founded by Ernest Oppenheimer in 1917. Thanks to the First World War, this businessman succeeded in supplanting German investors in financing – in association with American investors – the development of East Rand gold mines, east of Johannesburg, where deep deposits had just been discovered.[2]

In a few decades, what was originally a small mining business came to dominate the production of most of the precious minerals in the world, then became a major influence on the whole South African economy.

With the gradual acquisition – "amalgamation" – of numerous gold mines from the 1920s onwards, Anglo first became the leading South African gold producer, and at the same time, the leading world producer

---

   2   The name "Afro American" was originally considered for this business, bearing in mind the place where its activity was taking place and the origins of its investors. "Anglo American", however, was very quickly judged to be more presentable.

of this metal. Its annual production therefore was more than double that of its immediate competitor, the Canadian Newmont, with the gap between the known reserves owned by the two groups being greater.

While absorbing many of its domestic competitors, the Group also developed the new gold mines that were discovered in South Africa throughout the twentieth century: Western Reefs in the 1930s (which became Vaal Reefs); the Free State mines from the 1950s onwards; and finally, the Western Deep Levels mine, the deepest in the world, in the 1960s. It is the profit drawn from these mines that have financed its diversification. The powerful control that Anglo came to wield over the South African gold production was reinforced by its minority shareholding in other gold mines and by its preponderance within the Chamber of Mines, this sector's regulatory body.

Since the 1920s, Anglo has looked to expand its mining activities beyond gold mines, so as to partake in the exceptional wealth of the South African subsoil. The Group therefore bought De Beers Consolidated Mines, the world's leading diamond producer, in 1929. It then diversified into a third mining sector, coal, from the 1940s onwards, with this activity, however, expanding from the 1970s only onwards. It next became the leading global producer of platinum and uranium, contributing to three-quarters of South African production of each of these precious metals. The development of South African uranium production – a "fatal" product of gold mines – in the 1950s was in response to the needs of American and British nuclear military programmes.

Diamond mines, controlled by its "sister company" De Beers, occupy a privileged position in Anglo. Their importance holds no comparison with their relatively marginal share in global turnover. Firstly, apart from during crisis periods, they are the Group's leading source of profit. Moreover, to use the company's terms:

> *De Beers is the only South African company to have cultivated global brand awareness for its product, its corporate image and its country. Everywhere in the world diamonds are synonymous with De Beers and in turn with South Africa.*[3]

De Beers Consolidated Mines was founded by Cecil John Rhodes in 1888 through the merging of the two largest mines at the time, those of De Beers and Kimberley. From this date onwards, De Beers gradually took

---

3 Anglo American, 1997.

over all the independent mines in the years that followed. By the end of the previous century, Cecil John Rhodes thus succeeded in building up a monopoly that controlled almost all diamond production globally. South Africa's only real competitor was Brazil, where, since the beginning of the eighteenth century, the Minhas Gerais mines had been supplanting Indian mines, which had existed for two thousand years. But the production and reserves of Brazil and India were far more limited than those of South Africa. Whoever controlled the South African production therefore controlled the bulk of world production.

In this context, the narrow world market for diamonds – a luxury product confined mainly to an elite – necessitated the establishment of this monopoly, as the wealth of the South African subsoil and the regular discovery of new veins seemed to be leading to an inevitable tendency towards overproduction. Besides, the rush, which had started in Kimberley in 1869 after the discovery of the first diamonds, had led to a steep fall in prices, which was running the risk of continuing. The "amalgamation" of the diamond mines, and the control of prices and production it allowed therefore seemed to present the best solution for ensuring the gradual expansion of this sector to the largest possible profit of De Beers shareholders.

It may seem astonishing that this monopoly could have been maintained almost intact for over a century now. Through its London subsidiary, the Central Selling Organisation (CSO)[4] created in 1934, De Beers continues to control between 70 and 80 per cent of the global diamond market, which represents a turnover of around US$5 billion a year. Indirectly, the CSO in fact controls a market of US$50 billion worth of diamond jewellery, to which the much smaller industrial market has to be added. There is probably no other example of a monopoly of this size on the global scale. The long-term evolution of the diamond price is a resounding confirmation of the efficiency of this monopoly. Whereas all raw material prices – in particular that of gold – experience erratic and wide ranging fluctuations, this has not been the case for diamonds, whose price never falls, at least not that of quality ones. The average price of diamonds had therefore risen by half in ten years, before the onset of the Asian crisis in 1997.

This unique situation can firstly be explained by the preponderance of De Beers in global diamond production, whose total it represents 50 per cent through its mines in South Africa and especially in neighbouring

---

4   The Diamond Trading Company (DTC) replaced the CSO on 13/7/2000.

countries. The diamond mines in Botswana, discovered in the 1960s shortly after the country had attained independence, play a major role in the group's mining power. De Beers manages the local diamond mines as a joint venture in parity with the government-owned Debswana Diamond Company. The expansion of the Orapa mine and its processing factory has increased production in Botswana by a third since 2000, which already represent twice South Africa's production in terms of volume. This expansion has reinforced Botswana's ranking as the world's leading diamond producer.

The CSO, moreover, is benefiting from its hundred years and more of experience in manipulating the market and controlling its different players. Its market regulation relies on a system of production quotas allocated to each member. As soon as world demand falls, like when Japan, which is the second largest market in the world for jewellery diamonds, experiences an economic crisis that causes it to reduce consumption, the quotas of producers are lowered to avoid excess production. The CSO shares the cost of adjustment with producers – at the end of 1999, its stock reached a total of US$5 billion, or more than a year's turnover. Only considerable financial resources, amassed through no less considerable profits gathered for over a century, could allow such a policy to be sustained.

This very costly stockpiling resulted in a short-lived fall in profits for De Beers, less however, than a fall caused by the collapse of prices which would be sure to happen in a similar case in the absence of any market regulation. This allowed De Beers to maintain that:

> ... the CSO monopoly protects not only the shareholders of diamond companies, but also the miners they employ and the communities that are dependent on their operations.[9]

This reduction in demand is short-lived at any rate. During the 25 years that preceded the market crisis mentioned above, the turnover of the CSO multiplied tenfold (Graph 1), which corresponds to an average annual growth rate of nearly 10 per cent in value. This remarkable growth is an expression of the consumption boom of jewellery diamonds, the fruits borne from a formidably efficient marketing policy by De Beers, which has benefited the entire sector. This active policy aimed at widening the market permanently, has played a fundamental role in the success of this monopoly.

---

9 Pallister *et al.*, 1987.

Graph 1:
Annual turnover of the CSO (US$ million)

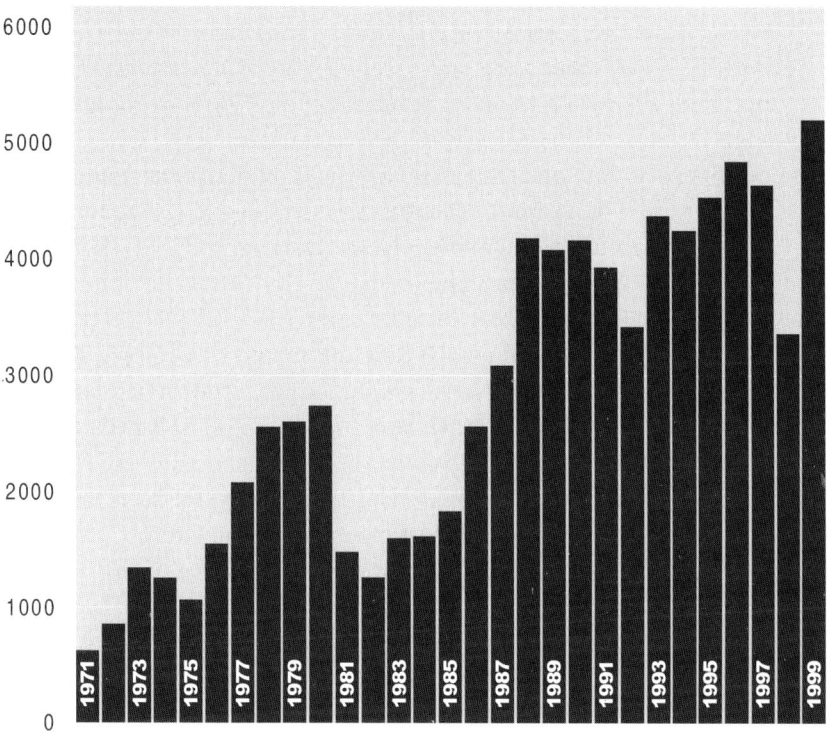

Source: De Beers

The way in which this company has succeeded in transforming diamonds into a mass consumer good in the United States and in Japan, while still retaining its prestige and character as a luxury product, is exemplary in this respect. Considering its size and wealth at the end of the Second World War, the United States was a priority target market.[5] Today, it represents about 45 per cent of the world market for jewellery diamonds. Besides, this is somewhat paradoxical – indirectly this country is by far the largest client of De Beers, whose executives cannot establish there on account of the breaching anti-trust legislation! After the United States, De Beers became interested in Japan, the world's second largest economic power, where the potential to develop its sales seemed particularly

---

5 "Diamonds are forever", title of the famous James Bond film, is in fact a publicity slogan launched by De Beers in the United States in 1948 to promote its products.

promising. Whereas only 5 per cent of couples there bought a diamond engagement ring at the end of the 1960s, in the 1990s this was the case for 70 per cent of them. As the weekly magazine *The Economist* wrote:
> As a worldwide dealer in enchanting illusions, Disney has nothing to De Beers, for the preciousness of the diamond is not a fact but a triumph of modern marketing.[6]

The discovery of diamonds in Russia and in several African countries in past decades, as well as more recently in Australia and Canada, poses a threat to the durability of the monopoly exercised by the DTC. However, even if one part of global production evades De Beers, no country has been able to break away totally from its control.

The attempt made by Zaire in 1981 in this regard was quickly aborted. The industrial diamond market on which Zairian production relied, suddenly experienced a situation of overproduction, following an influx of this type of diamond and the subsequent reduction of demand addressed to that country. At the end of two years, Zaire had to sign on with the CSO again. Following this episode, Harry Oppenheimer declared:
> I think that over the period ahead people who looked at the thing carefully may come to the conclusion that the Zaire experience should be looked upon as a warning rather than as an example.[7]

In 1996, the Australian-based Argyle mine, leading global producer in terms of volume, also wished to break away from the CSO monopoly. Subsequently then, the price of the lower quality diamonds produced by that mine (5 per cent of total world production in value) suddenly collapsed. There again, Nicky Oppenheimer, President of De Beers, declared rather cryptically:
> My belief ... is that if the Australians had signed a contract with us, the fall in prices that one has seen at the lower end would not have taken place.[8]

Without playing a truly coercive role and without assuming direct responsibility for the Zairian and Australian setbacks, De Beers has proven

---

6   *The Economist*, 20/12/1997.
7   Pallister *et al.*, 1987.
8   *The Economist, ibidem.*

by default the utility of its monopolistic power in these kinds of events. This is why the Australian group will probably be driven at one or another time to sign a new agreement with the DTC to commercialise at least part of its production, as Russia, has done.

An extremely diversified conglomerate

In the image of the Japanese *keiretsu* and the Korean *chaebols*, Anglo American belongs to a type of conglomerate that has become increasingly rare in the modern world. Its diversification principally got under way in the 1960s, thanks to the considerable profits made from the mines exploited by the Group during its first half century of existence. The withdrawal of numerous multinationals from South Africa, following the Sharpeville massacre in 1960, created a favourable climate for the compulsive series of acquisitions.[9] Anglo's expansion beyond its original business also benefited from active government support. Considering its financial power and the economic weight it had already acquired at the time, no company other than Anglo was in a better position to participate in the government's strategy to develop heavy and downstream industries, recommended by those in political power.

On the whole, beyond the mining sector, Anglo started controlling a large part of the South African economy. From their experience of a visit to Johannesburg, the authors of a book dedicated to the subject sketched the extent of the "Oppenheimer Empire" at the end of the 1980s in the following way:

> *Everything we pick out on the way is part of the Anglo empire, including those dumps, which Anglo is re-treating to extract the last vestiges of gold and uranium. At the other extreme is our Ford car, bought at one of the McCarthy showrooms and insured with Eagle. People are going about their daily business: shopping in the upmarket Edgars department store, buying South African Breweries beer, Fanta soft drinks and Boschendal wines from Solly Kramer's liquor store and food*

---

[9] In Sharpeville, a small provincial township situated about 50 kilometres to the south of Johannesburg, the police opened fire on a protest march against the pass law system, killing 69 and wounding 170 people. This event incited considerable emotion as far as both the domestic and the international scene was concerned. It was severe repression of the internal black opposition and led to the withdrawal of the country from the Commonwealth in 1961.

in one of the OK supermarkets. You could choose Farm Fare eggs and chickens, Olé sunflower oil, Yum Yum peanut butter, Carmel pickles and Denny mushrooms and asparagus. Cake could be picked up from the Blue Ribbon bakery chain, Jenny Wren fabrics and Scott's clothing store, Hush Puppies at the nearest ABC shoe shop, and any number of choices in paints, wallpapers and furniture.[10]

In brief, it is difficult for a South African to escape this conglomerate, which employs 400 000 people in this country. The old saying according to which "what is good for General Motors is good for the United States" is probably even more appropriate for Anglo and South Africa.

As a matter of fact, the list of Anglo's interests in South Africa is extremely long. The sprawling structure of the Group comprises an entanglement of cross-interests in two main categories of companies. In the terminology of the Group, "subsidiaries" refers to single companies in which it retains a majority interest. Traditionally the latter were few in number. In fact, until the recent restructuring most of the companies listed in its fold were minority subsidiaries called "associated" companies in Anglo's terminology. This minority interest nevertheless allowed it effective control of the company on the condition that the remainder of the shareholding was well dispersed. There would also be no hostile buy-out of any subsidiary, by virtue of the Group's financial power and the gentlemen's agreement between large South African Groups. Moreover, the companies of the Group are often "clients" as well, meaning that they receive administrative or technical assistance from their parent company, which is an additional way through which to reinforce its control over the latter. Anglo's diversification into the industrial sector has allowed it to reach a very high degree of vertical integration in its different economic sectors, from the production of raw materials by mines or agricultural plantations, to that of intermediary products used for their exploitation and trans-formation, through to mine construction, with the Group's bank financing these different activities.

Quite naturally, historically Anglo had first diversified into those activities necessary for the functioning of its mines or the transformation of mining products. African Explosives and Chemical Industries (AECI), originally held by De Beers and the British ICI, entered the group in 1929

---

10 Pallister *et al.*

when Anglo bought De Beers. Globally, it is the leading producer of explosives, over which it retained a near monopoly in South Africa. It is also one of the largest South African chemical groups, with a significant production of fertilisers, synthetic fibres, plastics, paint, and ferrosilicone for the Group's steelworks. Anglo furthermore has three main subsidiaries in the iron and steel sector. Highveld Steel and Vanadium Corporation was founded in the 1960s with technical support from British and American partners. Today it is one of the world's leading steel producers. This company is also involved in the production of vanadium, ferro-alloys, and aluminium canisters. It holds one third of the giant Columbus stainless steel plant, inaugurated in 1996 and which is the largest of its kind in the world. As for Scaw Metals, it specialises in the production of iron and steel products for the mining, automobile, energy and construction sectors. Its subsidiary, Haggie, is one of the world leaders in the production of metal cables. Finally, Boart Longyear, whose subsidiaries are present in many countries, is the world leader in drilling equipment. It is a heavy consumer of diamonds and tungsten, used in the manufacturing of this equipment, obviously supplied by the parent company.

LTA, created in 1965, is the largest South African building company. It is involved in most large public building projects in South Africa and even in the region. LTA is also involved in many of the group's mining projects, such as the Sadiola gold mine in Mali, or the Saldana Steel iron and steel project on the country's West Coast.

Anglo also dominates the paper industry through the Mondi paper group. The group owns large forest plantations and is the leading supplier of forest products for gold and platinum mines in South Africa.

Besides the above enterprises close to its core activities, Anglo has also diversified into the agricultural and food-processing sectors. In addition to food-processing factories (flour), textiles, and aluminium production, Tongaat-Hulett also owns sugar plantations in South Africa and in several countries of the region. Its subsidiary, Corobrick, is the leading South African brick manufacturer. The conglomerate also owns a minority interest in Bevcon, itself a shareholder of South African Breweries, the country's leading industrial group and the third largest brewery in the world. The diversification into automobile manufacturing (Samcor) was spurred on by the departure of Ford from South Africa during apartheid. Furthermore, the Anglo subsidiary McCarthy is the leading South African automobile distributor. Finally, Anglo also plays a dominant role in the financial sector. The group bought its South African subsidiary from

Graph 2:
Weight of Anglo's stock market capitalisation on the Johannesburg Stock Exchange (%)

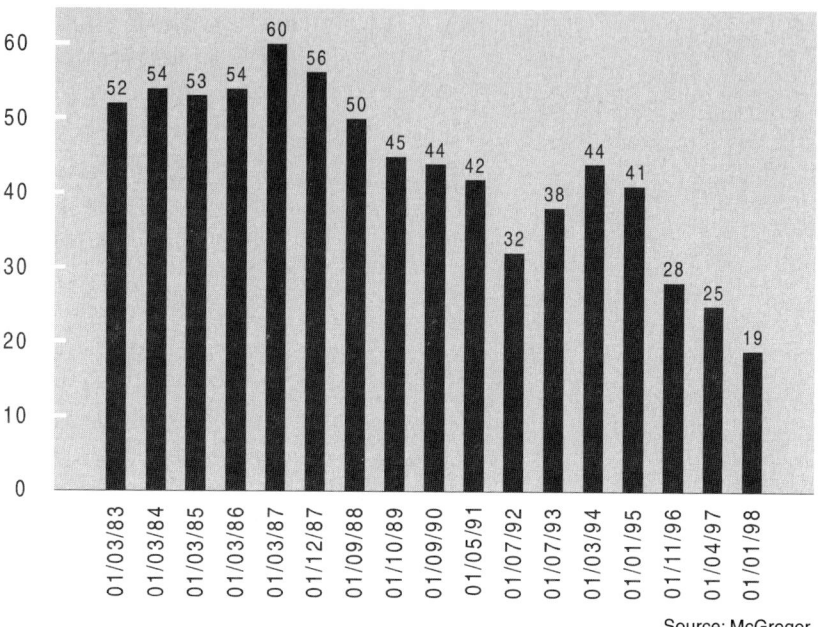

Source: McGregor

Barclays during the 1980s, when the British bank withdrew from the country during the implementation of sanctions against South Africa. This bank, renamed First National Bank, also had a majority holding in the life insurer Southern Life. In 1998, the merger between First National Bank and Rand Merchant Bank (and its subsidiary Momentum Life) gave birth to First Rand. This versatile financial institution is the first of its kind in South Africa. In the financial sector, the group also owns a minority interest in short-term insurer SA Eagle.

At the turn of the twentieth century, Anglo's expansion potential in its home country seemed largely saturated, considering the way in which it had started dominating the entire South African economy, and also because of the gradual depletion of local gold-bearing reefs, the historical basis for the group's wealth. A fall in its stock market capitalisation – which represented only a little less than 20 per cent of the capitalisation of the Johannesburg Stock Exchange the day before its departure to London, having exceeded half of it until the end of the 1980s – bore witness to this (Graph 2).

Even though it has been accelerated by a fall in the price of raw materials since 1997, this fall certainly expressed the realisation by economic operators of the price freeze, and probably also some anxiety about the future of the country where more than two thirds of the group's assets were still concentrated. Meanwhile, however, Anglo American has expanded its overseas interest by investing in mining interests in *inter alia* Australia, Great Britain and Canada.

Considering some negative market perception towards it and with the purpose of improving its profitability, Anglo was led to launch a process of unbundling, which ended with it selling all activities that did not belong to its core business. These operations, which were also inspired by the wish to deal with the hostility of the new government towards large conglomerates, coincided with a strategic reorientation to retain only those sectors of excellence where the group could reach a critical mass.

Three strategic sectors were subsequently identified. Most important, in the first place, are the mines, where the group is still earning the bulk of its turnover. Heavy industry, which Anglo has managed to integrate vertically, constitutes a second strategic sector. Finally, forest products are also considered part of its core business, taking account of the strong potential of this sector in which Anglo holds significant interests today.

Several interests in industrial and services groups, as well as in the agricultural sector (farms and tropical fruit plantations) have already been sold. The sale of some interests in AECI and Bevcon has also been announced, as well as that of some financial interests (First Rand), of those in the health sector, and of American subsidiaries Engelhard and Terra Industries. Besides, the European Commission has forced Anglo to resell its minority interests in the British conglomerate Lonhro, particularly present in Africa in the mining (platinum and coal) and agricultural sectors. Based on its preponderance in the domestic economy, Anglo's restructuring and the sale of its interests will have a massive impact on the restructuring of the South African economy.

Considering the amounts at stake, it is likely that only foreign multinationals will be able to purchase most of the companies put up for sale, which will have the simultaneous effect of increasing foreign investment and enhancing the opening up of the South African economy internationally. This relative disengagement has gone hand in hand with a strengthening of Anglo's activities in the mining sector in South Africa (the purchasing of a minority interest in Avmin, which owns the largest local diamond mine, of nickel mines, and so on) and especially with an expansion of investment abroad, described below.

Table 1:
Geographical distribution of Anglo's turnover (%)
(1995–1998; fiscal year terminates in March of the following year)

	By origin[1]				By destination[2]			
	1995	1996	1997	1998[3]	1995	1996	1997	1998[3]
South Africa	75	71	71	71	63	59	58	58
Abroad:								
Africa	9	9	9	8	1	1	2	2
Europe	8	9	9	10	20	25	23	21
North America	5	9	9	9	11	9	11	13
South America	3	2	2	2	2	1	2	2
Asia	–	–	–	–	3	5	4	4

Source: Anglo American
Notes: 1. Production location
2. Product sale location
3. Tax year

A South African multinational

Anglo is the only real South African multinational. Out of a consolidated turnover of about US$20 billion, made in 1998, only 58 per cent comprised goods sold in South Africa (Table 1). The rest, that is 42 per cent of the turnover, was made internationally, be it through exporting South African mining, agricultural and industrial products or through the activities of the group's subsidiaries abroad.

For no other large South African company is the share of turnover made by subsidiaries as important as for Anglo. The distribution of the turnover by geographical origin shows that 71 per cent of the total corresponds to the sale of South African products. The remainder originates in equal parts from the rest of Africa, Europe, and North America, with South America's share being very marginal.

Already under way for several decades, Anglo's internationalisation process has truly expanded rapidly in recent times. This has been stimulated by the search for new sources of growth and profit, which are no longer offered by its home country. Furthermore, the end of apartheid has allowed this rapid expansion as in most countries South African companies were now no longer undesirable, as they had been previously. Whereas before 1994 Anglo's investments could only be made through subsidiaries situated in third countries and were concentrated in "friendly" countries such as the United States, Great Britain or Brazil out of necessity, this is no longer the case today and henceforth no political obstacle stands in the way of the group's global strategy.

This strategy led the Group to direct the bulk of its investments towards core business sectors, and more particularly towards mining projects and the paper and packaging industry, where the Group is searching for critical mass at the global level. Huge investments have been made in these sectors in Africa, America and in Europe, as well as more marginally in Australia (manganese and diamonds). By contrast, until now the Group has not yet ventured much into Asia. These investments have meant a transformation of the geographical structure of turnover, which has seen South Africa's share shrinking gradually to the benefit of that of developed countries (particularly in terms of the origin of the turnover).

For a few years now Anglo's investment effort has been particularly important in Africa, where before hostility towards the apartheid government and its companies had been most pronounced. The development of Anglo's investments in these countries has moreover been favoured by their recent opening up to foreign investments. Investments here have been concentrated in the mining sector in which there are still considerable unexploited reserves throughout the entire continent.

Traditionally, Anglo has controlled the main southern African mines. It thus controls the entire mining production – diamonds, copper, nickel and coal – of Botswana. In Namibia, as in Botswana, De Beers manages local diamond production in the framework of a joint venture in parity with the government. The Group also manages the Navachab gold mine. In Zimbabwe its influence in this sector has been somewhat reduced by the nationalisation of its local coal subsidiary, which was operated by the government in the 1980s. Anglo still controls a large part of the gold, ferro-alloy and nickel production there.

Finally, Anglo has been exploiting the copper mines of the Zambian copper belt since the 1930s. Following the nationalisation of the operating mines by President Kenneth Kaunda in 1970, the Group no longer owned more than a minority share in these.

After the failure to privatise the main Zambian mines, which saw the withdrawal of the other candidates (Canadian, South African and Chilean), Anglo managed to buy back alone its mines that were nationalised thirty years ago. The Group is moreover the principal shareholder in the Konkola Deep project, which is anticipating investments in the order of US$1 billion to develop a new copper mine, which would allow Zambia to double its production of this mineral.

In the past few years, Anglo has invested in several mining projects in the rest of Africa. The Sadiola gold mine in Mali is one of its main investments on the continent. The projects to produce copper and cobalt in the Katanga region of the Democratic Republic of Congo are very ambitious in view of the civil war. The exploitation of several gold mines in Tanzania and diverse projects are also under examination in several other countries of the continent.

Outside of Africa the Group has pursued internationalisation since the 1960s. The exchange controls that existed in South Africa forced it to create a foreign subsidiary capable of procuring the finances necessary for the Group's international expansion policy. The advantage of such a subsidiary, provided that it seemed sufficiently independent from its parent company, was that it could maintain some discretion as to the international activities of the latter. This was especially necessary to avoid hostile reactions, which would be sure to arise vis-à-vis a company coming then from the country of apartheid. The establishment of Charter Consolidated in London in 1965 met this objective.[11] The activities of Charter Consolidated developed very quickly, to the point that, three years after its establishment, its capitalisation already equalled that of its parent company. In line with its usual strategy, most of the time Anglo took over minority interests in its new subsidiaries.

In 1970 the acquisition by the Zambian government of the majority capital of the Group's copper mines in that country earned it this start-up capital for Mineral and Resources Corporation (Minorco), which quickly replaced Charted Consolidated as the controlling vector of the bulk of Anglo's assets around the world, outside of Africa. Perfecting its discretionary strategy, while also aiming to minimise its tax rates, the Group based this new subsidiary in the fiscal paradise of the Bermuda Islands, before it subsequently transferred its headquarters to Luxembourg (delisted in May 1999). Through Minorco, Anglo became the leading foreign investor in the United States by the beginning of the 1990s, before being ousted by the massive wave of foreign investments that flowed into that country during the course of the 1990s. In North America, Anglo also has a presence in the United States (gold mines) and Canada (copper and zinc mines).

---

11 This company was formed through the merger between Central Mining, the initial parent company of Anglo, Consolidated Mines Selection, and finally the British South Africa Company founded by Cecil John Rhodes to finance the annexation of Rhodesia.

In Europe, the bulk of Anglo's activities are concentrated in the paper and packaging industry, as well as in construction material. In the European Union it therefore owns packaging factories in Germany, Austria, Belgium, Spain, France, Italy and the Netherlands. Over the past years it has made numerous acquisitions in this sector throughout Eastern Europe (Poland, Hungary and Russia). It started exploiting the Lisheen Irish zinc and lead mine in 1999, which counts among the largest in the world. In Great Britain, the Group owns the leading producer of construction material, acquired in 1999, the only British potassium mine, as well as the Johnson Mathey company, which – together with the American company Engelhard – dominates the global market in precious metal refining.

The Group's interests are equally significant in South America. Its first acquisition there was that of Brazil's largest gold mine, Morro Velho, located in the state of Minhas Gerais in 1975. In 1981, thanks to its acquisition of holdings in Empresas Sudamericanas Consolidadas, Anglo acquired an industrial and mining mini-empire throughout that continent. Furthermore, recent mining investments there have been quite numerous and varied – they involve as much the extraction of gold (Argentina and Brazil), as coal (Colombia), nickel (Venezuela) and copper (Chile and Peru). With production that could reach 350 000 tons of copper at optimum capacity, the Chilean Collahuasi mine, which it started exploiting in 1999, is one of the most ambitious investment in this area.

Anglo entered into a second qualitative phase of its internationalisation process when it set about transferring its headquarters and its main quotation from Johannesburg to London in 1999. This operation was officially justified as having the objective of facilitating the Group's financing and enhancing the value of its assets by giving it a more international image. Nicky Oppenheimer therefore quite surprisingly declared:

There comes a time when companies must, like human beings, leave the comfort of home and measure themselves against the best in the wider world.[12]

It is still difficult to give an accurate assessment of the consequences of this transfer operation for the South African economy. It certainly would not translate into immediate capital flight since its assets in South Africa are not being moved. On the contrary, the announcement of this transfer has been followed by important foreign portfolio investments on the Johannesburg Stock Exchange by index trackers who were seeking to

12 *Business Day*, 19/10/98.

purchase the Group's assets at the prospect of its quotation in London.[13] The payment of dividends to foreign shareholders, however, will tend to lead to a deterioration in the balance of payments. Similarly, one can expect an erosion of the Group's domestic fiscal base. Finally, the Johannesburg Stock Exchange will lose some of its importance. These questions, however, are minor compared with those affecting the geographical allocation of the Group's new investments in future, which, indeed, is the determining factor for the future growth of the South African economy. But, insofar as the transfer of the main stock exchange quotation in fact aimed to benefit the financing of the Group's international expansion, one cannot but expect this expansion to become a main priority. The large number of acquisitions made abroad since this operation confirms the validity of this argument.

Anglo's adoption of a new global strategy has been accompanied by a total restructuring of this conglomerate, with three main objectives in mind: to increase the efficiency of its management; to improve the transparency of its management structure in the eyes of international financial markets; and to open up access to the American market from which it has been barred quite openly until now because it was too closely connected to De Beers, which is still risking legal proceedings there, in accordance with anti-trust law.

The Group thus simplified its structures, substituting the geographical structure of the organisational chart with a structure based on business activities (Table 2). Mining assets have therefore been regrouped at a global level within several subsidiaries such as AngloGold (gold) and Anglo Platinum (platinum). Shortly after its establishment, AngloGold took over all the gold mines held by Minorco, which subsequently disappeared.

This restructuring has also provided an opportunity to end the entanglement of overlapping interests between Anglo, De Beers and their subsidiaries. De Beers thus sold its interests in Anglo's subsidiaries and kept only a 40 per cent interest in the parent company, which allowed it to reduce its vulnerability vis-à-vis diamond market fluctuations. De Beers headquarters and management also broke with Anglo, which was a prerequisite for the expansion of the latter's activities in the United States.

Moreover, whereas Anglo by and large retained a minority interest in most of its domestic assets, which, notably, has allowed this Group's omnipresence in South Africa to be largely concealed, it decided to secure

---

13 Index trackers are institutions seeking to equalise the composition of their stock market portfolios with that of the global index (Footsie) in order for it their performances to follow this index's accurately.

Table 2:
The structure of Anglo American (1999)

Sector	Subsidiary name	Share of interests (%)	Assets (US$ bn)	Turnover (US$ bn)	Share of turnover (%)
TOTAL	–	–	423	20,8	100
Gold	AngloGold	54	93	2,7	13
Diamonds	De Beers	34	20	1,5	7
Platinum	Anglo Platinum	51	43	1,3	6
Coal	Anglo Coal	100	11	0,9	4
Base metals	Anglo Base Metals	100	12	0,8	4
Industrial minerals	Anglo Industrial Minerals	100	7	1,1	5
Ferrous metals	Anglo Ferrous Metals	100	30	1,6	8
Forest products	Anglo Forest Products	100	28	2,3	11
Industry	Anglo Industries	100	106	8,5	41
Finance	First Rand	21	36	–	–
Various (services, etc)		–	37	0,1	1

Source: Anglo American

majority control in its main assets. When this control reached 100 per cent the concerned subsidiaries were removed from the Johannesburg Stock Exchange. This strategy is in line with a general effort towards transparency. It also allows better strategic control over these subsidiaries.

Anglo American is going through a critical phase in its history, the government change in South Africa having afforded it new international opportunities, while also imposing constraints on its domestic market. It still has to meet numerous and unfathomed challenges: to remain competitive in the face of its rivals, Anglo has to succeed in its internationalisation, which has been slowed down for several decades by the country's isolation; its sister company De Beers is seeing its global monopoly challenged by the entry of new producers; the Group has to reverse the tendency towards a downturn in its stock market capitalisation if it wants to have the necessary financial means at its disposal for its global strategy to succeed. Admittedly, Anglo's success remains vital for the future of the South African economy. But, for all that, it is unpredictable what the impact on this economy will be owing to the priority given to the Group's international expansion, with one of the inevitable results being the reduction of the share of new investments in its home country in the Group's total investments. In this sense, is what is good for Anglo still good for South Africa?

CHAPTER 2

Economic freeze

Contrary to the reality, the black majority is said to have inherited a magnificent country, which with the "correct" adjustments, can ascend into the ranks of the world's industrialised success stories.
— Samir Amin, President of the Third World Forum[1]

Until the mid-nineteenth century, South Africa had experienced only fairly modest development since the Dutch colonisers first settled in the Cape two centuries before. For Great Britain, this faraway colony – America is twice as close to Europe – and the dry climate held fairly limited interest. It was both strategic (the control of the Cape of Good Hope) and logistical: the Cape harbour thus served as a port of call on the route to the East since its origins. Economic activities were concentrated on food production, even if the exporting of mohair wool, wines, lemons, sugar and ostrich feathers showed some success.

Thus emigration to this country had been limited during the first two centuries of its existence. The geographical destination of British emigration flows to the colonies during the nineteenth century speak volumes in this regard: among the close to 40 000 emigrants that left Great Britain for the colonies in 1841, the large majority (or 23 950 people) had chosen Canada, a slightly lower number (14 552) Australia and New Zealand, and only 130 the Cape Colony.[2]

The discovery of the Kimberley diamond mines in 1867, then the Witwatersrand gold mines in 1886 turned the South African economy completely upside down. First, these discoveries led to massive immigration, comparable to the Gold Rush which took place in California a few years before: after doubling during the last decade of the nineteenth century, the

---
1 Foreword to Marais, 1998.
2 Houghton, 1964.

settler population exceeded one million by 1900. Next, the discoveries gave rise to importune desires in the context of the "Scramble for Africa", which took place at the end of the nineteenth century, leading to the Anglo-Boer War (1899–1902), followed by the annexation by Great Britain of the entire present South African territory. It also shaped labour relations, which were then extended to all economic sectors. Finally, it led to the establishment of large mining houses, which subsequently reinvested their profits throughout the economy.

At the beginning of the 1980s, the government realised the necessity of diversifying the economy, which had become excessively dependent on mining income. The process of import substitution industrialisation could take place thanks to a true symbiosis between public companies and private capital. Nonetheless, this development process remained unfinished, as witnessed by the gradual decline in the growth rate of the economy, which caused the per capita GDP to return to the level reached during the mid-1960s.

In contrast with the emerging Asian countries, which were able to maintain rapid economic growth for several decades as a result of a sustained investment effort and steady progress in factor productivity, one witnessed a fall in the investment rate, accompanied by a pronounced slowing down of productivity gains. At the time of the democratic transition in 1994, the South African economy, as well as the society, appeared largely at a standstill, not only because of a troubling political situation but more generally because the previous growth model that had proved increasingly inefficient was wearing out.

Limits of an import substitution policy

To understand the origins of this standstill and to analyse the actual problems of the South African economy, one has to go back to the 1960s when the first signs of dysfunction appeared as a result of the inwardlooking economic policy strategy, based on the political exclusion of the majority of the population.

In a certain way, this decade represented the "golden era" of apartheid in the social and economic spheres. First of all, economic growth continued at an exceptionally high rate: between 1960 and 1970, the Gross Domestic Product (GDP) growth rate amounted to 5,8 per cent a year, which allowed a steady rise in per capita income. (Graph 3)

Graph 3:
GDP and GDP per capita at constant prices (1960–1998)

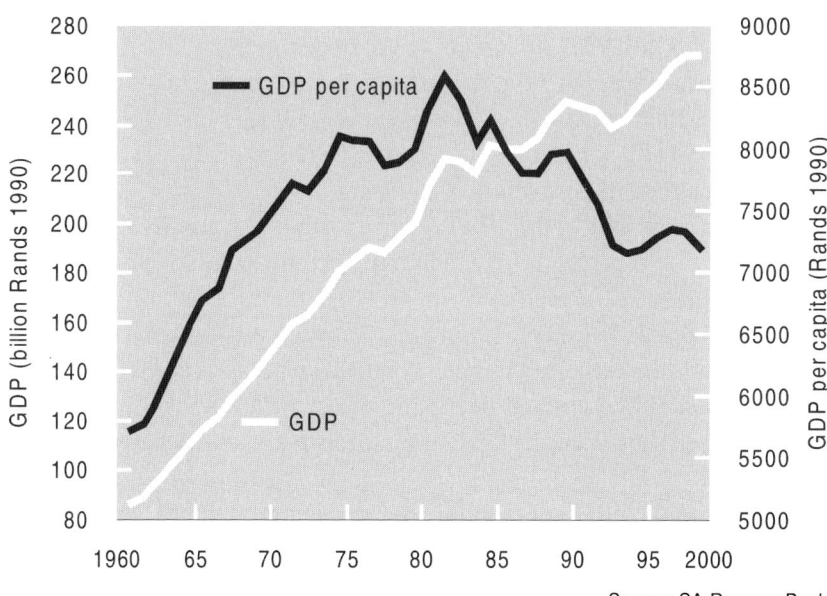

Source: SA Reserve Bank

This period was also characterised by remarkable social stability, particularly in the light of the two preceding decades. In the context of repression, the banning of the ANC and the PAC (which happened after the banning of the Communist Party in 1950), and the imprisonment of their chief leaders weakened political and social opposition over the long term. As a consequence, there were very few labour strikes in the following years.

The mining sector, which is historically the origin of the wealth of the South African economy, registered particularly high growth during this decade. Gold production, which had declined during the 1940s with the gradual depletion of reserves, started growing again after the discovery of the Free State veins at the beginning of the 1950s. Gold production and exports benefited from a stable price in the framework of the gold standard fixed at 35 US dollars an ounce since 1933. In 1970, South African gold production reached 1 000 tons, its highest volume in history, and a level that has not been rivalled since. This represented 60 per cent of the world production in the same year.

It was the manufacturing sector, however, that showed the most dynamism. Industrial value-added represented more than two-and-a-half times that of the mining sector in 1970 (or 22,6 per cent of GDP), after having more than doubled since 1960. Industry was by far the leading employment creator in the economy during this decade – 450 000 new jobs were created in this sector, as against only 55 000 in the mines. The rise in exports of manufactured products was also high. In 1967, exports of manufactured products surpassed that of gold for the first time.

The South African government encouraged the expansion of South African manufacturing since the 1920s. It realised at the time that the gold resources harboured in the country's sub-soil were being depleted and that it was necessary to diversify the economy to reduce the exclusive dependence on gold mining income.

The import substitution industrialisation policy implemented from the 1960s onwards contributed largely to the establishment and enlargement of an industrial base in this country. It relied on a very protectionist trade policy, a fiscal policy benefiting strategic projects (compare in particular the accelerated debt redemption allowance authorised by Article 37E of the fiscal code), and the direct involvement of the state in launching and financing projects through the improved lending and capital interest system practised by the Industrial Development Corporation (IDC).

In the framework of this policy, an arsenal of tariff and non-tariff barriers restricted the access of imported products to the domestic market in order to protect local production. South Africa's adherence to the General Agreement on Tariffs and Trade (GATT) in 1947 imposed tariff ceilings as far as customs duties were concerned. To respect these ceilings, while also retaining a high degree of domestic market protection, the system of import licences was gradually broadened. In relation to consumer goods imports, priority was accorded to primary products and final goods imports on which the import substitution effort initially depended to a large extent. The establishment and expansion of the automobile industry, created *sui generis* from the 1960s onwards, was thus privileged by the imposition of very strict import permits on Semi knocked down vehicles (SKD). This policy of substituting local products for foreign purchases allowed for a steady decline in the levels of industrial imports from the 1960s onwards.

The wealth of the South African subsoil, the abundance of natural resources and the low cost of domestic energy constituted the main comparative advantages in the context of the import substitution industrialisation policy. This has differentiated South Africa from most of the countries implementing a comparable policy, who rather wanted to take advantage of their low wage costs initially to expand the production and export of labour intensive products. Therefore, before praising the electricity production capacity of the country, which has made ESKOM one of the world's leading operators, the chairman of that organisation did not hesitate to declare in 1962,

In South Africa, instead of relying on so-called cheap labour, we believe in the use of energy.[3]

In the context of this "downstream" strategy, the state therefore established ESKOM in 1927 to supply cheap energy to domestic industries. The expansion of electricity capacity also allowed the accompanying economic growth through a policy of low tariffs and the avoidance of bottlenecks. The 1960s was also a period during which many large heavy industry projects were launched: aluminium, steel, chemicals (for the needs of the mining sector in particular), and so on. Beyond energy, the state thoroughly developed other public service infrastructure such as roads, railways, and telecommunications.

Finally, political considerations linked to the necessity of ensuring the country's autonomy in strategic areas led the state to invest directly in a number of key sectors. This policy was reinforced by the growing isolation of the country related to the policy of apartheid implemented by the government. The voluntary arms sales embargo decreed by the United Nations in 1963 following the Sharpeville massacre, and that embargo became compulsory in 1977, prompted the development of a national arms industry with the support of some developed countries. In 1950 the policy of energy independence led to the creation of Sasol, which specialises in the production of petroleum and chemical products from coal. The production capacity of this company was largely expanded during the 1970s, with the construction of two new plants. Despite the total absence of national resources in this area, these investments brought the level of petroleum independence to 50 per cent. Thanks to this policy (as well as to deliveries by some countries), South Africa did not really suffer from the petroleum embargo imposed on it by OPEC from 1973 onwards.

The economy's dynamism throughout the 1960s illustrated the capacity of the manufacturing industry to enhance South African growth and to substitute in part for the gold mining sector. However, doubts about the sustainability of this form of inward-looking growth started to emerge

---

3   Cited in Clark, 1994. It has been estimated that at that time ESKOM was the fourth largest operator globally. Today, it is the fifth largest in the world, after EDF (France), TEPCO (Japan), ENEL (Italy), and Korea Electric Power (South Korea).

during this period.

These doubts focused, first of all, on the possibility of continuing an import substitution policy, once the first stages (consumption goods, automobiles, intermediary goods) were exhausted. This policy seemed much more difficult to implement in the case of capital goods and high technology goods requiring higher training and incurring increased manufacturing costs.

Besides, the relatively small size of the domestic market constituted an obvious obstacle to the pursuit of higher industrial production in the framework of this policy since no interest was shown in the potential of foreign markets. Some economists detected this potentially stalling factor as early as the 1960s:

The limited size of the domestic market is partly due to the small size of the South African population compared to that of major industrial countries, and there is not much that can be done about this, if not extending the free trade areas into southern Africa. The size of the domestic market, however, is also limited because the majority of the South African population has a very low level of consumption. The three million whites have a relatively high standard of living on average, but the 13 million non-whites mostly live barely above the minimum subsistence level. If their average level of consumption were to be brought up to the present level of the white population, the size of the South African market would increase threefold. A close relationship therefore exists between improving the quality of life of the non-white section of the population and industrial production for the domestic market.[4]

Nevertheless, under apartheid one could not foresee a massive improvement in the income of the black population in relation to that of the whites. On the contrary, the essence of this policy was to maintain a profound inequality between the levels of income of the different population categories, through low education and qualification levels of blacks and through the policy of reserved employment. Under these conditions, the rapid growth rate of total consumption witnessed during the 1960s (equal to that of the GDP growth rate) could hold steady only with difficulty, even though the absence

---

4   Houghton, 1964.

of sufficient training of blacks was creating a shortage of qualified labour, which impeded the process of increasing capacity inherent to the import substitution policies. Indeed, Harry Oppenheimer confirmed this apprehensively in 1971:

> *We are approaching the stage where the full potential of the economy, as it is at present organised, will have been realised, so that if structural changes are not made, we will have to content ourselves with a much lower rate of growth. Prospects for economic growth will not be attained so long as a large majority of the population is prevented by the lack of formal education and technical training or is positively prohibited from playing the full part of which it is capable in the national development.*[5]

Moreover, in the South African case, unlike in that of the Asian countries, the import substitution industrialisation policy was hardly directed towards exports, but rather oriented towards the domestic market. From the 1960s, the foreseeable decline in the volumes of gold exports led to the realisation that the country risked being confronted with a new external constraint to its growth. Henceforth it became imperative to maintain high export growth (outside of gold mining) to be able to finance the import of intermediary and capital goods that are indispensable for the functioning of the productive apparatus. The report of the Reynders Commission, published in 1972, therefore insisted on the need to diversify South African exports, in order to reduce dependency on gold sales. The boom in raw materials that took place during the 1970s brought an unexpected godsend of foreign currency revenue. By lifting an external constraint, the boom temporarily relegated this problem to the background, before it was to re-emerge in a much more serious fashion from the 1980s onwards.

An outdated growth model

After the "boom" of the 1960s, the next decade marked the deepening of the South African economy's structural crisis, of which warning signs were already appearing during the preceding years. GDP growth amounted to an average of 3,3 per cent per annum between 1970 and 1980.

---

5 Cited in Gelb, 1991.

Moreover, it became more volatile. The growth rate of domestic demand was halved during this period: it went from 6,9 per cent to 3,6 per cent per annum. This slowing down process was even more pronounced if one excludes the revival in 1980, which was due to the temporary effect of the rise in the market price of gold. All the components of demand such as private and public consumption and investment experienced a sharp slowdown. The contribution of foreign trade to growth became negative, with imports growing faster than exports which contributed largely to a balance of payments problem.

The doubling of the petroleum price caused by an OPEC decision in 1973 had relatively little effect on South Africa. In fact, the negative impact of this event in terms of trade was more than compensated for from this date onwards by the increase in the prices of primary product exports. This increase especially affected the gold price, which started a very fast upward movement from 1973 onwards, when the gold standard was abandoned for good. Whereas its price increased to an annual average of US$52 an ounce in 1972, it doubled in 1973 (US$97 an ounce), then went up to US$160 on average between 1974 and 1975. After decreasing slightly in 1976, it again resumed its upward movement to reach US$307 in 1979, (the year of the second oil crisis) and US$613 an ounce in 1980 (or close to twenty times more than its price before 1972), before starting on a downward movement in US dollar terms from 1980 from onwards. Prices of raw materials went up similarly during the decade after the first oil crisis.

The impact of this phenomenon on South African exports and on the entire economy was considerable. The raw material boom caused a sharp increase in the dominance of raw materials and semi-transformed products in South African exports. The weight of gold in exports increased markedly, to the point where it represented 51 per cent of exports in 1981. From 1973 gold again outstripped manufactured goods exports. Growth in these goods was due especially to semi-transformed products. The net result was that the share of manufactured products in total exports, which had reached 41,1 per cent in 1970, was reduced to 35,1 per cent in 1980. The share of transformed products in total exports was halved (14,8 per cent in 1980) and at the beginning of the 1990s still remained below the level it reached twenty years before. The deterioration of the export performance of these products' has been attributed to the deterioration in their competitiveness, both compared with the past and with other products. In effect, a sharp appreciation of the rand was witnessed during this period, linked to the rise in raw material prices, according to the classical Dutch Disease phenomenon, which seemed to have hit the South African economy during this decade.[6]

Since the 1980s, all the structural problems faced by the economy for several years, but temporarily alleviated by the raw material boom of the 1970s, have reappeared, but much more acutely. GDP growth has again slowed down (1,5 per cent a year on average), and GDP per capita has started to decline.

The declining trend in investment rates since 1975 largely contributed to the deterioration of growth performance. Growth was increasing gradually until 1975: the average investment rate thus increased from an average of 21,8 per cent of GDP between 1960 and 1964, to 25,6 per cent of GDP between 1965 and 1969, and to 27,9 per cent of GDP during the first half of the 1970s, culminating in the very high level of 32 per cent of GDP in 1975. It is noteworthy that the domestic savings rate, that is the sum total of state, business and household savings rates, did not show similar progress and remained relatively stable, around 22–23 per cent of GDP, during that period. The increase in investment rates were only possible as a result of the return of foreign capital inflows flows since the mid-1960s, once political anxieties vanished.

After the Soweto riots in 1976, investment rates reversed again and started showing a marked decline. The fall in private investment could be explained by three main factors that came into play simultaneously: first of all, the private sector's loss of confidence with regard to the economy's evolution in an increasingly troubled political context; next, the constraint imposed by increasingly distressing prospects for in investment in substitution products; and finally, the absence of satisfactory export outlets, likely to offset the slightest dynamism in the domestic market. In contrast, it cannot be proven that the profitability of companies declined during this era, which could also have had a negative impact on their investment behaviour.[7] Whereas the state was confronted with growing budgetary difficulties (particularly an increase in state security expenditure), which

---

6   Bell *et al.*, 1998. Dutch Disease is a phenomenon that applies to raw material producers undergoing an appreciation of their real exchange rate because of wage increases in the primary sector. This appreciation takes place to the detriment of the industrial sector, which experiences a diminishing of its international competitiveness. The petroleum producing countries are the best example of this phenomenon. According to the normal definition, the real exchange rate is calculated as the actual exchange rate (as related to trading partners whose weight is counterbalanced by their share in trade), divided by the balance between national and foreign production prices.

7   Gelb, *op. cit.*, is therefore quite prudent on this subject.

led it to reduce its capital expenditures, public enterprises followed a similar turnabout after having over-invested during previous years. The rise in the cost of credit from the 1980s onwards, linked to the increase in international rates and then to the deflationary policies implemented after 1985 to ensure the balance of payment equilibrium, accentuated this phenomenon. The investment rate started declining fairly steadily, dropping below the 20 per cent benchmark after 1985. After the 1985 debt crisis and until 1994, the investment rate barely exceeded the savings rate, considering the fact that it was nearly impossible to borrow from outside the country.

The drop in the investment rate and the slowing down in the growth of capital stock that resulted from this were accompanied, paradoxically, by an acceleration of the process of capital substitution for labour. From 1970 to 1995, the capital to labour ratio grew at the very high rate of 10 per cent a year.[8] The speed of this process of capital substitution for labour can be explained both by heavy substitution at the level of each sector and by the additional effect of faster growth of the most capital intensive sectors (particularly heavy industries) compared with the more labour-intensive sectors. The slowdown in growth and the extent of the process of capital substitution for labour had the combined effect of almost interrupting job creation in the economy from 1981 (Graph 4). From 1981 onwards, only the number of public sector employees kept growing, whereas that in the private sector stabilised before declining after 1990. Industrial and mining jobs have been affected most by this reverse trend.

In the long term, productivity growth, together with the capital accumulation rate, constitutes the second most important source of potential growth in per capita income. However, several analyses have brought to the fore the major impact that the deterioration of productivity performance has had on the gradual slowing down of economic growth in South Africa during the past decades.[9] The pace of total factor productivity (TFP) growth across the economy has therefore declined markedly since the beginning of the 1970s. TFP has started diminishing from 1980 onwards (see Table 3). The net result is that total factor productivity has stagnated between 1960 and the beginning of the 1990s. Although South Africa's performance in this sphere is similar to that seen of in many other developing countries, it can clearly be differentiated from that of the top performing Asian

---

8   Bhorat *et al.*, 1998.
9   Compare particularly Fallon and Pereira da Silva, 1994.

Graph 4:
Development of non-agricultural employment (1970–1998)

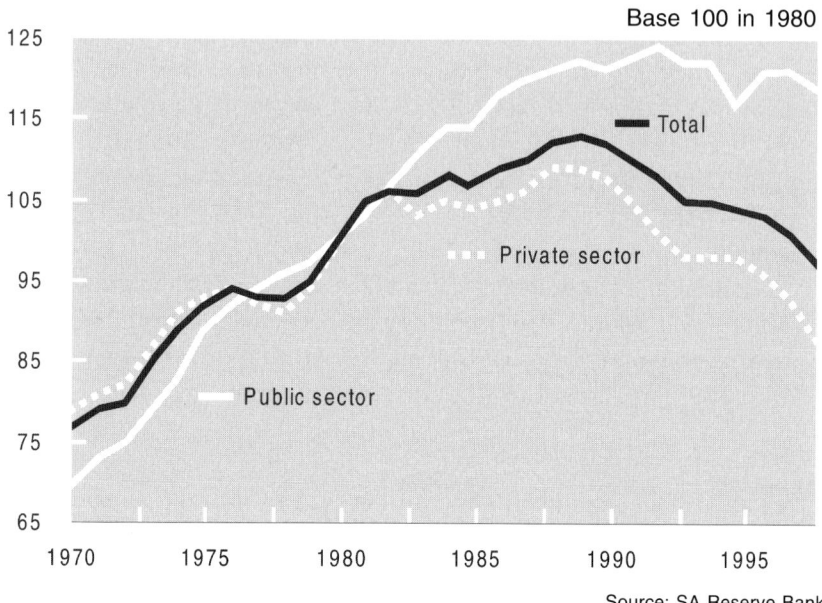

Source: SA Reserve Bank

Table 3:
Analysis of growth factors (1960–1992)

(%)	1960–1970	1970–1980	1980–1992	1960–1992 RSA	East Asia
GDP/employee	2,3	2,1	-1,7	0,7	4,1
Contribution of:					
– capital	1,1	2,0	–	1,0	2,8
– education	0,2	– 0,1	0,2	0,1	0,5
– total productivity factor	1,0	0,2	– 1,9	– 0,4	0,8

Source: Bosworth *et al*, 1995
Methodology note: In the framework of the usual analyses which measure factor contribution to growth (Solow's models), total factor productivity growth, considered to be the result of technical progress, is calculated as the residue of growth equation estimates.

countries, where productivity gains have contributed determinately to the fast growth in per capita income during the past decades (however, with investment having made a predominant contribution to growth).

Several factors explain the mediocre productivity gains:
- In the first place, investment allocation was often inefficient, particularly as far as public investment was concerned. Besides the fact that the latter was often inefficient for highly political reasons (industrial strategies), it also led to surplus capacity in several sectors (electricity, railway transport, iron and steel, petroleum, and so on).
- The policy of domestic market protection and the lack of international exposure also slowed down innovation and efficiency gains from the productive process, with the market size often too limited to allow for economies of scale.
- Finally, the shortage of skilled labour also slowed down productivity growth.

This last element has played a crucial role, insofar as the example of the emerging Asian countries shows that improving the skills of the labour force is an integral part of the development process. In the case of South Africa, this process could hardly take place because the apartheid system has to a large extent refused black people access to a higher education. On the whole, the South African labour force has a relatively low level of education and skills compared with the labour force of some east Asian countries at a similar level of development. This shortage of skilled labour has probably also prompted the development of capital-intensive production techniques to the detriment of labour productivity.

The elements described above have come into play to various degrees in different sectors of economic activity.

Total factor productivity in the manufacturing industry, which showed remarkable growth during the 1960s, has therefore stagnated, or subsequently declined. At the same time, one witnessed high capital growth, combined with a greatly reduced growth in production and employment. The decline in capital productivity evident between the mid-1960s and the 1980s was partly the result of huge investments that were made in the chemical sector. As in other sectors, the main factor at the origin of this decline seems to have been the adoption of increasingly capital-intensive production techniques and the preference given to investments in high capital-intensive sectors. The fiscal regime probably also contributed to this phenomenon. The highest rates of accumulation were therefore seen in the mineral beneficiation sectors, which benefited from cheap raw materials and energy, and from various fiscal advantages. The net result was that the industries with the weakest capital productivity also showed the highest growth in their operations during the period 1970 to 1990. The impact of the rise in labour costs, which were particularly steep after the legalisation of trade unions in 1979, on investment growth is difficult to assess, but it does not seem to have played a determining role. Growth in labour productivity was, however, almost nil from 1970 to 1985.

The government's strategy aimed at food self-sufficiency was probably detrimental to agricultural productivity. The effect of this policy, therefore, was an extension of the areas under cultivation for products that required large investments in irrigation systems. With production of around 10 million tons in good years, South Africa is an important producer and exporter of maize. This product, which covers more than a third of all areas under cultivation, is by far the most important national harvest. However, local climatic conditions are often hardly suitable, and the extension of cultivated areas for this cereal has corresponded to the semi-stagnation of yields. Benefiting from a very protected environment, white commercial agriculture moreover became highly mechanised despite the abundance of cheap agricultural labour. Agricultural performance, however, did not equal these investments. Finally, the government's traditional implementation of a policy of providing very generous subsidies to white farmers also contributed to discouraging efforts to improve production efficiency and to specialise in more profitable crops.

The mining sector benefited from high total factor productivity growth during the 1960s. It subsequently went through a steady decline, however, even though capital stock was growing rapidly. This largely reflected the gradual depletion of gold-bearing veins, which forced the extraction of lower grade minerals at increasing depths. But these "exogenous" factors cannot be invoked in isolation.

The productivity crisis suffered by some gold mines also revealed a crisis in the form of labour organisation that was based on the exploitation of an unskilled and lowly paid labour force.[10] This form of labour organisation reserved management jobs for whites mostly. This monopoly, combined with the growing complexity of mining operations, gradually led to the accumulation of hierarchical levels similar to those of geological strata. At the bottom of the ladder were the black miners, the majority of

---

10 Bomsel, 1998.

whom were illiterate, and who until recently, could neither gain access to skilled jobs, nor could they handle explosives.

In fact, the gradual decline of the ore reserves and grades in South African gold mines, already underway for several decades, would require a radical improvement in labour productivity, which would have resulted in a profound reorganisation of labour and a rise in skills that could not be realised under apartheid. In the absence of such reforms, labour productivity stagnation in the mines aggravated the crisis in the sector and eroded its profitability.

Collapse of the apartheid economy

Three major events that took place in the 1980s pushed the economy into recession and accelerated the end of the apartheid government.

First of all, the ongoing decline in the gold price in US dollars since 1981 reduced revenues in foreign currency and diminished the profitability of the gold mines. The gold price was declining fairly steadily between 1981 and 1985, reaching an average price of US$317 an ounce in 1985, the decade's lowest. This fall, which also affected other raw materials, led to a fall in exports and a depreciation of the rand during that period, while also sharply reducing budgetary income.[11]

Secondly, at the same time as the fall in raw material prices resulted in a serious impact on fiscal revenue, the budgetary cost necessary for the functioning of the apartheid system and the survival of a regime that was held in contempt by a large part of the population, became more and more exorbitant.

In order to function, the system needed a costly and overdeveloped administration, considering that a separate administration existed for each ethnic group in most areas, added to which was an administration for each of the homelands. The description below shows the extreme complexity of this system, the only one of its kind in the world:

> As a result of the existence of the separate administrative structures in each Bantustan and for each racial group in the Republic of South Africa, at least a dozen departments can

---

11 All the same, the gold price remained in fact at a relatively high and stable level throughout the 1980s: it registered only limited fluctuations (about 20 per cent), around an average of somewhat less than US$400 an ounce, which was still much higher than the price reached during the second half of the 1970s.

> *typically be handling the same function. Thus, both education and health are handled by fourteen ministries and four provincial administrations, agriculture by fourteen and welfare by eighteen ministries, industrial development by eleven ministries, ten development corporations, the Industrial Development Corporation and the Southern African Development Bank and economic policy by eleven ministries and many other official bodies.[12]*

The continuation of the policy of giving independence to the homelands and the implementation of a tricameral parliament, separating representatives from white, Indian, and coloured communities, contributed to the unexpected budgetary increase witnessed during the 1980s. From 1980 to 1988, the number of officials employed in the central administration thus increased by 57 per cent and that of officials employed in local and homeland administrations by 39 per cent.

The political cost of apartheid was also linked to shifting millions of black people to the homelands, to infrastructure and construction investments, and to fiscal measures to attract businesses in order to create employment and settle populations in these areas. The cost of investment subsidy policies, implemented in the framework of the Regional Investment Development Programme, quickly turned out to be difficult to control and thus mostly inefficient.

Finally, after the mid-1970s, growing internal opposition to the regime and the pronounced isolation of the country following the independence of the former neighbouring Portuguese and British colonies in southern Africa sparked off an increase in military expenditure and that necessary for the functioning of the police and judiciary machinery. The exponential growth in military expenditure from 1960 onwards weighed particularly on public finance: the latter first doubled during the 1960s (from 0,9 per cent to 2 per cent of GDP), before doubling a second time between 1970 and 1980, and since then has exceeded 4 per cent of GDP, which represents a share twice as high as the average in developing countries. The South African intervention in Angola in 1975, the fight against SWAPO in Namibia and more generally the "total" strategy of intervening in all the countries of the region, followed since the mid-1970s, explain why this increase continued steadily.

---

12 Lundahl and Moritz, 1994.

CHAPTER 2 Economic freeze

This policy resulted in a sharp increase in the share of public expenditure in GDP. To contain the budget deficit, public investments were sharply reduced from the mid-1970s. This did not prevent a rise in public debt, which however remained moderate (32 per cent of GDP in 1991, against only 27 per cent of GDP in 1983), and especially in debt servicing (because of the interest rate hike), and in the budget deficit. Almost zero in 1980, the latter rose almost without interruption from that date, reaching an untenable level on the eve of the first democratic elections.

The third element to take into account concerns international sanctions imposed on South Africa, which also had an undeniable impact on the difficulties suffered by the economy.

Private banks, increasingly anxious in the face of a deteriorating economic and political situation, decided to implement financial sanctions. The 1985 debt crisis was triggered off by the decision of the New York-based Chase Manhattan Bank to ask South Africa to reimburse its unpaid loans. This decision was announced shortly after a famous speech by PW Botha, which will live on in history under the name of the "Rubicon speech", during which the South African President announced that the principal tenets of his National Party's policy would be maintained, despite the general opposition which these were provoking both domestically and internationally. Following this speech, the disappointment of international financial circles resulted in an immediate fall in the rand of more than 10 per cent. The Chase Manhattan decision led, by contagion, to a general credit withdrawal on the part of all the American banks. Soon thereafter the country was obliged to declare a moratorium on its debt servicing under pressure from British and German banks which feared that the reimbursement of only American banks would work to their detriment.

This crisis was mostly of a political nature, insofar as the country's indebtedness was in fact very reasonable. Moreover, debt servicing represented only 7,5 per cent of annual foreign currency income in 1985, a very modest proportion.

Following the rescheduling of its debt, and until the change of government, which took place in 1994, South Africa no longer had easy access to international finance, public or private. This constraint led to the recording of a balance of payments surplus, whereas most developing countries recorded a running deficit, used to finance their economic growth. The reintroduction of a dual exchange rate system (which was abolished in 1983) was accompanied by a set of measures intended to fight capital flight, which accelerated after 1985 in any case.

Added to the impact of financial sanctions was that of trade sanctions. Of these, the embargo started by the United States in 1986 on the initiative of the Democratic majority in Congress played a determining role. It was a complete trade embargo parallel to forcing American companies to disinvest from South Africa. Many businesses from third countries with interests in the United States also withdrew to avoid incurring the risk of American retaliatory measures. The American embargo was decided upon at the same time as many countries were taking similar measures. In 1985, France had also decided to withdraw its public enterprises. The British Commonwealth countries (with the exception of Thatcher's Great Britain) and Ireland started implementing an embargo against most products originating from South Africa in 1985 and 1986, while the Nordic countries imposed a total trade embargo. Many countries prohibited the import of South African fruits. France, Great Britain, Ireland and the Netherlands stopped buying South African coal. No global assessment of the actual impact of these measures has ever been conducted. The products affected by the embargo imposed by developed countries represented 7 per cent of total South African exports. Even if part of these products could have been sold on other markets (or sold on these markets after a detour through third countries), the drop in the volume of exports witnessed in 1986 and 1987 was probably partly the result of this embargo.

Following the 1985 debt crisis, capital flight increased and in 1989 recession set in. It was interrupted only in 1993. Even though the process of lifting international sanctions was launched by the US after 1990, South Africa had to wait another three years to sign a final debt rescheduling agreement, which marked its return to the international financial community.

Incomplete industrialisation process

An analysis of the contribution of the main sectors of economic activity to the South African GDP over a long period of time allows one to weigh up the consequences of the difficulties described above. It brings to the fore the incomplete nature of the economic restructuring, with a short-winded industrialisation process, which in return has led to the continuing dominance of the primary sector in the economy.

The drastic reduction of the share of agriculture in the economy constituted the most important element of the economic restructuring.

Between 1960 and 1998, this sector's contribution to GDP was reduced from 11,1 per cent to 4 per cent of the total. The contribution to agricultural employment diminished in similar proportions, representing only 14 per cent of total employment. These proportions are extremely modest for a developing country. In countries at a similar level of income, agricultural employment generally represents between a quarter (Brazil) and two-thirds (Thailand) of total employment.

This trend has been accompanied by a growing concentration of agricultural property, the number of holdings having halved since 1960, consequently with a noticeable increase in the size of farms: 55 000 white farmers own most of the suitable cultivated land and produce the bulk of the commercialised agricultural produce.

Several factors explain why agricultural performance was mediocre for a long time. First of all, the dry climate has made a large part of the territory unsuitable for agricultural cultivation: the semi-desert Karoo area covers more than a third of the country. The World Bank, however, considers the low share of agriculture in the economy to be first and foremost the result of distortions created by the economic policy that was followed historically, which favoured large inefficient farms to the detriment of small farmers, many of whom disappeared.[13] Accordingly, there is a significant potential for agricultural development in this country.

The share of the mining sector in GDP experienced large fluctuations during the past years, which to a large extent have been determined by the fluctuation of raw material prices and particularly that of gold. After experiencing a continuous decline during the 1960s, it benefited from the rise in the price of raw material during the 1970s. It reached its highest level since the Second World War in 1980 (20,4 per cent of GDP), almost equalling the share of manufacturing in that same year.

Since 1980 the mining sector declined fairly steadily and represented only 6,6 per cent of GDP in 1998. Owing to the depletion of many gold reserves that were cheapest to exploit, gold ore production halved since 1970.

This indisputable decline, however, must be seen in perspective. The share of the mining sector remained a deciding factor in foreign exchange revenue (a third of the total, of which half came from gold), as well as to some extent employment. Moreover, an industry analysis leads to the realisation that, contrary to widespread opinion, dependency on the "mining-

---

13 World Bank, 1994a.

energy complex" – including mines, the electrical sector, and iron and steel, and chemical industries – has in fact increased: this complex represented 25 to 27 per cent of GDP since the 1980s, as against only 22 per cent in 1960.[14] Its components are highly interdependent both as suppliers and clients: thus, 90 per cent of electricity production is of thermal origin and the mining sector, and related foundry and mineral refining activities consume 43 per cent of electricity.

Finally, South Africa remains a mining giant on a global scale and the size of its reserves promises a brilliant future for this sector (Table 4). In 1998, therefore, this country was the world's leading producer of vermiculite (75,9 per cent), vanadium (61 per cent of production), chrome (47,8 per cent), and ferrochrome (44,1 per cent). Furthermore, today the South African subsoil harbours more than half the known global reserves of many minerals: this is the case for 80 per cent of global reserves of manganese, 68,3 per cent of that of chrome, and 55,7 per cent of known platinum reserves. What is more, these products are often rare minerals used in fast-growing high-tech industries. The global demand for platinum group metals, which is the second largest mining product exported for a total of US$2 billion, has therefore increased by an average of 5,5 per cent a year since the mid-1960s. Besides the manufacturing of jewellery, palladium is used to manufacture catalytic exhausts for automobiles and has many other industrial applications.

The share of the manufacturing sector in GDP stagnated since the beginning of the 1970s, after having grown very rapidly during the 1960s. It represented 18,9 per cent of GDP in 1998, a level somewhat lower than that of 1960 (19,9 per cent). This stagnation points to the inability of setting in motion (once the first stages of import substitution had passed) a genuine industrialisation process. If, until the end of the 1960s, growth in industrial production remained above that in other economic sectors, with this sector therefore playing the role of an engine for economic growth, this was no longer the case after the 1980s for the reasons described above.

The interruption of the industrialisation process after the 1970s reflects the general crisis of the South African economy, and more particularly the consequences of economic policy choices that were made: giving priority to the most capital-intensive heavy industries; specialising in those sectors that were hardly excelling at the international level and were subject to fluctuations in the prices of raw materials; the gradual wearing

---

14 Fine and Rustomjee, 1996.

Table 4:
South Africa's share in the global production and reserves of some minerals (1998)

	Production		Reserves	
	%	Rank	%	Rank
Vermiculite	75,9	1	40,0	1
Vanadium	61,1	1	44,5	1
Chrome	47,8	1	68,3	1
Ferrochrome	44,1	1	n/a	1
Platinum (PGM)	43,3	2	55,7	1
Zirconium	25,8	2	22,1	2
Titanium	22,6	2	21,0	1
Gold	18,2	1	35,0	1
Manganese	13,7	3	80,0	1

Source: SA Department of Minerals and Energy 1998/1999

out of the import substitution policy considering the limited size of the local market; and the impossibility of implementing the export-oriented growth policy promised from the 1980s onwards in the context of South Africa's international isolation.

The extraordinary high degree of concentration in the South African economy, which is found nowhere else in the world, has probably also contributed to these impediments, insofar as it has reduced investment opportunities for conglomerates, while also preventing the entry of newcomers to these highly protected markets. In fact, South African conglomerates control a large part of the South African economy. This is the result of the protectionism that has been applied for many years, as well as the disinvestments by foreign multinationals from the 1960s onwards.[15]

In 1994, five groups (Anglo American, Old Mutual, Sanlam, Rembrandt, Anglovaal, and Liberty Life), also known as the 'Big Five', represented 84 per cent of the capitalisation on the Johannesburg Stock

---

15 Anglo American has therefore successively acquired the subsidiaries of Ford, Barclays, and so on. Gencor has acquired the local subsidiary of Mobil, renamed Engen, Barlow that of IBM, and so on.

Exchange, according to the McGregor consulting firm's estimations.[16] They were exercising their control over a myriad companies through a system of holdings, characterised by minority capital interests in most of their subsidiaries. The leading three among them at the same time controlled a life insurance group, a merchant and commercial bank and/or a savings bank, an industrial holding and a mining holding, thus achieving a perfect integration between industrial, mining and financial capital. The Rembrandt conglomerate, symbol of Afrikaner capitalism, was also very diversified, owning mining, industrial and banking assets.

This alliance between industry and finance explained the substantial share of services in the economy, the level of development and sophistication of the South African financial system being a marked characteristic of the economy. The four main domestic banks (Amalgamated Banks of South Africa (ABSA), Standard Bank, First National Bank, and Nedcor) are also of an international scale. Furthermore, the size of the stock market (12th largest in the world in 1995) is unrelated to that of the economy at the global level.[17] The share of the tertiary sector in GDP rose from 50,6 per cent in 1960 to 64,3 per cent in 1998. Financial services have shown particularly fast progress during this period.

This chapter brings to the fore the gradual increase in obstacles at the heart of the South African economy during the past years, which led to the interruption of the development process embarked upon at the end of the nineteenth century. What is at stake after apartheid is how to overcome these obstructions in order to rediscover ways that would lead to high economic growth. This would at the same time be the precondition and the result of a policy that is necessary to reduce social inequalities and reconcile the dual society inherited from apartheid and colonialism.

---

16 The share of these groups was reduced to 54 per cent of the total capitalisation at the end of 1998, mainly because of the fall in Anglo's capitalisation.

17 The stock market capitalisation of Johannesburg has however diminished markedly during the past years, because of the fall in the prices of raw materials as well as the fact that major domestic groups have transferred their main listing to London.

CHAPTER 3

Two South African nations

> ... *South Africa is a country of two nations. One of these nations is white, relatively prosperous, regardless of gender or geographic dispersal. It has ready access to a developed economic, physical, education, communication and other infrastructure (...) The second and larger nation of South Africa is black and poor, with the worst affected being women in the rural areas, the black rural population in general and the disabled.*
> — Thabo Mbeki, President of South Africa[1]

Like Victorian England, described by Disraeli 150 years ago, South Africa seems to comprise two nations, coexisting in the same country, seemingly unconscious of each other.[2]

In fact, South Africa is one of the most unequal countries in the world. Most of the four million white South Africans (out of a total population of a little over 40 million inhabitants) benefit from a quality of life equivalent to that of a developed country. They are nearly unaffected by unemployment and enjoy mostly comfortable life styles and high salaries. At the other extreme of the social ladder are most of the black population and ethnic minorities.

This dual society registers very marked inequalities between ethnic groups in all areas. At the same time, the relatively low incomes of black people can be explained by their lack of appropriate skills and by the high rate of unemployment that prevails in this category of the population. These two characteristics are related to the way the labour market has

---

1 Mbeki, 1998.
2 In "Sybil or the two nations", published in 1845, Benjamin Disraeli wrote: "I have been told that the privileged and the people form two Nations, governed by different laws, with no common thought or sympathy, with an inability to understand one another. I believed that if this was effectively the case, the downfall of our country for all was imminent."

functioned historically. It reserved the highest qualified and best-paid jobs for whites, while most blacks had access only to unskilled and low salaried jobs. In addition, the development strategy implemented during the past years has led to a reduction in unskilled jobs, which has affected black people primarily, whereas, in contrast, the employment of whites increased.

Inequalities in living conditions are even more pronounced than those related to the income gap alone. In effect, the policy of apartheid, implemented from 1948, led to the displacement of several million black people to "homelands", where they were often housed under precarious conditions, while infrastructure expenditure in the urban townships was neglected to discourage blacks from settling permanently in the cities. This has accentuated regional disparities, and disparities between urban and rural areas.

The Reconstruction and Development Programme (RDP) is aimed at improving the population's access to housing and basic services, which in the past were reserved almost exclusively for the white minority. The scope of its objectives makes it the only one of its kind in the world. The government, moreover, is looking to increase the role of blacks in the economy through two types of policies.

First of all, affirmative action aims to promote a more equal distribution of employment at all levels of responsibility, while black empowerment tries to strengthen the participation of blacks in the business world.

The dual society

With a level of GDP per capita of around $3 500 in 1996, South Africa is considered a middle income country, and one of the richest countries on the African continent. However, this average is of little significance when one takes into account the scope of inequalities existing in this country: the South African reality is that of a dual society, be it in terms of revenue, employment, or more general living conditions. The measuring of "human development", done according to a method defined by the United Nations by adding a certain number of socio-demographic indicators (life expectancy, percentage of children in full-time education, and illiteracy) to income indicators therefore led to the classification of white South Africa in 19th position (out of 173 countries) globally in 1991, close to Germany, Italy, or Denmark. In contrast, black South Africa ranked only

CHAPTER 3 Two South African nations

117th, behind Swaziland, Albania, Bolivia, and so on. (The country as a whole ranked 86th.)[3]

The country is first of all characterised by an extremely unequal income distribution. According to World Bank estimates, the richest 10 per cent of the population – one might as well say whites especially – receive 47,3 per cent of total income, whereas the remaining 90 per cent of the population, that is to say blacks and all the other ethnic groups (coloured, Indian, and so on), share the other half of this income, with the poorest 20 per cent receiving only 3,3 per cent of total income.

The Report on Poverty and Inequality in South Africa, produced by the UK Department of International Development in 1998, furthermore shows that half of the South African population lives on less than US$2,40 a day, an amount considered to be the domestic poverty threshold. Sixty-one per cent of blacks were considered poor according to this definition, as against 38 per cent of coloureds, five per cent of Indians, and one per cent of whites. Sixty per cent of single-parent households headed by a female are poor. Nearly five million South Africans (more than ten per cent of the population) live on less than one US dollar a day[4]. By way of comparison, this proportion is less than two per cent in Thailand, a country with a lower per capita income. Even without disposing of recent statistics in this domain, it is obvious that the distribution of property is even more unequal than that of income.

Wage disparities, which reflect above all the inequalities in the level of qualifications between different categories of the population, are also very pronounced. According to the South African Institute of Race Relations, the average monthly salary in the manufacturing industry rose to R2 950 in September 1997. In the same month, the average monthly salary (R1 785) for blacks represented scarcely more than half the sector average and that of whites (R6 055) more than double the average. The salary of Indians (R2 885) was close to the average, whereas that of coloureds (R2 124) was halfway between the latter and that of blacks.

These considerable salary gaps between the different ethnic groups have tended to shrink for several decades now. During the past 20 years (1975–1996), the real wages of Indians have increased by 63 per cent in the industrial sector, those of blacks by 49 per cent, and those of coloureds by 27 per cent, whereas those of whites have stagnated.

---

3 Cited by DFID, 1998.
4 One US$ a day (at 1985 prices) is considered by convention as an international poverty threshold.

The origins and foundation of apartheid

Since it first originated, the Cape Colony utilised the pro-slavery movement on a grand scale. Instead of gradually modernising itself, by following the example of trends in the United States as well as in other colonies in the Americas, the system of segregating and oppressing the black population, which was implemented from the first years of the colony's existence, was on the contrary prolonged and was codified throughout the 19th and 20th centuries.

A certain number of laws, voted in immediately after the Constitution of the South African Union was adopted in 1910, laid the juridical foundations for this segregation, which were to be rationalised in the apartheid framework. One could cite, in particular, the Natives Land Act (1913), which set up the policy of territorial segregation, the Apprenticeship Act (1922) and the Mines and Workforce Amendment Act (1926), which established the colour bar, reserving skilled employment for whites, or even the Natives (Urban Areas) Act (1923). This latter Act aimed to exclude Africans from urban areas, except temporarily and to serve whites, and to separate black neighbourhoods from the city through the establishment of an autonomous financial administration (financed *inter alia* by an alcohol consumption tax!).

The juridical arsenal of apartheid, however, was supplemented after 1948, at the same time as the use of this term, which literally means "separation" in Afrikaans, was made official. The Prohibition of Mixed Marriages Act (1949) prohibited marriages between whites and members of other ethnic groups. The Population Registration Act (1950) assigned each person to a racial group. The sadly infamous (Section 10) Native Laws Amendment Act, which systematised the pass law system, gave only those blacks who were born there, who had lived there for 15 years without interruption or who had worked for the same employer for at least 10 years the right to live in an urban area. The Bantu Education Act (1953) laid down educational programmes for blacks, adapted to their needs as defined by the government. Later on, the Bantu Homelands Citizenship Act (1970) aimed to give blacks citizenship of one of the homelands, even if they had lived in a white area all their lives.

From the 1980s onwards, most apartheid laws were no longer respected. They were completely abolished in 1991.

CHAPTER 3 Two South African nations

This contraction of the wage hierarchy, witnessed in all economic sectors, had several causes.[5] The legalisation of black trade unions in 1979 probably played a major role in the process of convergence witnessed in the case of this population category, leading to inevitable diffusion effects for other ethnic groups. The increasing access of blacks (as well as other "non-whites") to skilled jobs during the past decades, which of course has to be seen in a relative light, also contributed to this development. But this movement has also affected non-skilled wage earners in all sectors of the economy. If the evolution of industrial wages is probably above all the result of the greater collective bargaining power that the black trade unions have acquired, that of wages in the gold mines also reflects economic considerations linked to the need to attract local workers with sufficiently attractive wages. This was the case in particular at the beginning of this period owing to the new labour policies adopted by the mining houses, which resulted in the large-scale substitution of South Africans for migrant workers, who had comprised the bulk of the labour force until then. In the same way, white farmers have been obliged to raise the wages of their agricultural workers substantially to face up to the shortage of such labour in rural areas.

Paradoxically, however, the catching up of wages did not result in a reduction of inequality among the races, at least not until the beginning of the 1990s, when one started observing the emergence of a black middle class: in urban areas, a relative convergence of income has been evident during the past years as is shown by the fact that the average income of a black household, which represented only 17 per cent of that of a white household in 1990, represented 42 per cent in 1995.[6] There is, however, no reason to believe that a similar phenomenon took place in most rural areas.

An analysis of the evolution of income gaps confirms the remarkable stability of these gaps since the beginning of the twentieth century, apart from structural economic fluctuations (Graph 1). In 1993, the average per capita income of blacks thus represented 8,5 per cent of the average income of whites, with the wages of coloureds and Indians also being very low. The latter seem to have succeeded to some extent in catching up from a level that was already higher than that of other groups since the 1980s.

---

5 Hofmeyer, 1996.
6 SSA, 1997. This ratio was 48 per cent for coloureds and 65 per cent for Indians. The per capita income gap remains much higher, taking into account a much higher average number of children in black households.

Graph 5:
Development of per capita income gap since the beginning of the century (Whites = 100)

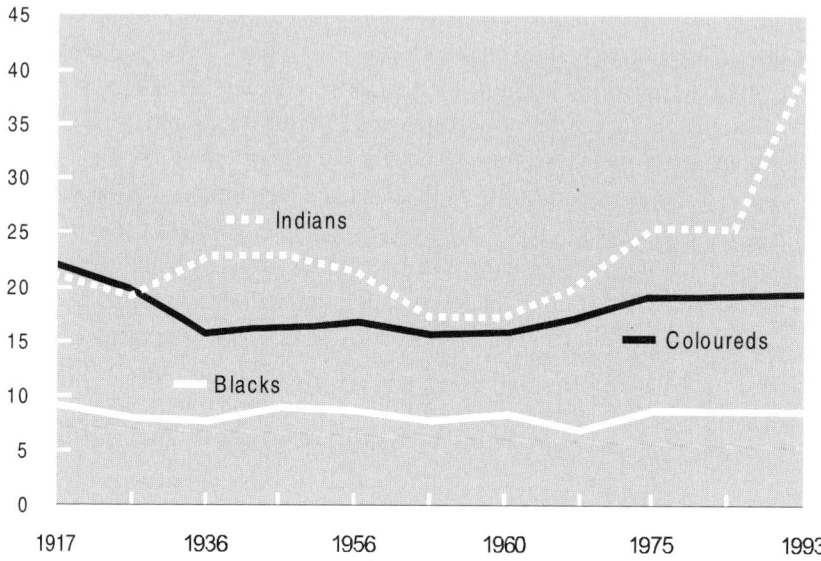

Source: Lundahl and Moritz, 1994, and Pillay, 1996

This apparent contradiction between the observation of some degree of contraction of the wage hierarchy and the absence of a similar phenomenon where incomes are concerned is mainly a result of the fact that, if the wages of blacks have caught up somewhat, the rise in unemployment in this population category has led to a growing inequality between a salaried minority and a majority that is unemployed or employed in the informal sector.

From 1970 to 1995, formal employment in South Africa increased by one million people, the bulk of this rise having taken place before 1980. During the same period, however, the number of blacks employed shrank by 200 000. Consequently, today blacks represent only barely more than half the employed labour force, a much lower share than their share of the total population. By contrast, the share of white employees (25 per cent of the total in 1995) has increased markedly, as well as that of Indians and coloureds, albeit to a lesser extent. Blacks have in effect suffered from the decline in the primary sector, which represented half of their employment in 1970, but only a quarter in 1995. The reduction in black employment therefore reached 60 per cent in agriculture and 44 per cent in the mining sector during this period.[7] With regard to annual demographic growth (more than 2,5 per cent for the black population since the beginning of the 1970s,) the latter therefore being subjected to a rapid increase in unemployment.

Employment inequality actually constitutes the second major characteristic of the social inequalities prevailing in South Africa. The household survey conducted by Statistics South Africa (SSA) Institute at the end of 1997 put the official unemployment rate in South Africa at 23 per cent of the active population. In accordance with the definition of the International Labour Organisation, the unemployed were considered to be all those who satisfied each of the following criteria:

- They had not worked during the week preceding the interview.
- They wanted to work and were available to start working the following week.
- They had started looking for work during the previous month.

According to this definition, the unemployment rate in 1997 was an average of 29 per cent for blacks, 16 per cent for coloureds, 10 per cent for Indians, and only 4 per cent for whites. If all those who fulfilled the first two criteria above, but not necessarily the third, were considered unemployed, the "extended" unemployment rate would rise to an average of 34 per cent of the population. The percentage of unemployed would be 43 per cent for blacks, 21 per cent for coloureds, 12 per cent for Indians, and five per cent for whites. Furthermore, long-term unemployment has affected blacks much more severely than other population categories: 42 per cent have been looking for a job for at least three years, whereas the proportions were much lower for coloureds (19 per cent), Indians (12 per cent) and whites (also 12 per cent).

In 1997, 1,8 million people, or 24 per cent of the economically active population in employment, admitted that they were working in the informal sector. Even if one does not have exact information on the evolution of this sector over a long period of time, all indications are that it has experienced quite a rapid expansion since the 1980s. The increase in the number of kombis (collective taxis), hawkers, street sellers, spazas (informal groceries), and shebeens (informal bars), among others, testifies of this. As a result, the informal sector today represents an important part of

---

7 Bhorat *et al.*, 1998.

employment and economic activity particularly in the area of trade. This remains much lower, however, than in most other African countries.

Without neglecting the vitality and the important economic role played by the informal sector, one has to underline the fact that the working conditions and income of workers in this sector are generally much less favourable – at equal levels of qualification – than those in the formal sector. In its study on poverty in South Africa conducted in 1994, the World Bank estimated that the income ratio between the two sectors was 1:2.[8] Although it contributes towards reducing the number of unemployed through the creation of precarious jobs, the development of the informal sector can only marginally alleviate poverty in the country.

Income and employment inequalities are also reflected in the heterogeneous living conditions of the South African population. The population census conducted in 1996 was the first to cover the entire population accurately.[9] It gave an accurate picture of the inequalities prevailing in this domain soon after the end of apartheid.

Firstly, it brought to the fore the acuteness of the housing problem in the country. The census listed 1,4 million shacks. This figure includes shantytowns put up in fields on the outskirts of cities, as well as hundreds of thousands of shacks constructed in the backyards of permanent houses. In total, taking account of the average size of households, it has been estimated that about five million blacks and coloureds were living in shacks in 1995. About a further one million people were living in overcrowded hostels for single workers, situated either in mining compounds or urban townships.

This situation is a consequence of the policy implemented by the National Party government during the past decades. A long-term goal of the apartheid ideology was to force the entire black population to live in one of the 10 homelands set up on South African territory from the remnants of former territories historically occupied by African tribes. It led to the deportation of 3,5 million Africans to these areas between the beginning of the 1960s and the 1980s, when this policy was finally renounced.[10] During this same period, several hundred thousand coloureds and Indians living in areas reserved for whites were also displaced. Those who were evicted from their homes, generally with at best a derisory

---

8 World Bank, 1994b.
9 Besides the fact that previous censuses had excluded the four independent homelands (Bophuthatswana, Ciskei, Transkei, and Venda), the quality of responses had moreover been influenced by a part of the black population boycotting or misrepresenting responses.
10 Report of the "Surplus Commission", cited by Davenport, 1991.

CHAPTER 3 Two South African nations

compensation, often built precarious housing for themselves in the homelands where they were sent. Others, who retained the right to reside in the city, came to inhabit the shantytowns around urban areas. Finally, since the 1960s the priority accorded to the homelands led the government to neglect the construction of housing for blacks in the urban areas where they were in any case supposed to reside only temporarily. In the 1980s, the gradual abolition of the pass law system resulted in the acceleration of the rural exodus, which even worsened the housing shortage. Together with demographic growth, these factors contributed to the rise in urban shantytowns and the worsening of the phenomenon of overpopulation in existing dwellings.

In a general way, the segregation policy accentuated the inequalities that exist in all third world countries between cities and rural areas. The bulk of economic activity, and therefore jobs, is concentrated in urban areas, where the higher income population categories also reside, especially the largely urbanised white population. Conversely, rural regions, where little more than half of the population lives, experience widespread poverty: according to DFID, 72 per cent of the poor live in rural areas and 71 per cent of the rural population is considered poor (as against 28 per cent living in urban areas). The lack of employment plays a significant role in this situation. Thus, the (extended) rural unemployment rate reached an extremely high level of 51 per cent, much higher than the average level in urban areas (33 per cent). This situation is the opposite of what is witnessed in most developing countries, where the rural unemployment rate is lower than that registered in urban areas.

The census shows that the country's two richest provinces, the main region of Gauteng (Johannesburg-Pretoria) and the Western Cape (Cape Province) are the most urbanised (Table 5). Their relative wealth can partly be explained by the effect of the over-representation of whites in their population. More than half the white South Africans live in these two provinces, which, however, account for barely a quarter of the country's population. But the main explanation of their privileged situation regards their level of development, since the two provinces in question generate more than half South African's GDP. For these reasons, the income of all the ethnic groups there are higher than those in the rest of the country. Gauteng is also the province which has the largest proportion of shacks: a quarter of the population, or more than a third of the black population, live in such housing. This proportion is also very high in the Western Cape.

Table 5:
Regional inequalities in South Africa (1996)

Socio-economic indicators (% of total population)	Two richest regions		Two poorest regions		Total SA
	Gauteng	Western Cape	Northern Province	Eastern Cape	
Poor*	17	28	59	71	50
Rate of extended unemployment	28	18	46	49	34
Rural population	3	11	89	63	46
Share/population country	18	10	12	16	100
Population living in shacks	1	1	32	41	18
Illiterates	10	7	37	21	19
Life expectation	66	65	63	64	64
Share of whites	23	21	2	5	11

* 1995
Source: Statistics South Africa and DFID
NB: North-west Province has a poverty rate of 62%, which would place it in second-last position before the Eastern Cape. This result, however, is not considered significant.

Conversely, the poorest provinces are those that account for the largest proportion of the rural population: this proportion is 89 per cent in the Northern Province and 63 per cent in the Eastern Cape. About two-thirds of the population there are considered to be poor, with half of them being unemployed. Among the former independent homelands, one (Venda) was situated in the first of these provinces, bordering Zimbabwe, and two (Ciskei and Transkei) were situated in the second, which is the poorest in the country. These former homelands formed true pockets of poverty. Little economic activity was developed in these territories, designed to serve as labour reservoirs for mines, farms or bordering cities. They generally had a very high population density, given that the government's policy consisted of saturating the receiving capacity of these territories, while at the same time limiting their size to a minimum, in order to prevent them from encroaching upon white parts of South Africa.

All other indicators confirm that extreme inequalities in living conditions divide the different population categories. Blacks had limited access to basic services: only 27 per cent had running water at home (as against 96 per cent for whites); 34 per cent had use of a toilet (99 per cent for whites), and 10 per cent of a telephone (89 per cent for whites). Their life expectancy is much lower than that of whites (63 against 73 years). Their infant mortality is three times higher than that of whites. Maternal mortality during labour was 400 out of every 100 000 for black women, as against six out of every 100 000 for white women.

The RDP – improving the living conditions of the population

Shortly before coming into power in 1994, the ANC defined the main orientation of its economic and social transformation policy in the framework of the RDP. This programme was in line with the Freedom Charter of the ANC, which was itself inspired by the philosophy of the post-war welfare state:
- All people shall have the right to live where they choose, to be decently housed, and to bring up their families in comfort and security;
- Unused housing space to be available to the people;
- Rent and prices shall be lowered, food plentiful and no one shall go hungry;
- A preventative health scheme shall be run by the state;
- Free medical health care and hospitalisation shall be provided for all, with special care for mothers and young children;
- Slums shall be demolished and new suburbs built where all have transport, roads, lighting, playing fields and social centres;
- The aged, the orphans, the disabled and the sick shall be cared for by the state.[11]

The RDP laid down a number of very ambitious quantitative objectives in both the social and infrastructure arenas, aiming to expand the population's access to housing and basic services by:
- constructing one million houses between then and the year 2000;
- providing electricity to 2,5 million additional households in the same years, thus doubling the number of households connected to the network (from 36 to 72 per cent);

---

11 African National Congress, 1955.

- providing running water and access to the sanitary network to the entire population in the long term;
- ensuring that everyone had access to healthcare and telecommunications;
- ensuring free medical care to all children under six years old and to pregnant women;
- extending the number of years of free and compulsory education to 10 years;
- redistributing 30 per cent of agricultural land to small black farmers.

The importance attached to this programme was concretised after the 1994 elections by the nomination of a minister without portfolio, responsible for the RDP in the government and by the establishment of a special fund to finance these projects. The clumsiness and bureaucratic nature of this mode of operation, however, became apparent very quickly. The technical ministries were therefore forced to distinguish – in a somewhat fictitious manner – between investment expenditures that came under the RDP and those that came under the remaining projects. The ad hoc ministry's position in government also remained vague. Without direct responsibility in managing the whole RDP fund, it only remained a co-ordinator to some degree, unable to correct shortcomings in project implementation. This ministry was abolished in 1996, and every technical ministry's programming of its investment programmes became much more flexible.

An analysis of the implementation of the highly ambitious objectives of the RDP shows that several of these were almost reached by the year 2000.

At the same time, the population's aspirations were probably most significant and most urgent in the area of housing. It is also the area in which the government programme experienced the most implementation difficulties initially, considering its complexity. The plan of action foresaw the allocation of a maximum subsidy of R15 000 (upgraded to R16 000 in 1999) a house, managed by the provinces. The decentralisation of the programme, as well as the granting of progressive subsidies according to income, turned out to be difficult to manage. After difficult beginnings, the programme was on track by 2000: 660 000 housing units have been built by mid-1998 and 900 000 subsidies approved, suggesting that the objective of building one million dwellings was well on the way to being reached. Admittedly, the mediocre quality and the scaled-down size of the houses that have been built, sometimes labelled as matchboxes, are being criticised. Even if one considers the size of the families, one should nevertheless bear in mind that five million South Africans who were previously accommodated under precarious conditions have acquired a house during the first five years of the realisation of this programme, which constitutes an undeniable success.

An equally significant effort has been made to develop other infrastructure. In his last parliamentary opening speech at the beginning of 1999, Nelson Mandela gave the following assessment of his presidency in this area:
- From 1994 to 1998 three million inhabitants of rural areas had been given access to a source of drinking water; whereas 30 per cent of the population had no drinking water in 1994, this had been reduced to 20 per cent.
- More than two million additional homes had been connected to the electricity network; henceforth 63 per cent of the population had electricity at home.
- 1,3 million telephone lines had been installed; by the year 2000, 35 per cent of the population own a telephone, against only 25 per cent in 1994.

Finally, in accordance with the orientation of the RDP, priority has been given to health and education: according to official estimates, the number of children attending school increased by 1,5 million from 1994 to 1995; five million children receive a free meal every day at their school; and 500 new clinics have been built, ensuring five million additional people a medical service close to where they live.

On the other hand, agrarian reform has shown very slow progress. Less than one per cent of cultivated land has been redistributed, which is very far removed from the declared objective, which, it is true, was obviously unrealistic. However, it could with difficulty be otherwise, insofar as the government chose a market-led redistribution approach, necessarily longer and more costly for the public purse. At the same time, this land redistribution benefit those who have been deprived of land, as well as the victims of forced removals, whether it concerns entire communities (the descendants of Bushmen, for example) or individuals.

Once infrastructure investments have been realised, the question arises of how to manage them and how users are to pay for services. The lack of creditworthiness of the intended beneficiaries of these new installations often prevents them either from paying their rental, or from making full use of these. Many households thus only use electricity for lighting. This casts doubts on the profitability of these investments and therefore on the continuation of current programmes. Added to this is the negative impact of the culture of non-payment prevalent in the country. Large boycott campaigns were actually launched under apartheid, and many people often have difficulty in changing their behaviour.

In addition, the investment plans of the large public electricity and telecommunications companies naturally concentrate new connections around those areas close to the existing network, which tends to exclude the poorest and most isolated regions. Thus, the Eastern Cape and Northern Province, which respectively have only seven per cent and three per cent of existing telephone lines, are allocated only a minute number of new connections each year, less than one per cent of their population. Many shantytown dwellers without property rights are obviously also excluded from these plans. Therefore, instead of reducing inequalities in living conditions and geographical disparities, these investments at times run the risk of accentuating these differences over the next few years, to the detriment of the poorest section of the population.

Affirmative action for equal opportunity in the workplace

In the framework of the apartheid policy, skilled jobs were almost all reserved for whites, with blacks allowed mainly unskilled, agricultural and domestic worker jobs.

The "Bantu" education policy, first implemented after the Second World War, aimed above all to create a servile labour force. Hendrik Verwoerd, Prime Minister from 1958 to 1966 and the ideologist of apartheid, stated it thus:

> *Of what use is it to teach mathematics to a Bantu child, if he does not need to use it in practice? It is absurd. There is no place for the native in the European community beyond the level of some manual work. They need to be taught that equality is not for them.*[12]

---

12 Cited by the Commission of Inquiry into Apartheid in South Africa, 1978.

At the end of the 1980s, despite the remarkable progress of this ratio during the previous decade, the expenditure on each black pupil represented only 25 per cent of the expenditure on each white pupil. To equalise the education expenditures between the ethnic groups by basing it on the expenditure for the white population would have required these to be raised to 15 per cent of GDP, compared with a percentage of about five per cent of GDP in industrialised countries, and close to seven per cent in South Africa.[13]

According to the 1996 census data, 24 per cent of black adults over the age of 20 years had never gone to school and 44 per cent of blacks (or about 7 million adults) could be considered illiterate, if one defines as illiterate those people who never finished primary school. This percentage indicates a distinct deterioration, compared with the beginning of the 1980s. This can be explained by the schools boycott by black students after the Soweto riots in 1976.

The low number of black tertiary graduates is an indirect consequence of apartheid and the inequalities in education. According to a survey conducted by the Human Sciences Research Council, in 1995 only 67 000 (14 per cent) out of 470 000 South African graduates were blacks.[14] Moreover, the majority of them held arts, philosophy, law or education degrees. Conversely, a minuscule number of blacks pursued scientific studies: the survey lists only 455 black engineers, and 69 economists. These characteristics persist despite the end of apartheid: in 1995, black students earned only 14 per cent of tertiary degrees awarded in the natural sciences, engineering, computer sciences and mathematics.[15]

The marked inequality in qualifications, dividing the labour force according to ethnic groupings (Table 6), is the direct result of this situation, as demonstrated by a household survey conducted in 1997, which used four categories to classify occupations: managerial, professional and technical or semi-professional; clerical, sales and service; artisan and operator; and elementary occupations. Whereas two-thirds of whites were employed in one of the first two categories, close to two-thirds of blacks are in one of two little or unqualified employment categories. Thirty per cent of black women and 10 per cent of coloured women who have a job were employed as domestic workers in 1997.

---

13 Lundahl and Moritz, 1994.
14 Cited by the South African Institute of Race Relations, 1998.
15 Sidiropoulos, 1997.

Table 6:
Labour distribution by employment category according to sex and race (1997)

	Blacks		Coloureds		Indians		Whites		Total	
	M	F	M	F	M	F	M	F	M	F
Managerial & professional	13,9	20,2	15,3	20,2	37,5	33,7	45,9	45,4	21,3	25,3
Sales, clerical & service staff	15,5	17,2	12,5	24,1	21,6	41,6	14,4	37,5	15,2	23,0
Skilled artisans & operators	39,9	10,7	36,7	11,5	22,7	12,7	23,9	4,5	35,5	9,8
Unskilled jobs	22,0	28,1	28,1	38,3	9,6	4,8	6,4	3,2	19,4	34,9
Sundry	8,7	6,5	7,4	5,9	8,6	7,2	9,4	9,4	8,6	7,0
Total	100,0	100,0	100,0	100,0	100,0	100,0	100,0	100,0	100,0	100,0

Source: Statistics South Africa, October 1997 Household Survey

The extent of these inequalities has led the government to realise the necessity of introducing a policy of "positive discrimination" towards the disadvantaged population.

The White Paper on affirmative action in the public sector, published in 1998, forced every government agency to develop a programme aimed at ensuring that the distribution of officials reflected that of the population: from 1999, 50 per cent of senior officials had to be black (African, coloured, and Indian populations all being considered "black"), 30 per cent had to be women, and two per cent disabled.[16] New targets will be set from the year 2000, which will be revised every three years.

The policy of affirmative action is by nature relatively easy to implement in the public sector, which has about 1,2 million officials. On the other hand, it will be much more complicated to enforce in the private sector. The Employment Equity Act, passed in 1998, provides the legal framework for this policy. Based on what is provided for in the public sector, it forces all companies of a certain size (more than 150 employees or R10 million turnover) to prepare a strategy to achieve employment equity. One has to bear in mind that about 10 000 companies could be eligible to apply this law, but only 3000 had registered by June, 2000.

---

16 At the end of 1997, 62 per cent of senior civil servants were still white, as against only 31 per cent of blacks. Similarly, although there were as many female as male officials, the former represented only 12 per cent of senior officials.

CHAPTER 3 Two South African nations

The law forces private sector employees to be classified according to their race. According to the five-year plan, every employer has to identify the under-representation of each racial group at the business level and for every level of responsibility, and has to fix targets for balancing the labour force demographically. An annual report has to be submitted to the Minister of Labour, supposedly to verify the implementation of the plan, with employees and trade unions also being invited to play a verification role in this regard. The law, in fact, is very vague on the quantitative targets which companies have to aim for.

The Employment Equity Act has been sharply criticised in employers' circles, all the opposition parties and by some liberal ideologists, such as the South African Institute of Race Relations. The imprecision of its targets has led to a fear of arbitrary action on the part of the Minister of Labour to ensure that this Act is respected. It has also been underlined that its implementation will place a constant bureaucratic burden both on companies and the government. From a more ideological point of view, the fact that the law is leading to the reconstruction of the notion of race, whose abolition was at the centre of the struggle against apartheid, is an indisputable paradox!

If one leaves behind the ideological terrain and practical questions of how to implement the Act, the main question that needs to be considered is in fact the following: can this law reach its objective, which is to improve the representation of blacks in the business world at all levels, without damaging economic efficiency?

The example of the United States is often cited to prove the success of affirmative action policies. According to an American study conducted in 1995, five million employees stemming from ethnic minorities and six million women have actually benefited from these programmes by having access to better jobs, which they would not have had in the absence of these policies.[17] The fact that there is currently a trend towards renouncing these types of policies in the United States[18] is hardly significant in this regard, insofar as it partly conveys the feeling that they have reached their main objectives.

The problem, however, is obviously very different in South Africa. First of all, affirmative action does not concern ethnic minorities – blacks,

---

17 *Financial Mail*, 14/11/1997.

18 The United States Supreme Court decided not to annul proposition 209, passed by a referendum in California, which prohibited the implementation of racial preferences in public sector employment, as far as education and public transactions are concerned. This decision implies the disappearance of affirmative action policies in that state, with others probably following suit.

71

Chicanos, Asians and so on – as in the United States, but the majority of the population. This means that, if the government has some determination to see them through, these policies will have a major impact on the employment composition and the economy in general. A second significant difference stems from the very low proportion of skilled blacks in the South African population, this trait being considerably more pronounced in this country than it ever was in the United States, even in the 1960s when these policies were first implemented. This shortage of skilled persons will take years to be remedied. During this period, the fear is that many blacks will be employed in responsible positions solely to observe quotas.

Only an intensive policy to train the labour force in the required skills will allow this pitfall to be avoided and this law to be implemented under appropriate conditions. The government is conscious of this priority, as is shown by the training levy paid for by companies since 2000.

Black empowerment – vector to reduce inequalities?

Together with affirmative action, black empowerment constitutes the second axis of the policy implemented by the government to accelerate the integration of blacks into the economy, and to remedy the effects of the segregation traditionally implemented against them as far as employment and participation in the business world were concerned. According to the usual definition, any acquisition or establishment of a business by black business entrepreneurs is considered a black empowerment operation.

The first company under black control was quoted on the Johannesburg Stock Exchange (JSE) in 1994. Five years later, 35 "black chips" (called thus by analogy with blue chips, a designation for the best performing companies on the stock market) were quoted on the JSE. If one adds to this the 76 quoted companies controlled by black business, the latter's share rose to R145 billion (about US$29 billion) at the beginning of 1999, according to Business Map, which represented 16 per cent of the total capitalisation of the Johannesburg Stock Exchange.

The exponential rise in companies controlled by black capital has led the latter to become involved in a large variety of economic sectors: finance, telecommunications and information technology, publishing and communication, industry, food processing, and so on. These companies

CHAPTER 3 Two South African nations

have very diverse origins. Thus, rubbing shoulders with traditional companies (New African Investments (NAIL), Real Africa Holdings) and former reconverted NGOs (Kagiso Trust Investments) are former ANC investment (Thebe Investment) and trade union funds (Mineworkers Investment, Kopano ke Matla, Hosken Consolidated Investments), etc.

The emergence of black business has been favoured, first of all, by the attitude of the large conglomerates, which understood very quickly the political necessity to increase the participation of blacks in the business world. The chairman of Johannesburg Consolidated Mines (JCI) thus stated in 1995:

> *In the new South African political configuration, it is unhealthy that all the levers of the economy are still in white hands. If the rise of black capitalism is too slow, the government could be forced to take unpleasant radical measures.*[19]

Besides, large Anglo-Saxon groups had set in motion a similar process when the Afrikaners, who had been excluded almost entirely from the business world until then, came into power in 1948. To reduce the natural hostility of the government and Afrikaner public opinion towards it, which could have given rise to a desire to nationalise this conglomerate, Anglo American facilitated the establishment of the Sanlam insurance group, to which it sold its subsidiary, General Mining.

The most important black empowerment operations have responded to an identical logic. The leading black group quoted on the JSE, NAIL, was formed in 1994 by Dr Motlana, a leading figure of the internal opposition (and Mandela's former doctor), through the purchasing of the Metropolitan Life insurance company from Sanlam. The second black group, in chronological order, Real Africa Holdings (RAH), was established in the same year when Anglo American sold off one of its insurance companies, African Life, to one of its former employees. More recently, in 1997 Anglo American sold its minority control in the Johnnic and JCI subsidiaries to two black consortiums established for the occasion, the first to the National Economic Consortium (subsidiary of NAIL) and the second to the African Mining Group (AMG).

Moreover, from the beginning, black empowerment has benefited from the active support of the government, which placed this process at the heart of its economic and social transformation policy. This support was conveyed in particular by the granting of public finance to facilitate

---

19 Statement to the *L'Humanité* journal, 29/11/1998.

the acquisition and setting up of companies. The Industrial Development Corporation and the Khula and Ntsika institutions (the latter two specialising in the financing of small and medium enterprises) constituted the secular arm of the state in this area. Furthermore, black business was accorded preference in public transactions going through the state, local communities and public enterprises, as well as in the privatisation framework: 10 per cent of telephone operator Telkom's capital will therefore be reserved for black groups; the concession for the fourth television channel was accorded to a company whose main shareholder is a trade union investment fund, and so on. This favourable climate for black business is prompting foreign investors to form a growing number of alliances with black partners when they make new investments, or indeed to open up the capital of their existing subsidiaries to them, which is contributing to the proliferation and external growth of these companies.

The speed of the process, which is an undeniable success of the government-driven transformation policy, is also its main weakness. Not having any start-up capital at their disposal, these groups were set up by incurring large debts. The high interest rates witnessed in South Africa have weakened the financial structure of these companies, even if the impenetrable nature of the latter prevents an exact appreciation of the scale of the problem. Moreover, the loans of the companies quoted on the stock exchange, which are often constituted as holdings, have generally been guaranteed on the basis of their stock market value. The latter has suffered from the market depression following the 1998 financial crisis. All these factors lead to the realisation that black business still finds itself in a precarious situation.

The example of the failed JCI acquisition, at the time hailed as a model of black empowerment even at the heart of the establishment, that is the gold mining sector, is a testimonial of the risks linked to these operations in an uncertain economic period. The acquisition of JCI in 1997 by the African Global Mining Group, headed by Musi Khumalo, former political prisoner, was in fact symbolic. This mining house that is over a hundred years old, founded by Barney Barnato (unsuccessful rival of Cecil John Rhodes for the control of South African diamond production at the end of the nineteenth century) was listed among the 10 leading gold producers in the world.

The entry of a black group into the mining sector, the symbol of black oppression since the discovery of the first South African deposits in the nineteenth century, in effect had some merit.

Unfortunately, this operation presented serious risks from its inception. In order to win the business from its rival, New Africa Investments, African Global Mining was first of all obliged to pay too much for the acquisition. The purchasing price of US$54 a share was in effect much higher than the market price. Whereas the gold price verged on US$350 an ounce when this deal was being negotiated, it dropped to less than US$300 an ounce one year later. Moreover, affected by the dissent between its leaders, the JCI group saw its price fall to US$13 a share in January 1998. Insofar as the acquisition was guaranteed by JCI's stock market value, company restructuring from then on was inevitable. Hardly a year after its purchase from Anglo, JCI therefore had to resell two of its most profitable gold mines, whereas its coal interests were sold to the Lonhro British conglomerate, and the CMI chrome producer was sold locally. The restructuring of JCI also resulted in most of the black investors withdrawing from its capital base.

The final issue that needs to be considered, is knowing who benefits from black empowerment. If it is only a matter of transferring wealth to a minority of black entrepreneurs, the objective of social transformation will not be reached. In fact, the large deals have been mainly of a financial nature and have not translated into a creation of wealth or additional jobs. In this regard one can contrast them with the example of many small and medium enterprises, led by blacks, which benefit from financial support on a much-reduced scale but probably have more social utility. Similarly, the risks of clientelism are not negligible, particularly where privatisation or public procurement is concerned. The preference given to black business in this arena can lead to much abuse if one does not guard against it: the fact that from August 1996 to the end of 1997, 47 per cent of public tenders have been granted to companies owned by black capital, compared with less than 5 per cent before 1994, is up for scrupulous interpretation.[20]

Aware of this risk, Cyril Ramaphosa, Johnnic chairperson and former secretary-general of the ANC, warned his fellow citizens:

The moment when a growing number of black South Africans acquire companies, it is necessary to show that the latter owes more to the economy than to the colour of their skin.[21]

At the same time, black business can play an active role in promoting the position of blacks in the firms. As Cyril Ramaphosa again remarks, its

---

20 Government's Report to the Nation, 1998.
21 *Sunday Independent*, 1/3/1998.

most useful social role essentially resides in this support for affirmative action:

> *The acquisition of a company by black businesspeople will have limited effect if it is not accompanied by other transformative measures. These include adequate resourcing of education and training within the organisation, affirmative policies of promotion and recruitment to redress demographic anomalies, as well as efforts to transform those elements and structures of the corporate culture that are racially or gender exclusive.*[22]

The potential impact of this should, however, not be exaggerated. To succeed, black business has to respect the laws of profit, in which respect solidarity objectives should be of secondary importance only. It is therefore illusory to expect that the behaviour of these firms towards their employees should be fundamentally different from that of other firms.

It is still too early to give a comprehensive assessment of the social policy implemented by the government since 1994, which will have to be judged over a long-term period.

Affirmative action and black empowerment policies, which have been implemented very defiantly in a very short time, can be considered a relative success. These policies incur two risks. The first risk is linked to the development of crony capitalism, the dangers of which were shown by the Asian crisis, forcing government to demonstrate extreme rigour in their implementation. The second is linked to the fact that, without reducing the social inequalities throughout the entire population, these policies risk contributing to heightening these within the black population. Even before the change in government, as black incomes started catching up with those of whites, this process has led to an increase in the disparities within this population category. Without recent data at one's disposal, everything, however, leads to the belief that this simultaneous process of a reduction in interracial inequalities and an increase in intra-racial inequalities (within each ethnic group) has been going on since 1994.

As seen above, the government's action can also be judged favourably as far as the improvement of the population's living conditions in the framework of the RDP is concerned. The anticipated increase in the access of the entire population to housing and public services is neverthe-

---

22 *Ibid.*

less stymied, on the one hand by how to finance investments from an unreformed fiscal base, and on the other by the fact that this programme affects a largely destitute population. More generally, the struggle against exclusion and poverty in a third world country cannot be satisfied merely through aid. In fact, a policy that will genuinely reduce social inequalities needs also to reduce the scourge of unemployment, which affects the black population in a massive way.

CHAPTER 4

An orthodox economic policy

The challenges facing the country were not hard to identify ... but their magnitude and their intractability were only fully revealed as the euphoric glow of the mid-90s faded. South Africa came to occupy its true status as a middle-order nation struggling to undertake complex and difficult economic and political reforms in a highly competitive world. Though the world wished South Africa well and wanted it to succeed, no special favours could be expected, and indeed none has been forthcoming.

— Julian Ogilvie Thompson, Anglo American Chairman[1]

The democratic transition entered into after many decades of struggle has given rise to tremendous hopes among the black population that they will experience an improvement in their living conditions. Confronted with this expectation, the ANC has been conscious that many predicted that it would fail following its coming into power. One of its most frequent anxieties was about the risk carried by a populist policy considered by orthodox economists likely to push the economy, already in trouble, into a serious crisis.

The ANC therefore found it imperative to ensure the credibility of its economic policy, both internally and externally, while rallying the largest possible majority of the population behind these objectives in view of ensuring national reconciliation. Its economic thinking has evolved very rapidly under the influence of think tanks and employers, the latter having led a fervent direct lobbying campaign. Presented on the eve of the 1994 elections as an integrated and coherent framework for economic and social policy, the Reconstruction and Development Programme (RDP) was abandoned as an overall strategy at the end of only two years.

---

1   Anglo American, Chairman's statement, 1998.

Having dismissed any hint of a social revolution project, the new government set itself the primary goal of increasing economic growth, and ensuring that it would create jobs. This appeared indispensable in the fight against the scourge of unemployment and to enable an improvement in the black population's living conditions.

The restructuring of a crisis-ridden economy was imperative to reach this objective. If international sanctions had played a role in this crisis, everyone was aware that a number of dysfunctions had become increasingly evident. In short, it was a matter of "normalising" the apartheid economy by transforming it into a modern economy, open to the outside world.

Launched in 1996, the Growth, Employment and Redistribution Programme (GEAR) forms the framework for the macroeconomic policy implemented by the government since that date. The "Washington Consensus" liberal ideology permeates this programme. Here, redistribution is of secondary importance, as is indicated by its position in the acronym. It is a structural adjustment programme, of which a significant aspect is macroeconomic stabilisation. This is ambiguous on two accounts: on the one hand, the new government views itself as being forced to remedy the effects of its predecessor's incompetence, even though the democratic transition has given rise to tremendous expectations on the part of the black population with a view to satisfying its needs; on the other hand, the ANC, historically in favour of a significant role for the state in the economy, has been brought to oversee the liberalisation of the economy, something that the apartheid government, while extolling the virtues of the market, was never in a position to do.[2]

From "growth through redistribution" to "redistribution through growth"

Since 1990, the liberation of Nelson Mandela and the unbanning of the ANC have pointed to this organisation's imminent accession to government. The period preceding the first democratic elections in 1994 saw intense debates unfolding on the direction that the policies of the new government to exit from the polls should take.

---

2   This chapter draws a lot on Cling, 1999.

Somewhat astonishingly for a political movement that is nearly ninety years old, the ANC did not have any distinct economic programme. The latter boiled down to the Freedom Charter, which advocated the creation of a type of mixed economy and the nationalisation of large mining groups such as Anglo American:

The People shall share in the country's wealth! The national wealth of our country, the heritage of all South Africans shall be restored to the people. The mineral wealth beneath the soil, the banks and monopoly industry shall be transferred to the ownership of the people as a whole. All other industries and trade shall be controlled to assist the well-being of the people.[3]

A first attempt to clarify the ANC's economic policy programme was made in 1990 in the framework of a "Discussion Document on Economic Policy". This document was based on a philosophy of "growth through redistribution". It was a question of stimulating economic growth through a policy of income redistribution aimed at satisfying the basic needs of the population. This policy of active state intervention covered all economic sectors.

Economic restructuring presupposed the dismantling of large conglomerates to increase competition and encourage the creation of small and medium enterprises. In particular, it envisaged a restructuring of the financial sector, judged to be too speculative. A rise in company tax was proposed. Somewhat naïvely, the document anticipated a rapid expansion of foreign investment flowing into the country, which it wanted to direct towards priority sectors. This hope can be explained by the belief that the disinvestments of the preceding decades had been due strictly to political factors.

That being the case, it would be enough to sort out these problems in order to receive a massive influx of investments. This Keynesian-inspired document immediately sparked off numerous critiques on the part of employers and mainstream economists.[4]

President Thabo Mbeki, then director of International Relations for the ANC, clearly set out the terms of the debate at the time:

---

3 African National Congress, 1955.
4 Marais, 1998.

CHAPTER 4 An orthodox economic policy

For many of the establishment economists their concern is clearly that, in the desire to meet the aspirations of the people, a democratic South African government will overstretch the resources and thus undermine the growth potential of the economy. For those economists committed to the democratic movement, their major concern has been the redistribution of income and wealth.[5]

Several factors have contributed to the ANC's gradual renunciation of this philosophy and to its conversion to more orthodox policies. First of all, the unbundling of the Soviet Union and the collapse of all the communist regimes in eastern Europe have played a major role in the evolution of this organisation's economic thinking. Many ANC leaders also wished to avoid repeating the errors committed in many African countries after their independence, having seen at close range, while in exile, the decline of countries such as Tanzania and Zambia that had followed socialist-inspired economic policies. Finally, the debates involving these subjects abroad and in South Africa itself have influenced the thinking of future leaders.

In 1991, the American political scientist Francis Fukuyama warned against the illusion that South Africa could follow a process similar to that in Germany, where the developed part of the country peacefully absorbed the less developed part and where, after suffering a temporary fall in revenue, it has caused the less developed part to catch up with its level of development.[6]

Besides the discovery that German unification took much longer and was much costlier than had previously been believed, this author observed that the comparison is fallacious for several reasons.

According to Fukuyama then, a widespread error of judgement to which many years of apartheid have contributed and which is shared by many blacks, has caused people to think of South Africa as a rich Western-type country, which has simply failed to distribute adequately its wealth among the black population. In fact, South Africa is a middle-income developing country.

Furthermore, wealth distribution bears no comparison to that of Germany where the richest and most developed part was also much larger than the eastern part. In fact, it is clear that whatever levy is imposed on

---

5   Preface to Howe and Le Roux, 1992.
6   Fukuyama, 1991.

the wealth of the four million white South Africans, it will not be sufficient to equalise the living standard of the rest of the population.[7]

The scenario fashion, introduced by Anglo American at the end of the 1980s with the so-called "High Road" scenarios[8] reached its peak at the beginning of the 1990s. In the 1993 social-democratic inspired "Mont Fleur" scenarios[9], different economic policy options are presented in the form of the flights of "Icarus", the "ostrich", the "flamingo", and the "wild duck". The "growth through redistribution" proposition, described by Fukuyama as the "Latin-American" scenario, in this becomes the "Flight of Icarus", where an increase of the budget deficit translates into an inflationary push, a decline of the current deficit, currency depreciation and finally, collapse of the economy.

The dramatic nature of these types of scenarios, as well as their simplicity and the "common sense" which seems to inspire them, helps to explain their considerable impact on the debates waged in South Africa. In this respect, they have reached their basic objective in all respects, which was to bring to the attention the serious consequences, according to them, of certain economic policy choices that might have been tempting to the new government.

The ANC presented the RDP, which showed certain similarities to a government programme, on the eve of the first democratic elections in 1994. As its name indicates, the RDP aimed to promote economic development at the same time as the redistribution of wealth – called reconstruction here – within the nation. This Keynesian-inspired programme concentrated on ways through which to accelerate economic growth and investment. Despite its declarations of intent, the RDP was a long way from being a coherent and clear economic policy programme.

The RDP was conceived as an integrated and sustainable programme, guided by the population, which aimed to provide peace and security for all, build the nation, and reunite the "first" and "third" world in one South African

---

7   Mbeki resumed this theme several years later, in a speech presented to parliament in May 1998. He denounced the white community as being hostile to any redistribution effort, contrasting them with the solidarity shown by the Germans at the time of their unification. According to him, the seriousness with which the German population has managed this unification process has manifested in the massive volume of resource transfers arranged by West Germany towards its poorer neighbour in the East. During the first five years of unification (1990–1995), US$586,5 billion in public funds were transferred from West to East in order to bring the two parts of Germany closer economically. In South Africa, then, only a "solidarity tax" was imposed for one year.
8   Sunter, 1987.
9   Le Roux, 1993.

society. Its objective was to link reconstruction and development, by opposing the perception according to which growth and development or growth and redistribution are contradictory, and to democratise South Africa.

To finance the massive cost of these programmes, the RDP anticipated, above all, a budgetary rationalisation that would be likely to generate new resources. The anticipated increase in growth was also in this direction. The RDP's economic policy section, however, was extremely general beyond the diagnosis of the weaknesses of the South African economy. This diagnosis touched on the serious structural crisis necessitating fundamental economic reconstruction, the wearing out of the import substitution regime, characterised by low productivity and wages, as well as the drop in public and private investment, the economy's inability to create jobs, and the excessive concentration of the productive apparatus.

Unlike the social and infrastructure areas, the envisaged economic policy measures remained extremely vague and cautious. The paragraph on the respective roles of the public and private sectors in the economy is testimony to the extreme caution exercised in this arena by the future governing party, which was not yet in a position to announce its conversion to economic liberalism on the eve of the elections:

> *In restructuring the public sector to carry out national goals, the balance of evidence will guide the decision for or against various economic policy measures. The democratic government must therefore consider:*
> - *increasing the public sector in strategic areas through, for example, nationalisation, purchasing a shareholding in companies, establishing new public corporations or joint ventures with the private sector, and*
> - *reducing the public sector in certain areas in ways that enhance efficiency, advance affirmative action and empower the historically disadvantaged, while ensuring the protection of both consumers and the rights and employment of workers.*[10]

The RDP White Paper, developed a few months after the elections, was subsequently regarded as the government's official programme.[11] First of all, the White Paper was much less precise and ambitious as far as social objectives were concerned than the previous base document. The

---

10 African National Congress, 1994
11 South African government, 1994.

only objective that had a figure put to it affected the financing of the programme: R5 billion budgeted for 1995/1996 (after R2,5 billion in 1994/1995), R10 billion for 1997/1998 and R12,5 billion subsequently, or the bulk of the capital expenditures listed in the government's budget. On the other hand, all the other quantitative objectives, particularly those concerning the satisfaction of basic needs, disappeared.

The White Paper, by contrast, was much more precise and coherent than the base document as far as economic policy was concerned. It emphasised the obstacles to growth and investment, such as public deficits and the excessive share of public expenditure in the GDP. The essentials of the GEAR philosophy could already be found in this document, which specified the government strategy in five points: maintaining monetary and fiscal discipline; establishing a favourable environment for economic growth; implementing industrial and trade policies aimed at opening up the economy to a greater degree; modernising professional training; and reforming the labour market.

The cabinet reshuffling which took place in 1996 when the National Party left the Government of National Unity provided the occasion to do away with the RDP ministry created in 1994. Without being officially abandoned, the RDP has been replaced *de facto* by the GEAR. Despite the government's systematic reminder since this date of the coherence between the two programmes and the fact that the implementation of the RDP is continuing in the framework of the GEAR, it is clear that its priorities have changed. In fact, the adoption of the GEAR sanctioned the conversion of the ANC to a market economy and the relegation of the objective of redistribution to a position of secondary importance.

Evaluating the GEAR

Developed with the assistance of the World Bank, the GEAR displays all the characteristics of a structural adjustment programme, albeit of a different scope; whereas it did take out a loan from the IMF[12] as soon as it came into power, the South African government has subsequently systematically refused to appeal to the Bretton Woods institutions. In this

---

12 This loan totalling US$850 million was intended officially to finance food imports. It has in fact never been used and was reimbursed in full in 1998. One might think, however, that this call upon the IMF responded to the same concern about "credibility", which the government sought for its entire economic policy.

CHAPTER 4 An orthodox economic policy

sense, the GEAR is without doubt a structural adjustment plan, but one that is self-imposed.

The GEAR starts off from the following basis: by continuing the tendencies witnessed since the government came into power, growth will reach no more than three per cent a year over the following years. This will not resolve the problem of employment and will prevent the financing of planned public investment programmes. In the best tradition of French five-year plans, the GEAR is looking for a way in which to realise a six per cent growth rate a year by the year 2000, when the programme will expire. This growth rate was supposed to allow for the creation of 400 000 jobs a year and a total of 1,3 million jobs from 1996 to 2000, or 830 000 more than in the base scenario.

Following a neo-classical inspiration, the GEAR considers savings to be the source of investment and therefore of growth in the long term. Now, the South African economy suffers from a lack of savings. The GEAR estimates that the sheer size of the budget deficit is the source of important crowding out effects that are to the detriment of private investment. It is therefore a question of gradually reducing the deficit to encourage private savings and of striving towards disinflation: the plan is thus to reduce the annual inflation rate to less than 10 per cent. Besides, in the continuation of the RDP, public finances are being called on to continue giving greater importance to social infrastructure and redistribution expenditures. The planned speeding-up of the privatisation programme is one way to finance the ambitious public investment programme in the area of public services.

The objective of increasing the job content of growth, according to the GEAR, would happen by launching job-intensive investment, greater labour market flexibility, as well as a modification of the tax system and a decrease in the relative cost of labour in relation to capital. The plan is also to aim for a gradual removal of exchange controls (the financial rand was finally abolished in 1995) and to continue reducing customs duties, to emphasise the opening up of the economy.

In principle, the government does not have direct influence on the monetary policy implemented by the Reserve Bank, whose independence is guaranteed by the new constitution. The GEAR, however, assigns responsibility to the Reserve Bank to keep the real exchange rate stable at a competitive level, while preventing a resurgence of inflation. This formulation is in fact close to that of the Bank's statutes, which stipulate its responsibility to protect the value of the currency.

This programme of growth through exports and investment rests on several strong assumptions: it first assumed a gradual reduction of real interest rates (up to 3 per cent), which is a condition of increased investment and a rise in savings; a second assumption was an increase in the private savings rate, as well as significant capital inflows (the objective is to reach 4 per cent of GDP), which are likely to lift the financial constraints on the economy and increase the global investment rate from 20 to 26 per cent of GDP.

The relief among employers' circles at the announcement of the GEAR resembled the scale of the anxieties created by the change in government and the ANC's previous radical position before it came into power. The accolades offered by Nicky Oppenheimer testify of this:

> *It is all too easy to forget where the African National Congress came from and what it stood for in its past history, and the extent to which it has, in a remarkably short time, matured into a government which understands and accepts the disciplines of the marketplace ... The Growth, Employment and Redistribution document ... both deserved and received the support of all elements of South African society.*[13]

Whereas the assessment of this programme was indisputably positive in terms of monetary and fiscal stabilisation, this is not the case as far as growth and employment are concerned, where results are much below the objectives. About 450 000 formal jobs have been lost in the South African economy between 1994 and 2000.[14]

It can be noted in this regard that the restructuring of the state and public enterprises has produced some initial results.

In this area, the liabilities left behind by the former government were particularly heavy: the budget deficit represented 10 per cent of GDP during the 1993/1994 financial year. This deficit, made worse by the recession that tended to reduce fiscal revenue, was also due to the integration into the civil service of former homeland officials, who were granted considerable salary benefits, as well as a remedial social policy which was activated on the eve of the democratic transition. Public enterprises were also hardly functioning efficiently, having served previously to help ensure full employment for the Afrikaner population.

---

13 South Africa Foundation, 1997.
14 SSA 2000.

CHAPTER 4 An orthodox economic policy

In other respects, the ratio of state expenditure related to GDP has experienced a downward movement since 1997 (their share of 31 per cent of GDP, witnessed in 1998/1999, is nevertheless still relatively high for a developing country).

It was thus possible to realise substantial savings owing to the end of apartheid, notably as far the military was concerned. A reduction in the size of the civil service, whose over-development was one of apartheid's legacies, was embarked upon. About 150 000 jobs have been axed between 1994 and 2000 with the government considering about 55 000 posts still to be superfluous. The sunset clauses written into the 1996 constitution, which obliged the government to retain the former regime's officials and prohibited massive redundancies, have acted as a brake on this restructuring.

Despite the drop in overall expenditure, the increase in social expenditure, which in 1998/99 accounted for 60 per cent of total expenditure (apart from interest charges), has continued. Greater importance has thus been given to education and health. At the same time, one has witnessed a sizeable increase in debt servicing as a result of the rise in interest rates.

The budget deficit has been reduced by two-thirds over a few years in the framework of this policy, with the current account balance (before debt repayment) showing a surplus. With a deficit initially estimated at 3,3 per cent of GDP, then revised to only 2,9 per cent of GDP in 1998/1999, the GEAR's objective (3 per cent of GDP) was reached despite the economic recession (Graph 6-a). The budget deficit for 1999/2000 was close to that of the previous year.[14] The reduction of the budget deficit has allowed public debt to be stabilised at a moderate level (50 per cent of GDP at the end of 1998).

The restructuring of public enterprises has also been embarked upon. Faced with opposition from trade unions, this only really took place after the 1999 general elections. The main transactions concerned the partial privatisation of the telephone operator Telkom, South African Airways, (20% to Swissair) and the South African Airports Company. The privatisation of Safcol, a company in charge of managing public forest

---

14 The downward revision of the 1998/1999 deficit can be explained by a new calculation of GDP presented in June 1999. The new assessment of GDP for 1999 was therefore 10 per cent higher than the previous one, which accordingly reduced the total deficit, expressed in GDP points (as well as that of public and in particular external debt). The anticipated deficit for 1999/2000, initially 3,5 per cent of GDP, also benefited from this revision.

estates, was launched in 1999. Public enterprise management contracts have been entrusted to private companies. That of the Post Office was therefore granted to a consortium comprising its counterparts in New Zealand. The management of the Aventura leisure group has been entrusted to a large local hotel group i.e. Protea hotels.

A second success has been achieved as far as inflation is concerned. It has gone down from an annual two-digit rate since the beginning of the 1980s to an annual rate in the order of only five to six per cent from 1999 onwards (Graph 6-b).

This distinct deflation process, which took place even faster than anticipated, was made possible by the reduction of the budget deficit, combined with a restrictive monetary policy, as well as the fall in the price of imported energy.

However, growth performance was much lower than predicted (Graph 6-c): the average growth during the period (about 2 per cent a year) only just allowed the GDP per capita to be stabilised.

The hint of economic recovery in 1993, confirmed in 1994, relied on a certain number of factors: a recovery in the confidence of economic role-players, linked to the prospect of democratic transition; an income increase made possible by the success of the social struggle; and the lifting of external constraints made possible by the end of financial sanctions.

Since this date, all the components of private demand registered a high growth: from 1994 to 1997, household consumption increased on average by 4,2 per cent a year and total investment by 7,8 per cent a year. The expansion in investment came both from public infrastructure investment and the private sector. This included above all replacement investments, which resulted in a rejuvenation of the average age of machinery, increasing their productivity more than the expansion of production capacity inasmuch as the degree to which they were used remained at levels far below their saturation point. External demand was also very dynamic as goods and services exports increased by 7,3 per cent a year (11,7 per cent a year for imports). The gap between exports and imports led to a downturn in the trade balance, which nevertheless continued to show a surplus, and a drop in the current account deficit, which registered a systematic surplus until then. The deficit, however, remained moderate (around 1,5 per cent of GDP).

This partly cyclical recovery after several years of recession was of short duration. Whereas the GEAR predicted a gradual increase in

CHAPTER 4 An orthodox economic policy

Graph 6:
GEAR forecasts and performance
6-a Budget deficit (% of GDP)

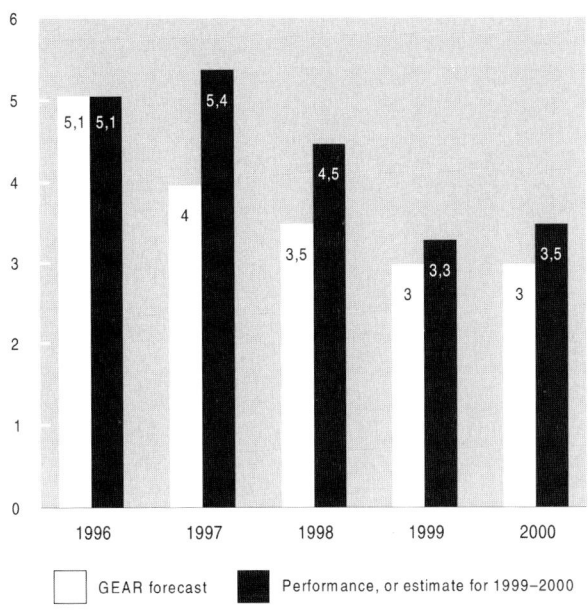

Source: Department of Finance

6-b Inflation (CPI annual average %)

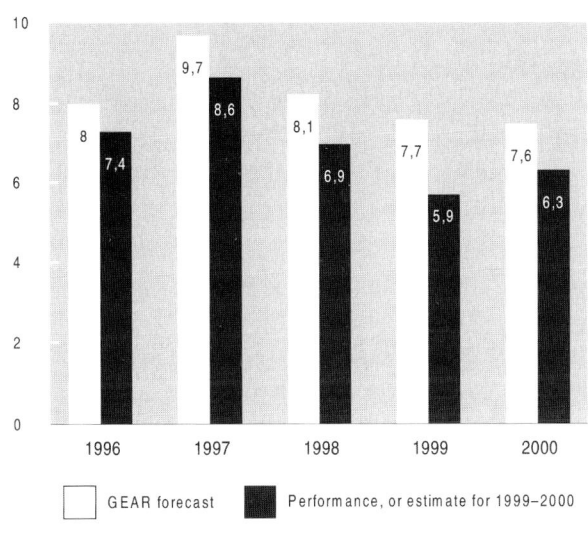

Source: Investec

89

From isolation to integration: the post-apartheid South African economy

6-c GDP growth (%)

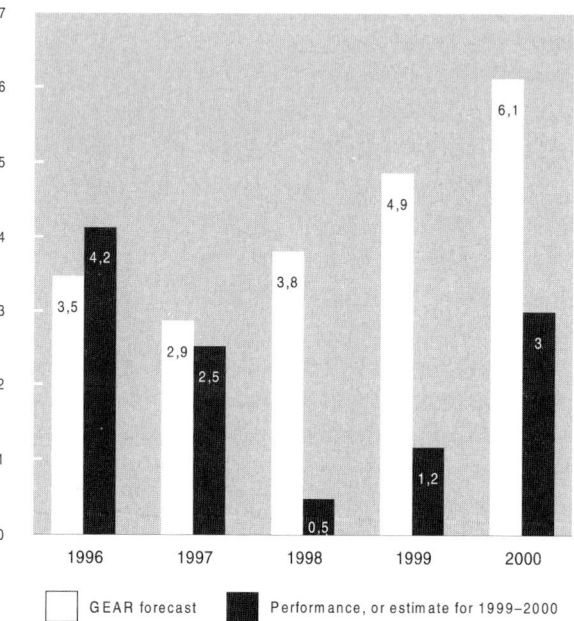

Source: Investec

6-d Employment variation (cumulative/thousand)

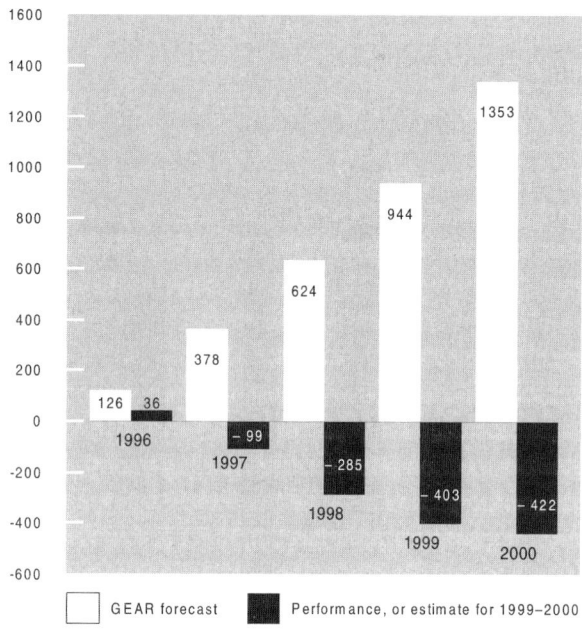

Source: Statistics SA and Investec

economic growth over the 1996–2000 period, the contrary has happened: a gradual slowing down in growth has been evident since 1997, with the soft landing in 1997 being transformed into stagnation in 1998. In spite of the economic recovery in 2000, the growth rate at the turn of the century was much lower than predicted. On the whole, despite its slight rise since 1994, the investment rate has remained too low (18 per cent of GDP in 1998).

As a result, the decreasing trend in total employment could hardly be curbed (Graph 6-d). The decline in employment has affected both the public and private sectors (industry, trade, construction, services sector and mines). Close to half the job losses have occurred in the mining sector, and more particularly the gold mines that have lost half their employees since 1990 (this is apart from the agricultural sector, for which there is hardly any reliable data available). Insofar as around 450 000 young people enter the job market every year, this has resulted in the continuation of a very rapid rise in unemployment.

Partly contradictory objectives

Several factors, both external and internal, can assist in understanding why the policy followed by the government failed to result in the expected economic growth.

Even though growth had already clearly started slowing down, the South African economy first of all partly suffered the consequences of the international crisis that started in Asia in 1997. It was affected in two ways mainly.

In the first place, it suffered a fall in the exchange rate partly due to the lower prices of its exports. The fall in the price of raw materials, linked to the depressing effect of the crisis on world demand for these products, severely affected the South African economy, with a large majority of its exports still composed of raw materials or semi-transformed products. Moreover, for the first time in 20 years, the gold price (gold being a leading export product) dropped to below US$300 an ounce, which represented a decline in the order of 25 per cent in relation to the average price recorded since the beginning of the decade. This decline, in fact, had started before the crisis. It accelerated, at first because of gold sales by Asian households in crisis, and then, secondly, when the International Monetary Fund and the British and Swiss Central Banks announced that they are selling part of their gold reserves. Job losses in this sector therefore accelerated, as many marginal mines were no longer profitable at this price level.

Moreover, South Africa went through a serious financial crisis in 1998, resulting from the contagion effect witnessed in most emerging markets. Whereas an inflow of capital had been registered at the beginning of that year (R35 billion in portfolio investment over a period of four months, or as much as for the entire 1997), one witnessed massive capital outflows from the moment that the deterioration in the international environment increased the risk aversion of international investors, a phenomenon described as flight to quality.

Capital outflows resulted in the depreciation of the rand to the order of 20 per cent to the US dollar over the entire year. The exchange losses of the Reserve Bank were subsequently considerable: they rose to more than US$2 billion, which represents around two per cent of GDP. These losses were focused on the Reserve Bank's Net Open Forward Position, which had increased by nearly US$10 billion in the spring of 1998 to come close to US$25 billion.[15] The Johannesburg Stock Exchange declined sharply, although the 40 per cent drop in share prices witnessed towards the middle of the year were followed by a marked rise.

The government's orthodox economic policy played a pro-cyclical role, by intensifying the process of economic slowdown that started in 1996.

The recessive impact of the restrictive budgetary policy implemented in 1994 has probably been underestimated. This impact has been reinforced by two factors. On the one hand, the government's reservations about foreign loans, be they in the form of bank loans or indeed from international organisations (particularly the World Bank) have emphasised the eviction effects of a rise in public debt; on the other hand, the high interest rate monetary policy, implemented in the mid-1995, has reinforced the budgetary policy's impact on growth.

Since 1994, the Reserve Bank in fact considered the South African economy to be "overheating", and a resurgence of inflation to be emerging. This policy prompted an appreciation of the rand, which was corrected suddenly in the first semester of 1996: the "first" crisis of the rand resulted

---

15 This mechanism of forward exchange cover has been used since the 1970s, and was activated with the implementation of sanctions in 1986: it is the supply of forward foreign exchange to importers and all dealers that have foreign exchange debts. Originally, this mechanism aimed to reassure domestic dealers and limit capital outflows.

in a devaluation of around 20 per cent of the domestic currency in relation to the dollar in a few weeks. Subsequently, the Reserve Bank maintained real interest rates at levels systematically higher than 10 per cent, which slowed down domestic demand considerably.

Just as monetary policy started becoming more flexible at the beginning of 1998, a second monetary crisis hit South Africa. Despite the efforts of the Reserve Bank to support the rand and fight against speculation, this resulted in a new depreciation of the currency. The Reserve Bank raised interest rates to discourage the short selling of the rand while intervening at the same time on the forward exchange market. The return differential between the American and South African government treasury bills thus increased sharply. The spread on five-year bonds, maturing in 1999, thus went from 70 base points in August 1997 to 517 points in September 1998, before going down again in January 1999. The inflationary acceleration following the devaluation was absorbed very quickly. In the first semester of 1999, the Reserve Bank was therefore able to announce that it had set itself as an objective a yearly inflation rate of between one and five per cent, an even more ambitious objective than that flaunted by the GEAR (6 per cent inflation in 1999 and 5 per cent in 2000). Interest rates took a year to come down to the already high level they had been at before the crisis. However, the Finance minister Trevor Manuel announced an inflation target of between 3 per cent and 6 per cent by 2002.

Finally, contrary to the predictions of the GEAR, the domestic savings rate continued to fall, in a continuation of the trends witnessed since the 1980s (Graph 7). Savings supply thus proved to be inelastic to the rise in interest rates. Whereas the domestic savings rate was supposed to rise for the duration of the programme to reach 22 per cent of GDP by the year 2000, owing in particular to the reduction in the budget deficit, the opposite happened. Since the end of apartheid, the easier access to credit by historically disadvantaged populations, as well as the rise in unemployment, are probably among the main factors responsible for this downward movement.

At its level of around 14 per cent of GDP, reached in 1998, the South African savings rate is among the lowest of all the emerging market economies. The savings capacity of the majority of the South African population is almost zero. The financial savings rate of South African households (that is to say, what they have left after having paid all their expenses and credit commitments) is thus less than one per cent on average. Indeed, in the long term the example of the emerging Asian

Graph 7:
Savings and investment rate (1980–1998)
% of GDP

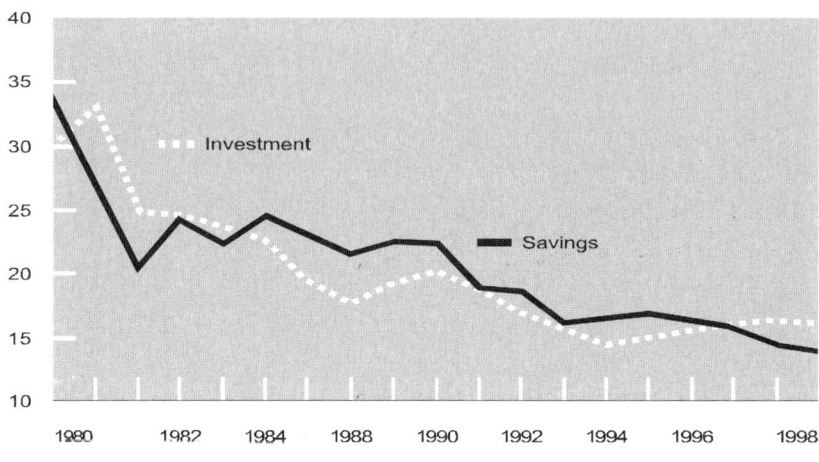

Source: Reserve Bank

countries shows that their development was based, above all, on strong domestic savings.

The fall in the savings rate resulted to some extent in a sharp progression in consumption, which supported economic growth for a while. In return, however, this led to a rise in household debt, which exceeded 60 per cent of disposable household income between 1996 and 1998, while also increasing the vulnerability of households to any interest rate hike: henceforth debt servicing absorbed 22 per cent of their income, whereas this proportion had been around seven per cent 10 years before.

In the absence of sufficient savings, the economy is hampered by external constraints and has to appeal to foreign capital to finance its growth, be it through accumulating foreign debt (external debt is lower than 30 per cent of GDP, which leaves a significant margin for movement) or by appealing to private capital in the form of investments. Although not negligible, capital inflows have nevertheless been modest since 1994, and in any case much lower than predicted by the GEAR: their average amount between 1994 and 1997 represented only two per cent of GDP. What is more, these were dominated by short term portfolio investments, by nature very volatile, making the economy very vulnerable to external crises.

The population's expectations vis-à-vis the GEAR have been strongest with regard to employment. It is also in this area where the gap between prediction and reality has been most distinct. This gap can be explained, firstly, by the fact that economic growth has been lower than the target. It can also be explained by the reduction in the "labour content" of growth, contrary to the predictions of the GEAR which were based on the assumption of an increase in this content.

This objective seemed extremely ambitious in the light of recent economic history, which had been marked by a trend towards growth in capital-intensive production processes.[16] In addition, the direction of industrial policy runs counter to the promotion of growth based on the development of labour-intensive industries, which shows that not all in government share in the philosophy of the GEAR in this area. The Minister of Trade and Industry defines his Department's strategy as follows:

Industrial policies are essentially aimed at promoting efficient investment, located in sustainable activity, spread across the enterprise system and geographically. It is this that will encourage labour-intensive growth, not trying to ensure that all productive activity is labour-intensive. Much modern production no longer lends itself to labour-intensive methods. Trying to force the economy in that direction would not create jobs. This reality gives the lie to the hare-brained proposals about low wages.[17]

The main line of the policy recommended by the GEAR is to increase labour market flexibility, and in so doing to follow the liberal theory according to which fixing the level of salaries under competitive conditions would lead to a reduction in surplus labour.

This means, firstly, that downward pressure is put on salary increases, based on the assumption of an inverse relation between the level of salaries and employment. The GEAR thus recalls the estimation according to which a rise in real wages of one per cent will reduce non-agricultural employment by 0,4 per cent, everything else being equal. Some recent analyses seem to confirm the existence of this relationship in the South African case.[18]

---

16 Natrass, 1998.

17 Erwin, 1999.

18 The imprecision of this type of result needs no longer be recalled. As for Fallon and Lucas, 1998, they considered that a rise in average real wages of 10 per cent is translated by a fall of 7 per cent in employment, whereas one of their previous studies resulted in an assessment of less than half the employment/wage elasticity.

This policy of wage restriction has had some success. On the whole, the rise in real wage costs (on average 3,8 per cent a year between 1994 and 1998) has been somewhat lower than that of productivity (4,4 per cent a year) in recent years. The relative stability of wages' share of GDP, which has been oscillating between 54 and 55 per cent since 1994, confirms the absence of cost inflation despite pressure in favour of social redress, encouraged by the change in government and one of the highest levels of trade unionisation in the world. In fact, a real increase in low wages is excluded in the short term, considering the choice that was made to open up and the objective to become internationally competitive flowing from it. At the same time, the salaries of skilled employees have been pushed upwards owing to the shortages in this labour category.[19]

Besides wage moderation, the GEAR also advocates institutional reform of the functioning of the labour market, whose lack of flexibility is considered by some local economists and the IMF as an important cause of unemployment in South Africa. Its propositions are very clear in this regard:

> *The government will pursue a policy of regulated flexibility in managing the labour market. This entails the regulation of the labour market in a manner that allows for flexible collective bargaining structures, variable application of employment standards and* ad voce *regulation.*[20]

This is akin to the proposal of big business contained in the document entitled "Growth for All", whose publication preceded that of the GEAR by a few months.[21] This document, which was particularly opposed to the institution of minimum wages, proposed that a two-speed labour market be implemented by making one part of the market more flexible and subject to relaxed legislation. It believed that the implementation of its proposals would be likely to create a million jobs in three years, an even more ambitious objective than that of the GEAR.

While advocating increasing flexibility, the GEAR also indicates its intention to extend the safeguards offered to workers. This relates in particular to the reduction of labour market fragmentation (an objective

---

19 This therefore increases the role of the state and its policy of indirect transfers. The theory of comparative advantage teaches that in the long term, opening up should lead to a convergence between the salaries of different countries.
20 Department of Finance, 1996.
21 South Africa Foundation, 1996.

CHAPTER 4 An orthodox economic policy

that largely contradicts the previous one), making labour relations less conflicting, and improving productivity through an increase in skills. The four Acts adopted since 1994 which constitute the foundation of the government's employment policy show that this second type of preoccupation has prevailed until now to the detriment of the first:

- The Labour Relations Act establishes the legislative framework for the running of labour relations by extending the rights that have until its inception been reserved for whites to all workers; it specifies in particular the conditions under which the freedom of association and the right to strike, allowed under the constitution, can be exercised; it created two specialised institutions, the Commission for Conciliation, Mediation and Arbitration (CCMA) and the Labour Court, to settle labour conflicts.
- The Basic Conditions of Employment Act lays down the working conditions applying, with exceptions, to the labour force; it limits the legal working week at 45 hours, and annual leave at 21 days; it also specifies the conditions under which sick leave, and overtime and night pay can be granted; it prohibits children under 15 years from working.
- The Employment Equity Act aims to adjust the composition of the labour force to that of the population; in particular it sets quotas for each ethnic group that all businesses of a certain size have to respect and report on.
- Finally, the Skills Development Act seeks to increase the skills of the labour force through an active effort of professional training financed by a training levy paid by companies since 2000.

Certain aspects of these acts probably constitute an obstacle to employment creation: this may apply to the extension of branch agreements to all the companies of a certain sector irrespective of their size, even if their representatives are not signatory to these agreements, or to the recent reduction in working hours. These measures, which increase labour costs in an indiscriminate manner, are to be relaxed. A criticism that is often expressed against labour laws pertains to the difficulties of dismissing workers. The sharp decrease in employment since the 1990s, however, indicates that companies have not experienced any difficulty in adjusting their size to the desired level and that this criticism is therefore largely unjustified.

The second line of the GEAR's proposals on the question of employment concerns the improvement of labour productivity. Unlike the policy of flexibility, this second facet was applied, with some measures taken under the GEAR framework having contributed to increasing the efficiency of the productive process and therefore to accelerating productivity gains.

The opening up of the economy, which has compelled companies to improve their international competitiveness, notably through better labour organisation, the putting in place of modern and more effective machinery, and an effort towards improved training, were steps in the right direction.[22] The same goes for the competition policy (compare the Competition Act adopted in 1998) which aims to fight against monopolies and the benefits accruing from the restructuring of public enterprises (the public transport company, Transnet, has thus reduced the number of its workforce from 65 000 to 41 000 since 1994). Finally, the stabilisation of the social situation, which resulted partly from the new social legislation put in place after 1994, has led to a considerable decrease in the number of workdays lost due to strikes, compared with the beginning of the 1990s, and therefore to an increase in the annual number of hours worked and in labour productivity.

Whereas economic growth in South Africa has traditionally been "intensive", that is to say it was more the result of growth in the factors of production than productivity gains, the opposite started to happen. Growth has become "extensive": characterised by an acceleration in productivity, but without a sharp resumption in capital growth.

From 1994 to 1998, annual labour productivity thus grew at the high rate of 4,4 per cent on average throughout the economy. Even if productivity growth is considered an essential source of economic growth and therefore of employment in the long run[23], such a high rate can only have a very negative impact on the evolution of employment in the short term in the South African economic situation, since at least equal GDP growth is necessary to interrupt the process of job destruction at the national level! This explains why studies evaluating the employment-creating potential

---

22 In the automobile sector, which is one of the best performing industrial sectors, the local subsidiary of Ford maintained that it had increased its production per employee by half (from 10 to 15 vehicles a year) thanks to putting in a considerable effort into training and better workplace organisation.

23 From 1970 to 1997, average labour productivity in the South African economy stagnated. It grew by 160 per cent in South Korea during the same period. Total employment did not increase in South Africa during this period, whereas it grew by half in South Korea.

of each economic sector believe that the main problem does not reside in industry, where productivity is growing even faster than the average, but in the service sectors (especially tourism and construction) where these efforts are less noticeable.

Presented from the beginning as "non-negotiable", the GEAR has been applied on the whole since 1996, with the area of employment, where reforms are politically very sensitive, the notable exception. The argument which holds that its lack of results as far as growth and employment creation are concerned is due to the government not respecting its GEAR commitments, is therefore not very convincing. Admittedly, transforming a moribund and inefficient economy into a performing economy that is opened up to the exterior cannot bring about immediate results. Moreover, the hope that a stabilisation policy would not produce recessive effects in the short term was illusory. The challenge at the turn of the century is purely and simply to put in place a new growth model that will generate, in all likelihood, strong growth and create employment. After a period during which control of the overall macroeconomic equilibrium constituted the main priority of economic policy, this demand for growth will become increasingly urgent. In an open economy, however, this objective can only be reached through successful integration into the international economy. This is the challenge posed by the new government's policy to join the global economy.

PART TWO

IN SEARCH OF A NEW INTERNATIONAL ECONOMIC INTEGRATION

CHAPTER 5

Economic opening up and globalisation

Governments and their policy advisors alike have to stop thinking of international economic integration as an end in itself. Developing nations have to engage the world economy on their own terms, not on terms set by global markets or multilateral institutions (...) Successful economies in the past have been those that have taken a strategic and differentiated approach to openness. There is little reason to believe that the future will look any different.

— D Rodrik[1]

After the abolition of international sanctions, the South African economy was quick to open up to the outside world. Breaking with the import substitution industrialisation policy practised for several decades, the government converted to an export-oriented growth model, which today is followed by most developing countries. South Africa has to avoid the main risk encountered by countries following this type of policy, which is to engage in "all-out" liberalisation as a substitute for true development and an international economic integration strategy.

Beyond macroeconomic factors (particularly the exchange rate), South Africa's prospects of reintegrating into world trade will be largely influenced by the quality of its international specialisation.

South Africa has traditionally been a "semi-peripheral" country in the international division of labour. Its international specialisation corresponds to a neo-colonial pattern: on the whole it is centred on exporting raw materials and semi-manufactured products and importing manufactured products. All the same, unlike other African countries, it occupies an intermediary position in this international division of labour: admittedly, it has not succeeded in becoming a significant exporter of manufactured products, in contrast with the countries of the centre or emerging countries, which have based their

---

1   Rodrik, 1999.

development on the export of labour-intensive products before gradually diversifying their exportable supply side. However, it has developed a dichotomy in its specialisation between its relations with developed countries, to whom it exports mainly intermediary goods, and those with its African partners, who constitute the principal markets for its manufactured products.

Firstly, it is a matter of improving this specialisation both geographically and as far as manufacturing sectors are concerned, to increase the growth potential of exports in the long term. The nature of South Africa's comparative advantages does not favour diversification into more labour-intensive products. In the absence of such diversification, pursuing "downstream" activities, as the government is looking to do, is not the sort of strategy that will help to resolve the unemployment problem.

Finally, even though it is a fallacy to base the eventual success of an export-led growth policy on the hope that there will be an inflow of foreign investment in the absence of sufficient domestic savings[2], the government continues to show great optimism in this area. Admittedly, the end of apartheid has allowed these investments to get off the ground again. But South Africa's attractiveness in this regard has suffered from its weak economic growth rate and its long distance from large markets. Conversely, the rapid expansion of direct investment abroad reflects the acceleration of the internationalisation of South African companies.

Rapid economic opening

The trade policy followed by the government since 1994 is in line with the liberal philosophy that has inspired its economic policy in a general way.

An increase in the opening up of the economy has been conceived of as a way in which to accelerate economic growth, in accordance with the export-led growth model. In the framework of this model, liberalising foreign trade is considered absolutely necessary to remove any anti-export bias, which raises the prices of imports and therefore production costs, and encourages companies to sell on the domestic market where trade protection grants them a competitive advantage. It is furthermore supposed to increase the efficiency of the productive process, by stimulating productivity through returns on scale, technology transfers and increased competition on the domestic market.

---

2   As Rodrik shows (*ibid.*) from the example of some recent success stories.

This last aspect is particularly important in the case of South Africa, where the ANC government, since its coming to power, has indicated its intention to reduce the monopoly power of large conglomerates. Other reasons specific to this country have also been of consequence.[3] In fact, protectionism has been associated with the National Party government and the isolation resulting from international sanctions, as well as the slowing down in economic growth witnessed since the 1980s. The opening of trade has therefore been envisaged as one of the ways in which to break away from the previous order in view of resuming an industrial and economic development process. For all of these reasons, the warnings of some foreign and local economists regarding the risks linked to this opening up – as far as employment in particular was concerned, some consumer goods-producing sectors having suffered dramatic losses in this area – and its uncertain benefits[4] have been largely ignored.

Besides these ideological reasons, the government has probably been encouraged to follow this path by some improvements in the economic situation and the country's image in the eyes of international investors as a result of the end of apartheid. This has prompted it to think that opening up trade would result in an increase in foreign investment in flows, which would prevent the emergence of external financing problems.

In the framework of the 1994 GATT agreements, South Africa has taken on the following main commitments for the period 1995–1999: reducing industrial customs duties by a third on average; consolidating 98 per cent of tariff lines (which consists of fixing maximum rates for each product category) and significantly reducing their tariff numbers; converting quantitative restrictions and specific duties (that is to say, calculated as a total amount per litre, tonne, and so on) to *ad valorem* duties (calculated as a percentage of the product's value); and the gradual elimination of export subsidies before the end of 1997.

These commitments have been implemented with some zeal, with most of them having even been exceeded. The lowering of industrial tariffs took place faster than expected: they went down from around an import-weighted average of 15 per cent in 1994 to 9 per cent in 1995. The number of tariff categories was unilaterally reduced to six (0/5/10/15/20/30 per

---

3   Bell, 1997.
4   As Krugman wrote in 1995 and as many empirical studies on the link between openness and economic growth have confirmed: "Trade liberalisation and other market liberalisation measures are certainly good, but the idea that they are going to generate an economic take-off represents a hope rather than a well-founded anticipation."

cent), with the exception of sensitive sectors. Duties on raw materials and semi-manufactured products, as well as on machinery would henceforth generally be included in the nil to 10 per cent margin, those on components between 10 and 15 per cent, and those on consumption goods between 15 and 30 per cent. The number of tariff lines (around 12 000 in 1993) has been reduced by half. The General Export Incentive Scheme (GEIS) was abolished as planned in July 1997, with almost all agricultural subsidies having been phased out since 1 January 1995, much earlier than required by the government's GATT obligations. The surcharges that affected close to a third of imports were removed as early as 1995.

Liberalisation has also been accelerated in the two "sensitive" sectors where South Africa was given permission to extend the timetable for the dismantling of customs compared beyond the usual five years. The timetable has been voluntarily reduced to eight years in the textile and clothing sectors, instead of 12. By the year 2002, customs duties on clothing should have come down from 100 to 40 per cent, whereas the Agreement anticipated a rate of 45 per cent at the end of the period. In the automobile sector, duties will come down from 100 to 40 per cent (for a commitment of 50 per cent) on assembled vehicles and, as foreseen, to 30 per cent on detached components by the same expiry date.

This policy came about as South Africa was putting an end to the international isolation imposed on it during the apartheid period. Consequently, significant trade expansion, particularly in manufactured products, has been seen over the past decade.

The increase in exports of manufactured products has been very rapid, such that it almost doubled in total between 1990 and 1998. It has exceeded those of raw materials to represent half of total exports by 1999 (Table 7). Besides the positive impact of reducing the anti-import bias, South African exports have benefited from several factors that came into play simultaneously: the general opening up of foreign markets, be it on account of the end of trade sanctions applied against them or to the external liberalisation implemented by African (especially Southern African) countries, played an important role; the significant depreciation in the real positive exchange rate of the rand between 1994 and 1998 (–21 per cent), which has gone down more than was desired, has markedly improved the competitiveness of South African companies, all the more so as regular studies have underscored that industrial exports have a strong price elasticity; finally, exports were stimulated by the sharp increase in world demand after the 1993 crisis.

Table 7:
Sectoral structure of exports (%)

Product	Share of total 1990	Share of total 1998	Average growth rate 98/90*
Raw materials	54,2	36,2	− 2,8
• Gold	29,8	16,2	− 5,3
• Coal	5,9	5,2	0,6
• Other mining products	14,1	10,8	− 1,2
• Agricultural products	4,3	3,9	0,9
Manufactured products	32,9	49,3	7,5
• Iron-steel	9,4	8,9	1,6
• Non-ferrous metals	4,4	5,4	4,8
• Industrial chemical products	2,6	4,8	10,4
• Automobiles (components)	1,3	3,8	3,8
Diverse non-classified	12,9	14,6	3,8
TOTAL	100,0	100,0	2,2

* Total converted into dollars
Source: Industrial Development Corporation

Moreover one has seen a diversification of these exports linked to the emergence of new export products. Sales of final products have been most dynamic, in particular of transport material and machinery, as well as of furniture and, to a lesser extent, chemical products. Despite the sharp increase in their sales, the first two sectors still hardly represent more than 20 per cent of total manufactured product exports. In contrast, exports of iron and steel and metallurgical products have suffered a relative decline, while still continuing to contribute to a third of total exports. Processed food exports (except for beverages) have increased slowly, with textile exports registering a decline in real value.

The decline in raw material exports has affected mining products especially (except for coal). The value of gold exports has dropped, reflecting a continuation of the simultaneous downward movement of export quantities and the price of this precious metal evident since 1980. The relative stagnation in agricultural exports has been partly the result of the elimination of export subsidies for these products.

CHAPTER 5 Economic opening up and globalisation

Benefiting from the reduction in the degree of domestic market protection, imports have increased at an even higher rate than exports. Within manufactured product imports, which represented the bulk of the total, a sharp increase in electronic product imports has been registered. On the other hand, there has been a decline in the weight of other machinery and transport material imports.

Trade opening has also resulted in a radical transformation of the geographical structure of trade, as well as a diversification of trade partners (Table 8). Even if external trade statistics have to be commented on with precaution, insofar as the trade embargo practised until 1991 led to many trade diversions, they do underscore some major trends.

The most dynamic export markets since 1990 have been those in Africa and North and South America (especially the United States, but also Brazil and Mexico), each of which saw their share in total exports practically double, as well as the European Union to a lesser degree. Despite the dynamism of sales to the European Union there has been a reduction in the global share of Europe, its most important client, which absorbed more than half of total exports in 1990. Asian exports too have been reduced, on account especially of the Asian crisis and this reduction is therefore of a structural nature, the share of this exporting zone having remained relatively stable throughout the 1980s.

Table 8:
Geographical structure of external trade (%)

	Exports		Imports	
	1990	1998	1990	1998
Europe	55,0	41,5	56,6	47,9
• European Union (15)	32,2	38,2	52,1	40,8
Asia	26,2	22,6	23,5	29,1
Africa	10,6	18,3	2,1	2,5
• Sub-Saharan Africa	n/a	17,9	n/a	2,3
Americas	8,0	13,8	16,7	20,5
• USA	5,9	9,5	13,1	13,6
Other	0,2	3,8	1,1	–

Source: South African Customs Service

Trade that is not classified by trading partner is excluded from the total. In 1990, it involved total SACU (Southern African Customs Union) trade with the rest of the world. In 1998, it involved only South Africa's trade, excluding its trade with SACU

Europe, South Africa's leading supplier, has lost some market share. Imports of Asian products, in contrast, have shown a sharp increase, contributing to close to a third of the total increase in imports since 1990. Imports originating from the Americas have increased somewhat faster than average, as well as those originating from Africa, which, however, remained very marginal.

As a result, the export rate, measured by the ratio of goods exports to the GDP, has increased by five points since its minimum in 1992, to settle at 29 per cent of GDP in 1998 (this increase is also an automatic result of the exchange rate effect). The import rate (the ratio of goods imports to domestic demand), which rose to 28 per cent of GDP, has increased even faster. Nonetheless, these ratios of openness remain moderate. They are less than the average ratios in middle-income countries (apart from petroleum-exporting countries), the category to which South Africa belongs.

The export rate in fact varies considerably between the different sectors of the economy. It is around 90 per cent for the mining sector, of which most of the production is exported, and only 10 per cent for agriculture, which still essentially remains turned inwards to the domestic market. The manufactured products export rate, which had stagnated after the 1970s, doubled between 1990 and 1998, going from 10,7 per cent to 20,8 per cent of production. During this same period, the import rate, which had decreased in the framework of the import substitution policy, increased from 19,7 per cent to 35 per cent of production.

Only two sectors (iron and steel, and non-ferrous metals), representing close to half the manufactured product exports, could be considered export-oriented in 1990. For the other industrial sectors, foreign markets were at most complementary, allowing them to maintain their activity when the domestic market was depressed. By 1998, export practice had expanded within manufacturing sectors. Besides the two sectors already mentioned, export rates are between 40 and 60 per cent for industrial chemical products, leather, furniture and non-automobile transport equipment.

With the relatively general opening up of many economic sectors, the same phenomenon can be seen regarding imports. Import rates now exceed 100 per cent in the few sectors where domestic production is almost non-existent, such as non-electrical machinery, telecommunications equipment, and so on. Sectors that are the least open to imports are "sensitive" sectors, which continue to benefit from customs protection, due to be reduced soon, and the intermediary goods sector (apart from chemicals) which holds a strong position in South African industry.

The factors contributing to the sharp increase in trade witnessed during the 1990s were limited or partly linked to the economic situation: hence market share that was lost during the sanctions period was largely recovered, and the elimination of GEIS significantly reduced the support given to exporters until then (assuming that the experience they had acquired internationally would allow them to some degree to get along on their own). Sooner or later, therefore, the sustainability of South Africa's export growth will have to depend above all on the structural competitiveness of companies. This is examined below in an analysis of sectoral and geographical export specialisation.

Disadvantageous international specialisation

At the global level, the economy's international specialisation is typical of a developing country exporting raw materials and semi-manufactured goods and importing capital goods necessary for the functioning of the economy:

> *South Africa's trade profile is not that of a newly industrialising country such as South Korea, but rather of an exceptionally well-developed exporter of primary products.*[5]

The main "revealed" comparative advantages, calculated according to the CEPII[6] methodology, relate to mining products (gold, coal, minerals, and so on), agricultural products (particularly tropical produce) and semi-manufactured products in the metal (iron-steel, non-ferrous metals and so on) and wood (paper, furniture) subsectors.

The main comparative disadvantages are in energy (petrol) and most complex industrial products: transport equipment (detached parts and automobiles in particular), capital goods (engines, specialised machinery, information and telecommunications equipment) and intermediary goods

---

5 O'Meara, 1996.
6 Centre d'Etudes Prospectives et d'Informations Internationales, based in Paris.

(electrical supplies, hardware, plastic articles). The fact that transport equipment is listed as a comparative disadvantage despite its share of exports is explained by the extent of this sector's trade deficit.

This specialisation seems particularly disadvantageous if one compares it to sectoral trends in the evolution of global demand over the 1990s, which are in all likelihood set to continue over the first decade of the twenty-first century.

Most of the comparative advantages relate to products that are declining in global trade,[7] be it because of a decline in their relative prices, or in the quantities traded. The only exceptions are furniture and paper, whose share of exports, however, is relatively marginal.

Moreover, South Africa demonstrates an absence of specialisation in those products that are most dynamic in global trade, such as those related to information technologies, machines, and transport equipment, which constitute its main comparative disadvantages. This differentiates it from the emerging Asian countries whose success was precisely based on specialising in these excelling sectors.

Splitting the export growth rate into a demand effect and a competitiveness effect for accounting purposes allows one to appreciate the impact of this specialisation on South Africa's external performance during the period 1991 to 1996. The results for all exporting countries of this analysis are set out by CEPII in a book, *The competitiveness of nations.*[8]

In the most favourable configuration (Malaysia, Mexico, and so on), countries gain market share as a result of specialisation focused on those sectors excelling in global trade and in the most dynamic geographical markets, and also through "pure" competitive effect. The emerging Asian countries also benefit from a positive geographical effect owing to the fact that a large share of their exports is directed towards their rapidly growing regional partners. Generally, the sectoral demand effect is negative for raw material producing countries (African countries, Brazil and Indonesia), considering the likely decline of the share of these products in global trade. South Africa is no exception to this rule. According to this estimation (which excludes gold sales), the sectoral structure of exports would have reduced export growth by 14,1 per cent during this time, with the geographical structure having experienced a less negative impact (–2,6 per cent).

---

7   CEPII, 1998 This classification is relatively stable over the long term.
8   CEPII, *ibid.*

This latter effect reflects the share in South African exports of European and African markets, where the increase in demand has been lower than the global average.

On the other hand, the fact that the competitiveness effect has been very positive (+43 per cent) conveys the positive impact of the ending of sanctions as well as the recent effort made by industrial companies to start exporting. This effect is an expression of the substantial gain in market share registered for manufactured products, which however, has been more than compensated for by the decline in South Africa's share of total world gold exports: the global market share held by South Africa (it accounts for around 0,5 per cent of world exports) therefore continued declining during the 1990s, albeit at a slower pace.

It is encouraging to note that recent developments in South Africa's sectoral specialisation seem to indicate a better adaptation to trends in global demand. The gradual reduction of the share of raw materials in exports is rather positive from this point of view, as is the increase of the share of manufactured products in return. Among the latter, the increase in the share of chemical products and the reduction in the share of iron and steel in exports are to be welcomed, while the increase in the share of non-ferrous metals is to be considered a rather negative development. The rapid expansion of automobile equipment exports (vehicles and separate parts) has resulted in a sharp improvement in the trade coverage rate of these products and therefore a decline in the associated comparative disadvantage. This is similar, although to a lesser extent, for several capital goods (especially machinery).

It is more complicated to comment on developments in geographical specialisation. Such comment has to be supplemented by an analysis of the sectoral structure of trade with different trading partners. Thus, the reduction in the share of exports going to Europe to the benefit of that going to Africa is essentially the corollary of the reduction in the share of raw materials and increase in that of manufactured products in exports.[9] In this sense, these developments seem rather reassuring, if it was not for the prevailing uncertainty about the African continent's growth prospects. Moreover, the massive trade imbalance with African countries means that it is hardly viable that exports to these countries will increase at the same rate as witnessed during the 1990s.

---

9   The decline in gold exports, however, did not influence the geographical destination of sales, as emerged from Customs Statistics. Actually, the latter do not break these sales down geographically.

The low percentage of sales to emerging areas, particularly as far as those of manufactured products are concerned, suggests that significant potential exists for increasing exports to these markets, which are probably going to remain the most robust in the world in future.

The expansion of trade with these emerging countries has until the end of the 20th century tended to reinforce South Africa's historical specialisation in exporting intermediary goods and importing manufactured goods. It is doubtful whether this country will succeed in thwarting this trend:

> *One could even ask oneself, if, far from moving South Africa away from its specialisation in the primary sector, trading with Asia would not already have initiated the unfolding of an alternative scenario, often evoked by prospective studies regarding Africa: the latter, because it has been the last to develop and because its traditional markets are showing weak growth, would be forced to turn towards Asia not to imitate it, but to take up again its traditional role next to it. It would have to resolve, if it has any respect for the game of comparative advantage, to use the opportunity offered to it by the economic take-off of countries, which, having exploited and sometimes even overexploited their own natural resources, are ready to take it on themselves to exchange increasingly industrial products for raw materials.*[10]

If one accepts this argument, it is only by improving their sales to the markets of developed countries that South African exports can improve their global competitiveness and exploit their seemingly comparative advantage in labour with regard to these countries.

Another way in which to evaluate the quality of South African specialisation is to break down manufactured product exports according to the production factor used most extensively.[11] This breakdown shows that the share of labour-intensive products in exports is marginal and even declining.

It is much lower than its level in China, Indonesia and even in South Korea, a country that has nevertheless passed the consumer goods export phase long ago. On the other hand, the export share of human capital-

---

10 Coussy, 1999a.
11 Tsikata, 1998.

intensive goods (notably transport equipment) in South Africa is higher than that of emerging Asian countries, with that of natural resource-intensive goods (semi-manufactured goods) being equally high. Finally, high-technology products (machinery, chemical products and so on) represent a marginal share of exports, but are showing a relative increase as a result of support from public agencies, which have launched assistance programmes to promote innovation and the electronic sector, while still maintaining high customs duties to protect domestic production.

This specialisation, which is atypical for a developing country, reflects that of the production apparatus and industrial policy choices made in the past, which have resulted in a concentration of exports in heavy industry and more recently, in finished goods and automobiles. The continuing expansion of exports in those sectors using highly skilled labour (human capital-intensive goods, but also most high-technology products) risks, however, being thwarted eventually by the shortage of this type of labour in South Africa, which is probably not to be resolved for a considerable time.

The low labour content of exports is the result of this specialisation. Thus, whereas an average of 11 000 employees (direct) are needed to produce a billion rand of industrial value-added, only 7 000 are needed for the same total of value-added in the iron and steel sector, 6 000 in the production of non-ferrous metals, and 5 000 in that of chemical products, these products constituting the three most important export items. These ratios can be compared with the 11 000 employees necessary to produce non-electrical machinery and telecommunications equipment and the 9 000 needed to manufacture automobiles, which are the most significant manufactured imports. (In the case of clothing, a very labour-intensive sector, this number reaches 32 000.)

Using input-output matrices, which take into account the indirect employment necessary to produce intermediary consumer goods that are incorporated into the production of each product, allows one to calculate a global indicator measuring the job content of manufactured goods trade. An average export-import ratio of 0,96[12] means that a balanced increase in manufactured goods trade of R10 billion (around 10 per cent) will result in the loss of about 4 000 jobs, all things else being equal.

What is more, this ratio would tend to drop, owing to the modification of the trade structure, characterised by a decline in the relative export share of the most labour-intensive products to the benefit of more capital-

12 Natrass, 1998.

intensive products[13], and in reverse, by an increase in imports largely of the most labour-intensive goods (especially electronics, and clothing to a lesser degree). Asian competition, which is of great concern to industrialised countries in these products, therefore also negatively affects South Africa, which has seen a decline in its prospects for creating unskilled jobs in the industrial sector. This trend is in accordance with the conclusions of the estimations of the Industrial Development Corporation assisted by a general equilibrium model, for the implementation period of the GATT commitments.[14]

The nature of all large projects launched recently serves only to reinforce this characteristic. The Hillside aluminium plant, built by the Billiton group in Richards Bay on the shore of the Indian Ocean, is exemplary in this regard. Inaugurated in 1996, it produces 500 000 tons of aluminium a year, which makes it the third largest aluminium plant in the world. It employs only 1 200 employees for an annual turnover of around US$600 million, all of it exported.

The Columbus and Saldanha steelworks, which constitute the two other big projects inaugurated since 1994, display the same highly capital-intensive industry profile, producing semi-manufactured goods while benefiting from the low cost of energy in South Africa, whose electricity rates are the lowest in the world.

An analysis of South African labour costs shows that it is illusive to aim at growth based on labour-intensive industries such as textiles and clothing, electronics, etc. Even if wage levels in South Africa are no higher than those in countries at a similar level of development[15], they cannot possibly be compared with those of countries that have very low labour costs (China, India, other African countries, and so on). Probably because of lower productivity, the wage cost per unit produced seems higher than that of many countries in these economic sectors. Thus, the production cost of a yard of fabric would rise to US$0,79 in South Africa as against only US$0,69 in Italy, US$0,64 in Japan, US$0,38 in Brazil, US$0,35 in South Korea, US$0,34 in Thailand, and US$0,22 in India.[16] In this context, the only successful examples of exporting these types of products (furniture,

---

13 The increase of Africa in exports has also played a negative role in this regard, insofar as South Africa's comparative advantage in labour with regard to developed countries does not apply with regard to African countries.
14 IDC, 1997.
15 SRI, 1998.
16 Tsikata, 1998.

CHAPTER 5 Economic opening up and globalisation

automobile leather articles, and so on) are based on "niche" strategies that are difficult to discuss generally.

Taking note of this fact, and refusing to implement a low wage policy, the South African government has implicitly abandoned the aim of expanding the exportation of labour-intensive consumer goods, modelled on the growth path historically followed by the Asian countries.

Its policy priority in this area consists of reinforcing production networks, in order to increase the degree of product transformation and to exploit more the economy's comparative advantages as far as the abundance of raw materials and low energy costs are concerned.[17] This policy is, to some extent, in line with the continued implementation of interventionist policies by the South African government,[18] combining financing granted by development institutions (Industrial Development Corporation, Development Bank of Southern Africa), subsidising mechanisms, and a trade policy that remains oriented towards supporting sectors that are considered as being strategic.

The rapid expansion of automobile production and exports constitutes an undeniable success of the industrial clustering policy advocated by the government. In this sphere, it again started prioritising this sector, which comprises German, Japanese, and American vehicle assembly operations, to which is added a significant production of component parts.

Protected for a long time by tariff barriers higher than 100 per cent, it very recently started opening up internationally, while benefiting from the Motor Industry Development Programme (MIDP) support programme since 1995. In particular, this programme allows for the exemption of customs duties equal to 27 per cent of the price of a new vehicle for the components necessary to assemble it. It also allows for the exemption of customs duties for new vehicle imports on condition that an amount equivalent to total vehicle imports is exported to compensate for the latter. This last measure has stimulated the rapid expansion of downstream automobile products (catalytic exhausts, leather accessories, and so on).

The MIDP has promoted a rapid expansion of automobile exports – insignificant in 1990, today they rank third in exported manufactured products. German car manufacturers, very well established in South Africa, have largely contributed to this process by integrating this country into the international division of labour as part of their global operations: both BMW

---

17 Erwin, 1998a.
18 Coussy, 199b.

and Mercedes have thus entrusted their subsidiaries with the sole mandate to manufacture certain of their right-hand drive models.

South Africa has undertaken, in the framework of the GATT, to make changes to the MIDP after 2003, which will lead to it putting into place new automobile support programmes. To encourage productivity increases and rationalisation in this sector, public assistance may only be granted above a certain production threshold for each model.

Negative foreign direct investment balance

The liberalisation of capital movements has taken place parallel to the opening up of trade. Several restrictions on foreign investments were thus lifted: institutional investors are now allowed to invest up to 20 per cent of their South African assets abroad and local companies to repatriate their foreign exchange income after six months and invest up to R250 million in SADC countries and R50 million in the rest of the world.

Non-existent before 1994, direct investment flows to South Africa have increased, reaching R6 billion or a little under US$1 billion a year on average (Graph 8). These flows, however, remain modest compared with those received by the most attractive emerging markets, and especially as regards the country's financing needs.

Various factors explain these investment flows:
- First, the privatisation of public service enterprises has been at the base of several of the major recent deals. The partial privatisation of Telkom in 1997, 30 per cent of whose capital was sold to Telkom Malaysia and Southern Bell Company (SBC), thus provided US$1,2 billion. This deal explains the exceptional rise in investments during this year compared with the recent average. Swissair's 20 per cent participation in the partial privatisation of South African Airways also gave rise to significant investment.
- Some multinationals decided to invest in high-potential sectors (public works construction, food-processing products, finances) where local presence is indispensable in order to penetrate the South African market.
- Since 1994 multinationals (Coca Cola, IBM) have repurchased many of their subsidiaries sold during the disinvestment era.
- Finally, the unbundling operations undertaken by large

CHAPTER 5 Economic opening up and globalisation

Graph 8:
Foreign Direct Investment flows (1990–1997) (R billion)

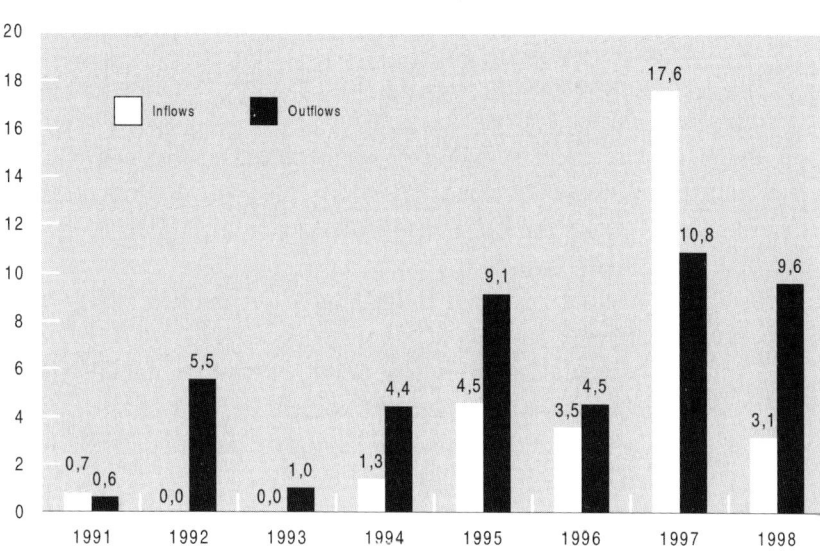

Source: South African Reserve Bank

conglomerates have resulted in the sale of many subsidiaries, often acquired by foreign groups owing to the weak absorption capacity of the local investors' market.

However, there have not been many greenfield investments, which are linked to the setting up of new factories or the expansion of existing factories. Several reasons explain the general hesitance of international investors with regard to South Africa: anxieties regarding the political future of this country and its neighbours could play a role, but it is probably above all the long-term growth potential that is creating doubts.

In fact, the experience of the last few years is hardly encouraging in this regard.

The above comment refers to the general competitiveness of the economy. In 1999, the World Economic Forum has ranked South Africa in 47th position out of a total of 59 countries, behind El Salvador and before Vietnam. In fact, this type of absolute classification is of little significance, considering the heterogeneity of the countries concerned and the arbitrary nature of the way in which many tens of quantitative and qualitative indicators, supposed to measure this competitiveness, are weighed. The fact that these qualitative indicators are calculated from opinion surveys conducted among local business circles introduced an additional source of uncertainty, insofar as response behaviour differs from one country to another.

This having been said, this survey does provide assessment criteria regarding South Africa's strong and weak points, which essentially reflect how these are perceived by South African businesses and confirm the ideas entertained in this domain. If one limits this comparison to African countries only[19], then the main assets of the South African economy, according to the relevant survey, lie in its degree of openness and the quality of its financial system, infrastructure, universities and general business environment.

South Africa reached the very first ranks according to these criteria. Nonetheless, it appears in a very mediocre position as far as certain aspects of the state's functioning (tax system), labour market (social relations, shortage of skilled labour, and so on), goods markets (oligopoly situations) are concerned and because of the very high level of crime.

Finally, it can be noted that, as far as direct investments are concerned, the most attractive developing countries have benefited either from the size of their domestic markets, or from their proximity, albeit relative, to a large developed market. China is exemplary of the first case. Examples of the proximity effect, are quite numerous: Mexico was able to expand its exports of manufactured products towards the United States through a regime of open border areas, the *maquiladoras,* in this way; similarly, Asian countries prioritised the Japanese market; finally, the eastern European countries border on the European Union.

South Africa does not find itself in any of these beneficial situations. Firstly, the size of its domestic market is relatively limited. Next, it is very far away from most large developed markets. Resulting from this are high logistical costs, which are compensated for neither by the size of the domestic market nor that of regional markets.

Hein Marais describes this handicap as follows:
South Africa cannot wish away its geographical location on a continent which barely features in the world economy."[20]

---

19 In 1998, the World Economic Forum conducted a survey on the competitiveness of 23 African countries, of which the results are presented here. South Africa was classified in seventh position, behind Mauritius, Tunisia, Botswana, Namibia, Morocco, and Egypt, or in fourth position when limiting the survey to sub-Saharan African countries.

20 Marais, 1998, p 126.

CHAPTER 5 Economic opening up and globalisation

This geographical situation can have an effect in two different ways. Presently, the attractiveness of South Africa to investors is certainly suffering from its proximity to countries experiencing serious political difficulties. In contrast, however, this country would be the main beneficiary of an improvement in the regional environment and in southern Africa's international image. This would be all the more so since foreign investors in South Africa often aim to use their local subsidiary as a "springboard" into the region, or indeed, into the entire African continent.

Conversely, the rapid expansion of South African investments abroad, of which the average total since 1994 has been higher than that of foreign investment into the country, was made possible by the end of sanctions against South Africa. Today, South African companies, which were previously *persona non grata* in most countries of the world, are welcome everywhere. The phenomenon of catching up in the 1990s has also been made possible by the gradual lifting of exchange controls.

The challenge for large South African groups is to diversify their risks, while at the same time ensuring their position in the global market. All the mining groups have thus launched a multitude of projects in Africa, Australia, and Latin America. There are also numerous industrial, financial, and commercial investments, particularly into Europe.

The transfer by Old Mutual, South Africa's leading pension fund, of its headquarters and main quotation to London, following that of the Billiton (ex-Gencor) and Anglo American mining groups, Sappi and of South African Breweries, third largest brewery in the world, is completely symbolic in this regard. Officially justified by the need to finance the expansion of these groups more easily, these transfers are integral to a globalisation strategy that will inevitably lead these companies to reduce the share of South Africa in their turnover and their investments.

The exchange of interests that took place in 1998 between Rembrandt and British American Tobacco (BAT), which has resulted in the South African group taking control of the world's second largest cigarette producer, is in line with this same logic of internationalisation. Moreover, through its Richemont subsidiary based in Switzerland, the South African group has become one of the large global players in the luxury goods industry.

On the whole, if the investment inward stock in South Africa has multiplied by 3,8 from 1990 to 1997 according to the balance of payment statistics, South African outward stock abroad has multiplied by 3,5. At the end of 1997 the latter had risen to R133,7 billion according to Reserve Bank estimates, which represents one-and-a-half times the former, valued

Graph 9:
GDP per capita and ratio between foreign direct investment and investment abroad in each country

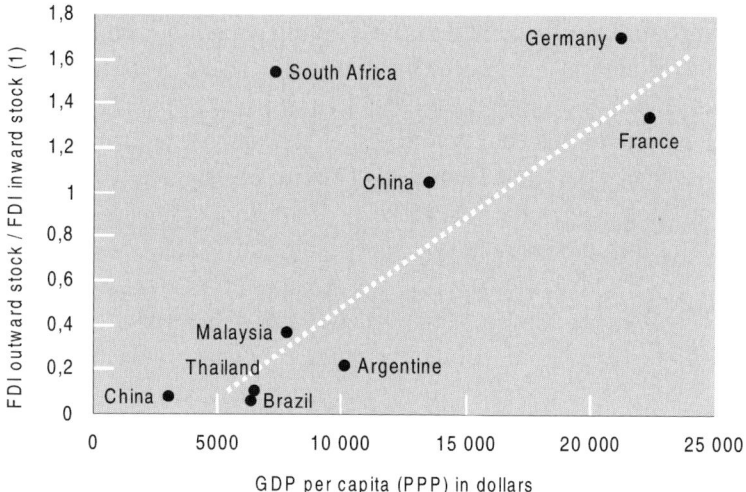

GDP per capita (PPP) in dollars

Source: World Bank and UNCTAD
(1) This ratio is equal to 1 if the country's investment outward stock is equal to the investment inward stock in the country.

at R89,3 billion. This characteristic is almost unique among developing countries (Graph 9).

According to the same statistics, which need to be interpreted in a qualitative way, three-quarters of the investment inward stock is held by European investors (Great Britain especially, whose share showed an increase when several large groups moved their headquarters to South Africa, and were henceforth considered British subsidiaries), with the United States also being a significant investor. This foreign capital is concentrated in the industrial (food processing in particular) and services (telecommunications and finance) sectors. The bulk of outward stock is situated in Europe, followed by Africa and the United States[21], with no sectoral breakdown of this having been published.

---

21 Balance of payment statistics do not provide a precise geographical breakdown of these stocks since it is limited only to the link between South African companies and their subsidiaries or foreign parent companies. This hampers measuring investments abroad. Thus, after Great Britain, Luxembourg (headquarters of Minorco) and Switzerland (headquarters of Richemont) were respectively considered to be the countries receiving the second and third largest amount of South African investment, even if the headquarters of the subsidiaries in these two countries were situated there for tax reasons only.

In the long run, the success of South Africa's international integration policy is a challenge that will contribute to the realisation of economic development and employment creation objectives. The above analysis shows the successes that have already been achieved as well as the difficulties encountered in implementing this policy. In particular, it confirms the fact that if this opening up is necessary, its success is not guaranteed. The following three chapters complement this analysis by examining the new modalities of the economic and trade relations that are in the process of being established with the main trading partners, which are Africa – more particularly southern Africa – and the European Union.

CHAPTER 6

South Africa and the "African Renaissance"

Rwanda is our nightmare, South Africa is our dream.
— Wole Soyinka, Nobel Prize for literature[1]

By an accident of history, two major events simultaneously shook the African continent in the spring of 1994. The Rwandan genocide, characterised by the massacre of close to a million Tutsis in the span of a few weeks, was the first of these events. This tragedy reinforced those who believe that Africa is returning to darkness, or that the rise in barbarism and civil wars in Africa is the inescapable consequence of the end of the cold war and the growing disinterest of the large powers in the continent. In contrast, the fact that at the same time, the National Party government regime, which was in power in South Africa for close to half a century, peacefully handed over power to the black majority, after an exemplary process of democratic transition, constituted a serious reason to believe in the future of this continent.

These two examples show that great uncertainty exists regarding the prospects of African countries over the coming years. Whereas some of them seem ready to experience some improvement in their economic and political situation, a large number will probably continue to stagnate, with some finally suffering the ravages of destructive conflicts.

As a result, the "African Renaissance" concept, launched by Nelson Mandela soon after his election as the first president of the new South Africa[23], which echoes the discourses of Nkrumah and Nyerere during the independence era of the 1960s, is to some degree an act of faith. It

---

1   Cited by Reader, 1997.
2   Nelson Mandela declared at the Heads of State Summit of the Organisation of African Unity (OAU) in June 1994: "Thus, do we give reason to the peoples of the world to say of Africa that she will never know stability and peace, that she will forever experience poverty and dehumanisation and that we shall be forever knocking on somebody's door pleading for a slice of bread. We know that we have it in ourselves, as Africans, to change all this. We must assert our will to do so. We must say that there is no obstacle big enough to stop us from bringing about an African Renaissance", (Mills, 1998).

establishes a bold parallel between the period of rapid economic expansion and intellectual surging experienced in Europe during the fifteenth and sixteenth centuries and the revival currently experienced on the African continent in a number of areas.

According to an ANC document:

This approach is underpinned by our commitment to, and active promotion of, the African Renaissance: the rebirth of a continent that has for far too long been the object of exploitation and plunder. For us, this African Renaissance is both a strategic objective and a call to action.[3]

This definition synthesises the three basic ideas underlying this concept, according to the vision of those that promote it:

- The first touches on the witnessing of a relative improvement in the situation of the African continent, both in the political and economic spheres, to which South Africa has contributed.
- The second is the belief that South Africa is an entirely African country, which means that this country experiences problems similar to those of other countries on the continent.
- Finally, flowing from the above argument, the future of South Africa is inextricably linked to that of the continent, to which this country has to make a decisive contribution.

Precarious economic recovery

During the past decades, most African countries have experienced almost uninterrupted economic decline. Thus, the per capita GDP of most has stagnated at a very low, indeed often reduced level since the beginning of the 1960s. Only a few countries such as Botswana and Mauritius have succeeded in increasing their per capita GDP in significant proportions. The nature of the African "poverty trap" has also been characterised by a falling behind in relation to the rest of the world and more particularly in relation to other developing countries. The per capita GDP of Ivory Coast, which was higher than that of South Korea in 1960 expressed in purchasing power parity, today is almost four times lower. In 1996, total African GDP of US$295 billion represented less than one per cent of global GDP.

---

[3] Kornegay and Landsberg, 1998.

These mediocre growth performances have been accompanied by a gradual marginalisation of Africa in world trade. Sub-Saharan Africa's market share was therefore reduced by more than half (from 3,8 per cent to 1,4 per cent) between 1960 and 1996. This was due to a collapse of African market share at the global level for its main exported products, as well as a specialisation in hardly buoyant primary sectors[4].

In this context, the economic recovery experienced on the continent during the second half of the 1990s gave rise to great optimism, inasmuch as one could believe that African countries have succeeded in halting their process of marginalisation and impoverishment. This revival interrupted the long period of declining per capita income which marked the entire decade of the 1980s and the first half of the 1990s. Thus, the International Monetary Fund posed the question: "Has Africa reached a turning point?" to which it has prudently responded in the affirmative.[5]

The general improvement in the political environment in a number of countries is a key factor in explaining this revival. This is particularly the case in South Africa, where the economic recession under way at the end of the 1980s was interrupted and where a significant improvement in the economic situation since the end of apartheid was witnessed. This event also had a major impact on the entire southern Africa, a sub-continent that has suffered the longest and most serious conflicts since the 1960s. The countries of the region have in fact suffered profoundly from the South African policy of destabilising its neighbours and their own civil wars.

The end of the civil war in Mozambique in 1992 was partly the result of South Africa ceasing its support of the Renamo rebel movement.[6] This civil war, among the most brutal on the continent, has been at the basis of the destruction of almost the entire infrastructure of the country and the displacement of half its population. Thus, since the end of the civil war, Mozambique is experiencing a double digit economic growth rate, among the highest on the continent.

However, the hope created by the end of apartheid that South Africa could constitute the "growth engine" of the African continent has partly been disappointed until now. Since 1994, despite the interruption of the recession in South Africa, the economy's average growth has been lower

---

4   Yeats *et al.*, 1997.
5   Fischer, *et al.*, 1998.
6   The former neighbouring Rhodesian government created this movement during the 1970s, while the South Africans took over their support after the independence of Zimbabwe, which took place in 1980.

CHAPTER 6 South Africa and the "African Renaissance"

than that of all the sub-Saharan African countries and more particularly that of most of its southern African neighbours. Moreover, its protectionism with regard to its trading partners as far as their main export products were concerned (textile and especially agricultural products) prevented them from benefiting from the growth recovery of the largest regional market to their full extent.

Nigeria, which follows South Africa as the second largest African power, has also recently experienced a favourable political evolution following the disappearance of the dictator Abacha in 1998. The holding of elections in 1999 has facilitated the pursuit of democratisation of the regime in a country that has practically known only military dictatorships since its independence in 1960.

The improvement in the political environment on the continent, however, is both fragile and largely contradictory. A United Nations report found that 14 African countries out of a total of 53 – or more than a quarter – were affected by armed conflicts in 1996. These conflicts, which have caused 8 million refugees to leave their homes, were responsible for half the war-related deaths registered in the world during that same year. The civil wars in Sudan, Somalia, Liberia and Sierra Leone have brought about massive destruction and widespread famines. Similarly, the resurgence in 1998 of the civil war in Angola, the longest known on the African continent, is a major tragedy. Finally, whereas the fall of Mobutu gave rise to many hopes in the Democratic Republic of Congo, this country is torn by the first large-scale war the African continent has known since the independence era, involving about ten belligerent countries.

The economic recovery witnessed in sub-Saharan Africa also has to do with the international economic situation. As shown in Graph 10, which compares economic growth and the index of international raw material prices (in the absence of reliable statistics on the terms of trade), a tight correlation exists between the rise in the prices of the main raw materials exported by African countries between 1995 and 1997 and an acceleration in the growth of African economies during this period.

In fact, price increases have strongly stimulated these countries' GDP growth and exports. They have affected both food (coffee, cocoa, tobacco) – which sometimes experienced considerable increases – and industrial (most minerals) raw materials, as well as petroleum, in the context of strong growth globally. This favourable development has temporarily interrupted a trend of decline in their terms of trade, which affects all raw material exporting countries and more particularly African countries. South

Graph 10:
GDP growth in sub-Saharan Africa and raw material prices
(1990–1999)

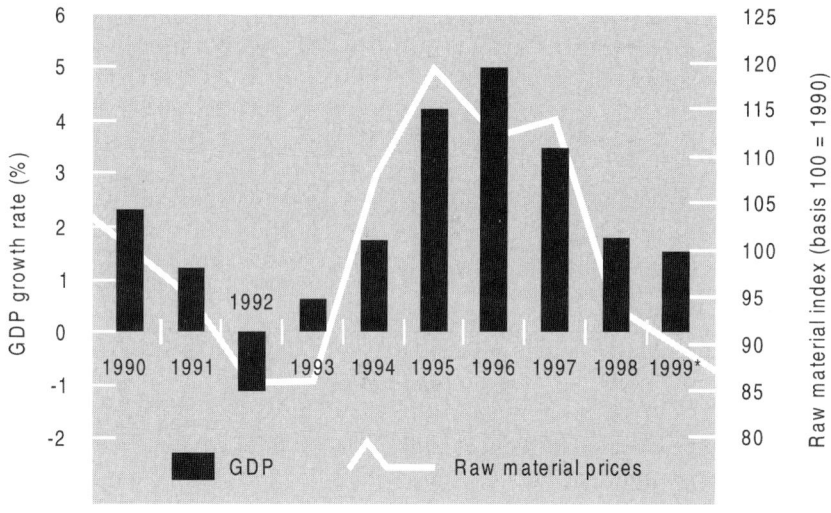

* estimate
Source: World Bank and *The Economist*

Africa, the world's leading exporter of many minerals, also benefited from this increase, which stimulated its growth.

Conversely, the slowing down of African growth witnessed at the end of the 1990s is the direct consequence of the international crisis which slowed down global demand for raw materials. The fall in the price of raw materials which resulted from this, affected African countries quite differently.

This analysis shows that the continent's economic performance at the beginning of the 21st century continues to depend largely on the future development of raw material prices.

A last factor explaining the recovery is the widespread improvement in the economic policies implemented by African countries.

Here again, South Africa has participated in this improvement. Actually, the new government broke with a policy that led to complete economic stagnation and severe recession. Whatever one's judgement of the macroeconomic policy followed since 1994, one is forced to acknowledge that it curbed the soaring public expenditure and reinforced the international competitiveness of companies, a necessary condition for accelerating growth in the long term.

CHAPTER 6 South Africa and the "African Renaissance"

In the CFA franc zone, the 50 per cent devaluation of the currency in January 1994 allowed the correction of an overvaluation, which contributed largely to the recession registered by these countries since the 1980s. Furthermore, more generally, the governments of most of these countries, often under pressure from funding agencies, took pains to abide more strictly by a number of good management principles that were often foreign to them, especially as far as budgetary matters were concerned. Moreover, the conversion of these countries to an export-oriented growth model, promoted by the Bretton Woods institutions, has led to a general reduction in customs duties and non-tariff barriers, a standardisation of exchange rates, and the suppression of many export monopolies, proving their inefficiency.

The business environment therefore became more favourable, as confirmed by surveys conducted on the opinions of local business people, such as the survey of the World Economic Forum.[7]

In the long run, the lack of productive investments and their global inefficiency, which explains the mediocrity of African economic performances during the previous years, still remain impediments to sustainable growth.

Weak capital growth in sub-Saharan Africa is the result of an investment rate that is weaker than in the rest of the world. Moreover, this rate declined following the implementation of structural adjustment programmes, before stabilising at a low level at the beginning of the 1990s. With an average level of less than 18 per cent, it is much lower than that of all other developing regions.

Three factors help to explain this shortcoming:
- Over a long period, a weak domestic savings rate restrains the investment rate. The Asian example during the past decades, however, shows that the savings rate increases as countries develop according to a virtuous circle in which strong growth leads to strong domestic savings. The fact that this rate is higher in Latin America and especially in Asia above all reflects this difference in development level and displays a tautological character to some degree.
- Insufficient domestic savings give foreign capital contributions a determining role. But sub-Saharan Africa attracts little private capital and, with the notable exception of South Africa, depends above all

---

7 World Economic Forum, 1998.

on tendentiously declining international aid. Between 1994 and 1997, the direct investments flowing into the entire African continent, almost all of which were directed at South Africa and some petroleum producing countries (Angola and Nigeria especially) amounted to only US$1,4 billion a year on average, or hardly more than 2 per cent of total flows received by all developing countries, and less than the total amount received by Malaysia. On the other hand, the continent has been suffering significant capital flight owing to countries not being attractive in terms of investment, which has negative implications for foreign investors.

- The constraint of over-indebtedness often made net resource transfers to these countries negative. This is structural, insofar as it is common knowledge that these countries will not be able to alleviate their debt significantly without external aid; in fact, two-thirds of the debt stock increase has been due to payment arrears; the Highly Indebted Poor Country Initiative (HIPC), launched by donors in view of annulling part of their debt could improve the situation.

Furthermore, African countries suffer from a number of drawbacks such as a lack of human capital, lack of water, the occurrence of frequent climatic hazards, and vulnerability to erratic fluctuations in raw material prices, whose impact on growth, however, is difficult to assess accurately.

This last aspect is reinforced by the export concentration of most African countries for whom two to three types of raw materials generally represent almost all exports. Indeed, the example of the Asian countries shows that export diversification cannot be bypassed in the framework of a development process.

Finally, AIDS is among the numerous scourges suffered by sub-Saharan Africa. At the end of 1999, 70 per cent out of 33,3 million HIV-positive people in the world lived on this subcontinent.[8] This pandemic is totally uncontrolled in this region, as is shown by the exponential increase in the number of people infected with the virus. A drastic reduction in life expectancy has already been witnessed in the most affected countries situated in southern (South Africa, Botswana, Namibia, Zimbabwe) and eastern (Uganda) Africa. The economic and social consequences of this pandemic in these countries are catastrophic.

---

8   UNAIDS, 1999.

Therefore, whereas life expectancy at birth has increased by 15 years in southern Africa, going from 44 years at the beginning of the 1950s to 59 years at the beginning of the 1990s, this scourge has destroyed half a century's worth of social and sanitary progress: according to the United Nations, life expectancy should in actual fact decline in the relevant countries to 45 years between 2005 and 2010.

These well-known structural shortcomings, as well as the clinging to power of some corrupt regimes and the practising of still bankrupt economic policies contribute to the growing heterogeneity characterising the African continent. Since the 1960s, the dispension of per capita income levels has doubled.[9] This recovery has accelerated the divergences between a few performing countries, countries with average growth, and those who are experiencing a prolonged decline.

No country can escape these problems completely. Those that have succeeded in reducing their dependency on the raw material cycle by diversifying their productive apparatus and export supply to the advantage of manufactured products have an important asset at their disposal in the long term. Only three countries, South Africa, Mauritius, and to some extent Zimbabwe find themselves in this situation. The latter, however, is suffering from drawbacks that may prevent it from benefiting from this characteristic over the next few years. In contrast, the majority of African countries that are classified as least developed countries (LDCs) continue to display a weak development potential and reduced appeal. Whereas the possibility of any structural recovery in the economic situation is naturally very fragile, considering the lack of diversification of their economies, numerous structural constraints limit growth prospects in the long run.

More than ever, Africa can count only on itself above all to ensure its development, and it urgently needs some countries to act as a driving force for this development. As the IMF study observes:

Economic prospects for the region as a whole would look very different if growth in Nigeria and South Africa were to rise significantly, not only because of the very large share of these countries in the GDP and the population of the continent, but also because of the considerable potential for favourable spillover effects in neighbouring countries.[10]

---

9   Measured by the standard GNP per capita deviation assessed in 1985 purchasing power parity (Author's calculations).

10 Fischer *et al.*, 1998.

Africa for Africans ...

Close to four decades after the beginning of the independence era, the end of apartheid concluded, to some degree, the continent's colonial period. After the oppression of the black majority came to an end in the last African country still to be ruled by a white minority, African sovereignty could be exercised throughout the entire continent.

In this sense, the "African Renaissance" marks the reintegration of South Africa among its peers and the recognition of the fact that this country, which has the largest white population in Africa, is also above all an African country. This is why, after having used this concept for the first time at the presentation of the new constitution in 1996, Thabo Mbeki stridently affirmed: "I am an African". Removed by almost three centuries, this declaration echoed that of the Huguenot settler Hendrik Bibault who declared himself an "Afrikaner" in 1707 and no longer Dutch,[11] thus refusing to be considered a foreigner in this country, and claiming his status as a legal inhabitant of the continent.

With this quote, Thabo Mbeki first of all put an end to the illusion, fostered by the apartheid government, of a South Africa that belonged to the developed world and was isolated from a continent in distress.[12] This illusion also consisted of viewing South Africa, where whites only represent a minority share of the population, as equal to the Maghreb at the other extreme of the continent, a world apart closer to Europe and other industrialised countries than its sub-Saharan African neighbours, or as a white enclave whose location on the African continent was purely accidental. The homelands policy was in line with this thinking, since it aimed in the long run to transfer the entire black population to theoretically independent territories (but in fact never recognised by the international community) while splitting it from its South African nationality.

To consider South Africa as an African country seems obvious if one takes into account its geographical location and the composition of its population. Without neglecting the specificities of its economy, be it in terms of size, level of development or potential, this declaration emphasises its similarities with other African countries.

These similarities relate in particular to contemporary economic history. A comparative study[13] has shown that South Africa's economic

---

11 Davenport, 1991.
12 Friedman, 1997.
13 Hawkins, 1997.

CHAPTER 6 South Africa and the "African Renaissance"

performance between the first oil crisis and the beginning of the 1990s was hardly different from, and even worse than, that of the whole of sub-Saharan Africa. In all cases it lagged far behind the average performance of developing countries. Thus, whereas the GDP per capita of all developing countries increased by 2,3 per cent a year on average between 1973 and 1992, it fell by 0,4 per cent a year in sub-Saharan Africa and by 0,6 per cent a year in South Africa during the same period. In both instances, the latter did not increase since the 1960s. The same observation can be made for the development of exports. Finally, the marked decline in South African investment rates has brought these to a level comparable to that of the average rate in sub-Saharan Africa from the second half of the 1980s.

In short, South Africa has not escaped the process of economic decline and marginalisation in global trade that has affected all of sub-Saharan Africa. What is more, its mediocre economic performance can to a large degree be attributed to the same factors that are at the basis of the same occurrence in other African countries, be they a matter of bad governance, inefficiency of resource allocation under the National Party government (the stagnation of total factor productivity witnessed in South Africa was also the case in the rest of sub-Saharan Africa), incapacity to attract foreign investment, inappropriate monetary and fiscal policies, lack of investment in human resource development as far as a very large majority of the population was concerned, high level of protection of the domestic market, "white elephant" investments[14] aimed at ensuring the country's self-sufficiency, and so on. A notable difference lies in the country's low level of debt.

In the latter half of the 1990s, the economic recovery registered in South Africa also displayed some points of comparison with that experienced in the rest of the continent.[15] In the context of rapid external and internal liberalisation, this was achieved more by an acceleration in productivity gains and a better utilisation of production capacity than by a significant increase in investments in most of the countries concerned.

The fact that the economic difficulties encountered by South Africa, despite their specificity, are on the whole similar to those encountered by other African countries means that the challenges are also comparable.

---

14 The term "white elephant" refers to the many large projects launched throughout Africa since independence, often oversized and inefficient, and which sometimes have never even functioned.
15 Berthélemy and Söderling, 1999.

In fact, South Africa as much as the rest of the continent, needs to create employment and reduce the poverty of its population, but also to improve its international competitiveness in view of increasing its growth potential and reducing its vulnerability to the international economic situation.

This "Africanness" is quite obviously bound to become more pronounced with the gradual access of blacks to the commanding heights of the South African economy promoted by the state, the emergence and expansion of a black bourgeoisie, the broadening of the informal sector, as well as the slow social and geographical mixing, which is sure to take place.

All the same, South Africa is bound in all likelihood to stereotype itself as resembling more and more just another African country, while at the same time emphasising its specificity as a continental power.

Not satisfied to declare their "Africanness", the instigators of the "African Renaissance" also claim to be a model for the whole continent. To do so, they rely on the exemplary nature of the South African transition, be it in the political or the economic sphere.

In a world governed by power relations and the use of violence, South Africa has demonstrated that it is possible to resolve conflicts in a relatively peaceful way: without resorting to the route of arms, but to that of reason; not through force, but through negotiation.

On a continent that usually transformed the presidential office into lifelong employment for decades, the voluntary departure of Nelson Mandela on the occasion of the 1999 presidential elections showed that true African statesmen, who are not only preoccupied by their own interests and personal enrichment, but who possess a true sense of state and of governing a country, do exist.

South African role modelling applies equally to economic matters. In fact, even if the economic transition turned out to take longer than expected, developments in South Africa have refuted those who predicted the economic collapse of the country after the change of regime that took place in 1994.

Moreover, South Africa is the only African country that can be compared with the emerging Asian and Latin American countries in some respects, and can hope to set in motion a development process similar to that of those countries over the next years. Besides being listed in 28th position globally in terms of Gross Domestic Product, it ranks 9th among developing countries (apart from the OECD), before Malaysia.

CHAPTER 6 South Africa and the "African Renaissance"

As Jenny Cargill writes:
Without neglecting the scale of poverty in South Africa, it is appropriate to underline that the infrastructure worthy of the first world, which exists in this country, makes its transition different from all the comparable processes witnessed throughout the world, be it in Africa or elsewhere. No other country in recent history has emerged from a revolutionary conflict with an intact and sophisticated financial infrastructure, and such a sizeable capital stock and qualifications – admittedly still inadequate.[16]

Finally, the fact that the South African transition took place without external intervention (unlike the example of neighbouring Namibia and Zimbabwe, for instance) is an incentive for letting Africa become responsible for its destiny. Whereas many leaders revel in attributing their countries' difficulties to the colonial heritage, this success reinforces the significance of the discourse on "good governance" advanced by South African leaders. For African people it is a question of taking responsibility and accountability for their future and granting themselves the means to real development without external interference. The corollary to this is the indispensable democratisation of African regimes that have to be accountable for their policies and the economic results of these to their populations, whereas many despots have been able to remain in power for decades despite their catastrophic results in this domain.

"Africa for Africans" also signifies acceptance of the specificity of African culture, which is not an inferior culture unsuitable for development, contrary to an argument that historically has served to justify colonialism and apartheid. To support his vision, Thabo Mbeki cites the Egyptian pyramids, the city of Carthage and the Zimbabwe ruins, as well as the universities of Alexandria, Fez and Timbuktu. Here again, South Africa and its new leaders are a driving force in this domain.

According to Karl Maïer:
Much has been written about the iron will and sacrifice to free his (Nelson Mandela) people from subjugation; but his genius, and one of the many reasons he evokes such admiration around the world, is his ability to bring African values to bear on the problems of late twentieth-century

---

16 Business Map, 1999.

values such as the pre-eminence of the interests of the community over those of the individual, respect for traditional culture, and at times unbelievable capacity for forgiveness.[17]

Taking this "pan-Africanist" logic to its conclusion, some reject imported economic policy models and are looking for an appropriate route that is not imposed by the Bretton Woods institutions.

According to the ANC:

This Renaissance is a rejection of both inefficient and sometimes corrupt post-colonial bureaucracies and of the absolute hegemony of technical structural adjustment programmes imposed by imperialist countries and their institutions.[18]

This discourse is not entirely unfounded in the case of South Africa, which until now has succeeded in avoiding defeat by a structural adjustment programme, even if the economic policy implemented in the framework of the GEAR closely resembles such a programme. Moreover, South Africa is the only African country in a position to finance the bulk of its infrastructure investments itself, with only marginal support from donors. It is also the only one where private capital represents the bulk of external financing. By contrast, for most of the least developed African countries, which seem condemned to subsist in the future mainly thanks to international aid, hope of a more autonomous development can remain only an illusion.

Similarly, the desire to reinforce south-south co-operation to escape the influence of the big powers and their multinational corporations, risks being followed to little effect. The impact of the 1998 financial crisis on the future of this co-operation is ambivalent. On the one hand, the crisis showed that developing countries, particularly South Africa, suffered from the excesses of globalisation, without the developed countries having shown their capacity to prevent the recurrence of such crises. This urges developing countries to come together in order to defend their interests. Conversely, the Asian crisis proved the weaknesses of the development path followed by the Asian countries. In particular, the Malaysian model, until now often cited in Africa as an example, has lost much of its glory.

---

17 Maïer, 1998.
18 Kornegay and Landsberg, 1998.

... or Africa for South Africans?

As the application of the "African Renaissance" – if there is a Renaissance – only to South Africa would empty this concept of all significance, one must consider the role that this country can play in the framework of this process. The inevitable consequence of asserting South Africa's entrenchment in the African continent, according to the political scientist Steven Friedman, is recognition of the fact that the future of South Africa cannot be disassociated from that of the rest of Africa and that this country therefore has to play an active role to influence the latter.[18]

This can firstly be justified by the economic dominance that South Africa exerts on the continent, where it is a true "Gulliver in Lilliput" (Table 1). South Africa accounts for 41 per cent of sub-Saharan Africa's GDP in 1996, an equivalent proportion of its exports, and 76 per cent of electricity production. The total number of automobiles owned in South Africa represents 48 per cent of that owned on the continent; 45 per cent of all telephone lines installed in Africa are situated there, and so on.

This assertion can also be justified by South Africa's higher level of development, which vests this country with a "civilisation" mission, according to this concept. Forty million South Africans produce almost as

Table 9:
The weight of South Africa in sub-Saharan Africa (1996) (%)

(1996)	South Africa	Total sub-Saharan Africa	Share of SA/total sub-Saharan Africa	Share of sub-Saharan Africa/world
GDP (US$ bn)	126,3	305,1	41,4	1,1
Exports (US$ bn)	28,7	72,3	39,7	1,4
Population (m)	40	596	6,7	10,3
Stock market capital (US$ bn)	232,4	257,4	90,2	1,3
Electricity production (kWh bn)	186,8	245,8	76,0	1,9
Total automobiles (thousands)	4028	8344	48,3	1,6
Number telephone lines (thousands)	4000	8940	44,7	1,2

Source: World Bank, World Trade Organisation

---

19 Friedman, 1997.

much on their own as the 560 million inhabitants of other sub-Saharan African countries. It is the only African country that has research and development potential of an international standard at its disposal, and that owns high-tech industries in the aeronautical, information technology, spatial, and other spheres. Its universities already welcome tens of thousands of students from all over Africa.

Despite its failure to assume the role of a driving force expected of it at the end of apartheid, South Africa can, however, contribute to the continent's development in different ways. Its role as an engine of growth – especially at the regional level – could above all result from its policy of co-operation with its neighbours in economic and trade matters, through education and technical assistance, and through the impact of its companies' internationalisation strategy.

In this sense, the "African Renaissance" also constitutes to some degree both an actualisation and a rationalisation of South Africa's hegemonic discourse as regards the continent.

Aiming to continue the process of colonisation towards the north, starting from the southernmost tip of the continent, Jan Smuts responded to the question "What is South Africa?" at the establishment of the South African Union in 1910:

South Africa is a geographical term that we advisedly do not define. It would surely cover any part of the continent south of the equator.[20]

South African expansionism has asserted itself since the end of the nineteenth century, when Cecil John Rhodes, then Prime Minister of the Cape Colony, had conquered a territory larger than the current South Africa on behalf of the British South Africa Company, which became Zambia and Zimbabwe. As soon as the South African Union was formed by a merger of the two former British crown colonies (the Cape and Natal) and the two former Boer republics (Transvaal and the Orange Free State), annexed after the Boer War, South African leaders expressed the wish to expand their country's borders. The constitution thus called for the three bordering British colonies (Bechuanaland, which became Botswana; Basutoland, which became Lesotho; and Swaziland) to join the Union to enlarge the "tribal reserves" and the agricultural territories monopolised by the white settlers and their descendants. Even if opposition

---

20 Cited by Parsons, 1982.

by the local population caused these plans to fail, South Africa did not cease applying pressure to this end on Great Britain until these colonies attained independence during the course of the 1960s. Following Germany's defeat in World War I, the mandate given to South Africa of South West Africa (which became Namibia) by the League of Nations allowed South African companies to lay hands on the vast mining resources of this country the size of France. Finally, despite intense lobbying, Southern Rhodesia, conquered in 1890 by a party of South African pioneers, rejected the proposition to become the fifth South African province in a referendum in 1922.

Subsequently, these ambitions found their natural economic extension through the pursuit of an effort to penetrate the African continent commercially. At the beginning of the Second World War, the same Jan Smuts expressed his vision of the role that his country had to play as follows:

If we wish to take our rightful position as leader in Pan-African development and in the shaping of future policies and events in this vast continent, we must face the realities and the facts of the present and seize the opportunities these offer. All Africa may be our market if we will but have the vision, and farsighted policy will be necessary if that is to be realised.[21]

Whereas the gradual retiring of colonial powers favoured an increase in South African influence, the apartheid system that was put into place immediately after the Second World War has prevented South Africa from reaching its goal of continent-wide leadership. The country's isolation increased as African countries gradually attained independence, with South Africa not only being excluded from all regional organisations but over time also being made the object of increasingly severe sanctions.

The end of apartheid, which allowed South Africa to reconcile with the rest of the continent, also granted it the opportunity, for the first time, to realise its secular ambitions there. Even if the size of the African market is limited, equivalent to that of Argentina or Belgium, and displays weak growth prospects on the whole, it is of major interest to South African firms. Here they actually have undeniable comparative advantages in terms of proximity, price, and product type, which is more adapted to this market

---

21 Cited by Vale and Maseko, 1998.

that those coming from developed countries. As was crudely stated by a South African businessman:

Africa is a huge market: it may be turbulent sometimes, but it eats and it uses toiletries every day.[22]

All the firms are participating in this "scramble for Africa" primarily directed at southern Africa, for reasons of geographical and cultural proximity, but which is increasingly extending beyond it.

Trade has registered a very rapid increase (Graph 11). South African exports to its African partners (aside from SACU) went up from R4,4 billion in 1990 to a total of R20 billion in 1998. Even though the bulk of exports are destined for southern Africa, the rest of the continent is absorbing an increasing share. South African imports have also increased very rapidly (from R0,8 to R3,6 billion, of which half is coming from southern Africa). South Africa exports five times more merchandise to its partners than it buys from them, with this ratio not having changed since 1990.

Admittedly the increase in exports partly conveys a catch-up effect: until the 1960s, the era during which South Africa's exclusion from the international community started, around a fifth of its exports were directed towards Africa, or a proportion very near to that reached at the end of the 1990s. It is clear, however, that this phenomenon is bound to continue and expand, as soon as the downturn in trade witnessed in 1998, linked to the international crisis, has been absorbed.

For their part, direct investments have benefited from the recent opening up of South Africa to foreign investment, the launching of public enterprise privatisation programmes, and the granting of concessions to some public services, as well as in some cases from disinvestments by European investors, whose presence rose again to that of the colonial period. To some degree, South Africans are taking over from European firms, whose investments today are concentrated in the countries of the Asian triad and their peripheries.

Large South African multinationals are the most active. Mining projects abound in southern Africa, but also in the rest of the continent. Investments in the commercial and banking sectors are of essential strategic importance, insofar as they constitute the means of reinforcing South African commercial presence on the continent. South African retail chains have introduced large-scale distribution in countries where they had been

---

22 *Ibid.*

Graph 11:
Development of trade between South Africa and Africa (1990–1999)

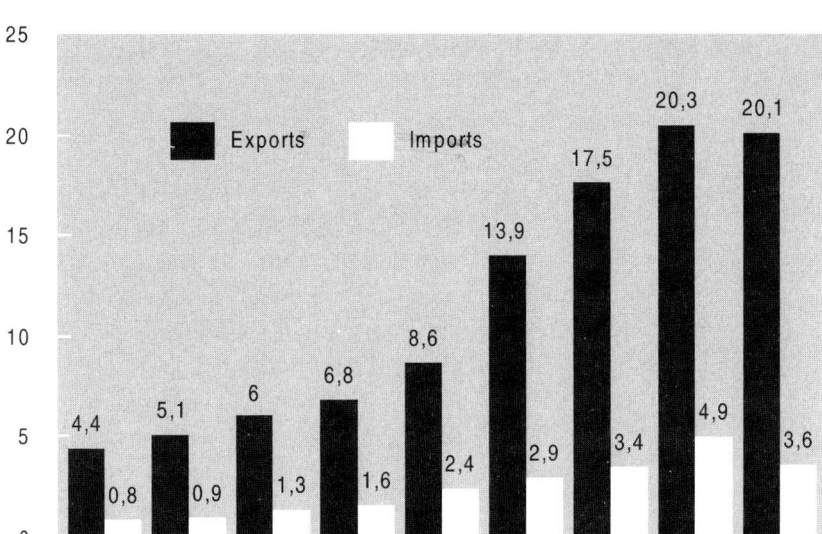

Source: South African Customs

unknown until now, benefiting from their trade and introducing new consumption patterns in so doing. Since buying several subsidiaries of the Meridien-BIAO bank when it collapsed, Standard Bank has a network covering 15 African countries. Furthermore, thanks to its recent investments, today South African Breweries is present in 11 southern and eastern African countries. More recently, one has seen the South African sugar-producing group Illovo buying the interests of British conglomerate Lonhro in this sector in Malawi and Swaziland. The oil producer Engen has recovered the Petrofina and British Petroleum distribution networks in Burundi and Rwanda and is now operating in a joint venture with the leading oil producer in the Democratic Republic of Congo, and so on.

The opening up of the telecommunications, transport, energy and even the health sectors to the private sector is also offering opportunities to South African operators. MTN, operating one of the cellular telephone networks in South Africa, was granted an operating license in Uganda, Rwanda and Swaziland and is negotiating a license in Nigeria. In Cameroon, Spoornet may soon manage part of the railway network in collaboration with a French company. The project to build a transport corridor between South Africa, Tanzania and Uganda resumes Cecil John Rhodes's unfinished project to build a railway from the Cape to Cairo. It consists of linking the Tanzam line connecting Zambia to Tanzania, built by the Chinese to allow Zambian copper to be exported through Dar-Es-Salaam, to the Tanzanian network to Uganda. By avoiding transporting merchandise by boat, this railway corridor will cut the delay in carriage between Johannesburg and Kampala in half. The electricity operator Eskom also intends to internationalise its activities. Finally, Netcare, South Africa's leading private hospital group has taken advantage of the collapse of the public health system in Africa to sign public hospital management contracts in Angola, Gabon, Uganda, Rwanda, Swaziland and Zimbabwe and to negotiate new agreements in about ten other countries.

These investments have caused the capital stock held by South African firms in Africa to double since 1993, increasing from R2,8 billion to R6,4 billion at the end of 1997. Africa's share in total investment outward stock (4,8 per cent) nevertheless remains limited.

Does the "Africa for Africans" slogan therefore not run the risk of becoming a geographical transposition of the Monroe Doctrine decreed by the United States at the beginning of the twentieth century, which in reality would mean "Africa for South Africans"?

This risk cannot be dismissed, especially in the case of southern Africa. But it is without doubt inevitable compensation for the role South Africa could play as a growth engine in developing the region and indeed the entire continent beyond that.

CHAPTER 7

A regional power

The future of South Africa in an increasingly globalised world economy is intrinsically linked to that of its neighbours (...) South Africa can hope neither to be an island of prosperity in a sea of poverty, nor to compete efficiently on the global market while ignoring its regional partners.
— Alec Erwin, Minister of Trade and Industry[1]

South Africa occupies a dominant position in southern Africa. Its GDP is three times higher than that of all the other countries of the region combined. Although it is considered to be a medium-income country, most of its neighbours, with some close exceptions e.g. Botswana, are categorised in the least developed country group.

The heterogeneity in size and level of development between South Africa and the rest of the region explains the very specific nature of economic and trade relations between this country and its neighbours.

Southern Africa represents an important market for the exports and investments of South African companies, as well as a source of raw materials and a relatively cheap labour reserve. The end of apartheid has not fundamentally challenged this pattern of unequal relations. On the contrary, it has allowed companies to resume their expansionist strategy, interrupted by decades of international isolation.

At the same time, South Africa's entry into new relations of co-operation with its regional partners indicates a break with the destabilisation strategy implemented by the previous government, which regarded the poorest countries with disdain and showed interest only in developed countries, considering them alone to be peers. These relations stem from the fact that the development of countries to the north of the Limpopo[2] is indispensable to that of South Africa, to guarantee the enlargement of its

---

1 Erwin, 1998b.
2 The Limpopo River demarcates South Africa's northern border with Zimbabwe and part of Botswana.

export markets on the one hand, and on the other, because it is the only way in which to limit massive immigration from its neighbours.

South Africa's accession to the Southern African Development Community (SADC), which demonstrated the importance it attached to this co-operation, has conferred a true regional dimension on this organisation while also giving it new momentum. Regarded to an excessive degree as a key element of a regional industrialisation strategy, the regional free trade area process in fact will only be able to succeed if it forms part of a more global economic integration project.

Generally, South Africa's partners want it to play the role of a "substitute metropolis" at the regional level[3], and to contribute to the development of countries that have recently often experienced a sharp economic decline. At the same time, the dominance that South Africa exerts over the region, as well as recent history marked by its regional destabilisation policy, has intensified antagonisms and fears of a growing dependency on it.[4]

Southern Africa, South Africa's hinterland

South Africa exerts such economic dominance over all southern African countries that this region can be considered its true hinterland, according to an expression of Cecil John Rhodes.

Historically, relations between South Africa and the countries of the region have been in keeping with a neo-colonial pattern, which corresponds to the theory of comparative advantage in its most elementary form: South Africa exports manufactured products and imports raw material and labour-intensive manufactured products; its most abundant production factor relative to its partners – its capital – tends to move to its partners in the form of direct investments, in exchange for their most abundant production factor, that is their unskilled labour, which tends to emigrate to the most developed country in the region.

Trade between South Africa and its neighbours essentially consists of the exporting of manufactured goods (mainly capital goods, transport equipment and chemical products) in exchange for purchases of intermediary goods necessary for the functioning of its economy: minerals, textiles, and so on.

---

3 As expressed by Bach and Cohen, 1993.
4 This chapter draws a lot on Cling, 1998.

The ranking of countries according to the significance of the South African share of their markets brings to light three highly distinct groups. In the "main circle", comprised of Botswana, Lesotho, Namibia and Swaziland, described as the "BLNS" countries, the South African share of their markets is in the order of 80–90 per cent. Even if this percentage is probably somewhat overestimated, insofar as many goods that are considered imported from South Africa in fact originate from third countries[5], it has to be related to the fact that these countries belong to a customs union dominated by South Africa, the Southern African Customs Union (SACU). South Africa's share of the market is also very high in four other countries of the region (Malawi, Mozambique, Zambia, Zimbabwe) that also form part of its sphere of direct influence. Here, imports of South African products represent between a third (Malawi, Zambia) and half (Mozambique, Zimbabwe) of total imports. South Africa's market share is somewhat lower in the other countries of the area.

Since the beginning of the 1990s, South Africa has largely benefited from the end of the embargo and its neighbours' rapid removal of custom duties in the framework of their structural adjustment programmes. South African exports toward the whole of southern Africa thus practically multiplied fourfold from 1990 to 1998, going from R4 billion to R15,3 billion, which represents 14 per cent of its total exports.

As a consequence, the trade imbalance between South Africa and its regional partners has become enormous. South African exports are close to eight times higher than its imports from the region. Not a single southern African country has been spared this upsurge, which has allowed South Africa to become the main supplier of almost all of them.

The sharp increase in exports was partly related to the recapturing of market positions that were lost during previous decades, when its neighbours had looked to reduce their dependence on the country of apartheid. But this phenomenon goes beyond that and also relates to the conquering of new markets, as was shown by the fact that South Africa has recently become the main supplier of Mauritius, Seychelles and Tanzania, to the detriment of the former colonial powers or neighbouring countries (Kenya in the case of Tanzania), which saw themselves being relegated to second place.

---

5   In the case of Botswana, 30 per cent of products considered to be imported from South Africa only transit through there according to Imani, 1998.

This trade advance has increased the dependence of South African firms on regional markets. Moreover, it has to be underlined that the total amount of exports to southern Africa is highly undervalued by official customs statistics:[6] if one adds to it sales to the SACU, which are not taken into account by these statistics, the total amount doubles in relation to the normal estimation. Furthermore, the share of southern Africa (including the SACU) in South African manufactured product exports is much higher than its average share in all products put together. Zimbabwe, South Africa's sixth client overall, is the fourth client of its industry but also the main client of many industrial sectors. This is particularly the case for chemical products, rubber, plastic products, glass, non-metallic minerals, metals, machinery, and capital goods products, and radio, television, and communication appliances and instruments.

The dominance exerted in trade matters is also evident in investment matters. Hence, large South African conglomerates largely control the economies of the neighbouring countries. Their subsidiaries are often the main taxpayers and are responsible for the bulk of the country's foreign exchange earnings.

Through its mining subsidiaries in Botswana (diamonds, copper-nickel, etc), the Anglo American group realises 70 per cent of the exports of that country and contributes close to half its fiscal revenue. The situation is similar in Zambia where Anglo controls a large share of copper production, which represents the main exports. South African firms also largely dominate the Zimbabwean economy, which is the most diversified in the region. The country's leading group, the Delta conglomerate (food processing, hotel industry, distribution, and so on), is controlled by South African Breweries and Old Mutual. Similarly, Anglo American controls all sugar cane production in Zimbabwe directly and through its Tongaat-Hulett subsidiary. Moreover, its subsidiaries carry out a large share of mining production (gold, zinc, iron-alloy). South African companies are also omnipresent in other countries of the region.

The upsurge in trade has been accompanied by a rapid expansion of direct investments in the area, which concerns all the large South African groups as well as many small and medium enterprises.

Large South African mining groups are among the most active in this domain. They aim to partake in the enormous potential of the region's

---

6   According to this country's national sources, the SACU exports, that is mainly from South Africa, added up to the following amounts: R7,6 billion to Botswana; R4,4 billion to Lesotho; R6,9 billion to Namibia; R4,6 billion to Swaziland.

CHAPTER 7 A regional power

subsoil, which still has barely been exploited until now, besides in South Africa. Anglo-American's projects in Zambia (copper), Katanga in the DRC (copper) and Tanzania (gold) are numerous. Billiton, second largest South African mining group, has also launched several projects in Mozambique in the iron and steel and aluminium industries.

South African investments are equally significant in the agricultural and food-processing sectors, which constitute, together with the mining sector, the second largest resource of these countries. The South African Illovo group has bought Lonhro's sugar interests in Malawi and Swaziland. Moreover, together with its competitor Tongaat-Hulett, it is driving the rehabilitation and development of Tanzanian and Mozambican plantations, neglected for several decades. Despite a highly favourable climate, Mozambique saw its annual production fall to 30 000 tons after two decades of civil war, which has left it a net sugar importer. Thanks to the current investments, production could increase to 370 000 tons by the year 2005, hence regaining pre-independence production levels. South African Breweries, for its part, has acquired local breweries in Mozambique, Zambia and Tanzania when they were privatised (in fact, in the first two cases it was a question of repurchasing subsidiaries that had been nationalised in the 1970s), and so on.

As in the rest of Africa, there have been numerous investments in the services sector. ABSA, one of South Africa's leading banks, took control of the leading Tanzanian bank when it was privatised, as well as a Zimbabwean bank. Large South African commercial retail chains have also expanded rapidly in neighbouring countries. In partnership with the National Company of Belgian Railways (SNCB), the South African public railway transport company, Spoornet, has been managing the Katanga railways in the DRC for a short while and is part of a consortium negotiating to resume the management of the Johannesburg-Maputo railway.

Traditionally, southern Africa fulfils a second function for South Africa, which is to serve as a source of raw materials and cheap labour.

The countries of the region thus provide South Africa with hydroelectric energy. The construction of the Victoria Falls power station on the Zambezi at the border between Northern and Southern Rhodesia (today Zambia and Zimbabwe) at the beginning of the twentieth century aimed to supply power to the South African gold mines on the Witwatersrand, which had just been discovered. The construction of the Cahora Bassa dam, also on the Zambezi river, at the beginning of the 1970s, partly financed by South Africa, was essentially intended to supply

South Africa. The constitution of the Southern African Power Pool (SAPP) at South Africa's initiative is also in line with the framework of this strategy. The aim of this body in bringing together regional electricity operators is to co-ordinate the management of electricity resources at a regional level and to contribute to completing the interconnection of national networks. The Democratic Republic of Congo's accession to the SAPP would allow the entire region, South Africa most of all, to benefit from the immense resources of the Zaire River, by expanding the Inga Dam power station, situated close to the river's mouth downstream from the capital Kinshasa. In Mozambique, which, with the Democratic Republic of Congo, owns the bulk of the region's hydroelectric resources, the Mepanda Uncua Dam could also increase the supply of cheap electricity meant for South Africa.

The Lesotho Highlands Water Project is a second example of the supply of raw materials to South Africa by its neighbours. This "Pharaonic" project, costing several tens of billions of rands, allows for the Gauteng region to be supplied with water from the Lesotho highlands, a few hundred kilometres away. The first phase, inaugurated in 1998, resulted in the building of the highest dam in Africa (Khatse Dam) and the digging of a 50-kilometre tunnel, as well as a water transport canal up to the Vaal River.

South Africa traditionally has used a large number of unskilled labourers from the countries of the region, which has helped to reduce the salary costs of its companies. From the beginning, South African mines resorted to the labour force of neighbouring countries to a very high degree. This allowed them to increase labour flexibility, with the immigrants being hired on fixed contracts generally for less than a year, to push down labour costs in this sector and increase profits in return, and finally nearly to do away with labour conflicts (immigrants did not have the right to strike).

This use of immigrant labour also suited large white farms, since it prevented the reduction of the rural labour surplus that would have resulted from employing local workers. At the beginning of the 1970s, close to 80 per cent of the 380 000 blacks employed in the mines were immigrants, mainly from Botswana, Lesotho, Malawi, Mozambique and Swaziland; of the neighbouring countries, only Rhodesia (now Zimbabwe) refused to send emigrants to the mines. Today still, the revenue transferred by Lesotho migrant workers, mostly employed in the mines, represents close to half the GDP of this small mountain kingdom completely surrounded by South African territory.

Owing to the decline of the gold mines since the 1980s and the gradual rise in unemployment in South Africa, the use of foreign labour became less and less necessary. However, there has been a somewhat rapid expansion in the employment of immigrants (official or clandestine), and today it is practised on a grand scale in some economic sectors: agriculture, construction, hotel-restaurant industry, domestic services, and so on. According to population census estimates, South Africa has one million official immigrants. The number of illegal immigrants, however, could be several million, since there is no precise estimation of this figure.

In the context of the general poverty in most of the region's countries, a number of factors explain the unprecedented increase in the scale of this phenomenon in the past years:[7] first, the abolition of apartheid has resulted in less control over internal population flows; furthermore, the general opening up of the country to its neighbours has been accompanied by an increasingly strict closing off of borders in developed countries. Despite the scale of unemployment in South Africa, an immigrant willing to accept any unskilled employment can earn at least five times more in South Africa that he or she would have earned in his or her country of origin, considering the development gap between South Africa and its neighbours.

Despite a number of actions having been taken to reduce the massive immigration from the region, which is worsening the domestic social situation, the South African government realises that only an acceleration of growth in neighbouring countries can create employment there while diminishing the attractiveness South Africa holds for these immigrants. This country's implementation of a regional co-operation effort and increasing economic integration at a regional level since the democratic transition, aimed at contributing to the development and the industrialisation of the whole region, is in response to this concern, as well as to the objective of enlarging markets for its companies.

The implementation of this strategy has been realised by South Africa's entry to the Southern African Development Community (SADC) in 1994. In 1992, this organisation, whose headquarters are in Gaborone, the capital of Botswana, replaced the Southern African Development and Co-ordination Conference (SADCC) established in 1982.

The SADCC, which aimed to reduce the dependence of the "frontline" states on South Africa, in fact no longer had grounds for its existence in the light of this country's democratic evolution. Whereas the SADCC had functioned mostly as an organisation co-ordinating and

---

7 Pérouse de Montclos, 1997.

canalising international aid for regional co-operation projects, at the outset SADC set itself a much larger objective, namely to establish a true regional community engaged in a regional integration process.

Following the inclusion of South Africa and of Mauritius (in 1995), the SADC now groups together all the countries of southern Africa,[8] with the exception of Madagascar. If one bears in mind that Tanzania has belonged to this organisation since the beginning, and the Democratic Republic of Congo's accession in 1997 (at the same time as that of the Seychelles), SADC extends beyond even the sub-continent's strict geographical field as it is usually defined. The resumption of the civil war in Angola and in the Democratic Republic of Congo in 1998, as well as the political dissent between the countries of the region resulting from this, at one point raised the fear that SADC was about to split, but this did not happen. Despite these antagonisms, realism has prevailed and co-operation has continued without the two countries at war participating in most projects.

Each member country is responsible for a particular sector in SADC: Angola for energy, Lesotho for water, Mozambique for transport and telecommunications, and so on. The establishment of the "finance and investment" sector in 1995 as South Africa's responsibility completed the diversification of this organisation's tasks. This sector is clearly different from those mentioned before. It aims for better co-ordination of macro-economic policies in southern Africa. Member countries' finance ministers and central bank governors have started consulting one another on this theme. In the long term, this sector could reinforce South Africa's leadership in the macroeconomic arena at a regional level. The recent signing of several sectoral protocols by SADC countries provides a framework for the harmonisation and integration of national policies and infrastructure in affected areas. Of particular interest are the water (1995), transport-meteorology-communications, energy (1996), and mining resources (1997) protocols. The trade protocol (see below), signed in 1996, has broader but not less significant implications.

Since joining SADC, South Africa has tried to solicit the support of its partners to engage in an in-depth restructuring of the SADC, in particular the reduction of the number of sectoral co-ordinating units in order to improve their functioning efficiency, and the modification of their tasks.

---

8   South Africa, Angola, Botswana, Lesotho, Malawi, Mauritius, Mozambique, Namibia, Democratic Republic of Congo, Seychelles, Swaziland, Tanzania, Zambia and Zimbabwe.

CHAPTER 7 A regional power

This has become even more necessary as the increasing contribution of the private sector to project financing is reducing their traditional function of co-ordinating donor funding. Nevertheless, South Africa's three years at the presidency of this organisation (1996–1999) did not lead to the achievement of any results in this sphere, as member countries are loath to abandon their sectoral responsibilities.

Moreover, South Africa has remained a member of the SACU, formed in 1910 at the time of the establishment of the South African Union. This customs union had been renegotiated following the independence of Botswana, Lesotho and Swaziland in the 1960s and has functioned in its current form since 1970. Since Namibia joined the SACU at its independence in 1990, it comprises five member countries: South Africa, Botswana, Lesotho, Namibia and Swaziland.

It is a customs union allowing for the free circulation of merchandise between its members, accompanied by a common external tariff and a formula for distributing the customs revenue among the different countries.

The SACU was of significant political benefit to South Africa from the 1960s until the end of apartheid, insofar as it allowed South Africa to break its international isolation. The SACU countries also offered South Africa a means of circumventing sanctions. Since the democratic transition, the SACU has represented no more than a captive market for South Africa.

For the BLNS countries, the loss of fiscal autonomy has been compensated for by an increasing transfer of income from South Africa corresponding to the redistribution of customs revenue according to a distribution formula which is largely in their favour. Whereas these countries received only three per cent of the pool when the current mechanism was put into place in 1970, this share has gradually increased to close to 50 per cent of the pool today, while their imports represent less than 10 per cent of the SACU total, including South Africa. In this context, the latter paid a total of R7,1 billion to its partners in 1999, that is 46 per cent of the customs revenue.

This subsidy was originally justified by the necessity to compensate for the negative effects of the SACU on the BLNS countries. These are a priori of three kinds: a trade diversion effect, linked to the tariff policy implemented by South Africa to protect its own industry which has resulted in a higher price level than in the absence of a customs union; loss of fiscal autonomy, insofar as South Africa unilaterally sets the customs duties that apply to the whole of the SACU in line with its own interests (some economists nevertheless believe that the loss of fiscal autonomy has been a significant factor in Botswana's economic success, which according to World Bank estimates, has experienced the highest GDP growth in the world since the 1960s); finally, a trend towards the concentration of industrial development in South Africa to the detriment of its partners.

The SACU's mode of functioning has provoked increasing hostility on the part of the BLNS countries since the 1970s, with the latter believing that the Union's trade policy has been conducted by South Africa to suit its interests only without consulting its partners. South Africa, for its part, reckons that the mechanism for redistributing customs revenue collected in the union today is working to its disadvantage. Negotiations aimed at renewing the SACU were embarked upon in 1994. This renegotiation set itself three objectives: putting into place a new distribution formula; democratising the organisation's mode of functioning, which could result in the establishment of a SACU secretariat based in one of the BLNS countries; defining a common industrialisation policy aimed at adapting the industrial policies followed by the member countries jointly to determine development objectives.

Predictably, the main difficulty was agreeing on a new distribution formula. South Africa proposed to its partners that the basket serving as a basis for redistribution should be simplified at the same time as they are trying to stabilise their revenues at their current level. An agreement on a new distribution formula has been concluded in 2000, South Africa having accepted to increase its financial contribution. South Africa did not wish to join the Common Market of Eastern and Southern Africa (COMESA), which groups together 21 southern and eastern African countries.[9] This refusal can be explained by the problem of the overlap between the tasks of COMESA and those of the SADC, whereas the heterogeneity of this vast regional ensemble casts doubts on its chances of success. Like SADC, COMESA foresees having in place a free trade area (by October 2000, a much earlier date than SADC), and a customs union by the year 2004. Most of the member countries, however, are far behind schedule.

The decision taken by the SADC countries in 1994 to leave COMESA for the time being has been implemented only by Lesotho and Mozambique,

---

9 COMESA groups together the following countries: Angola, Burundi, Comores, Democratic Republic of Congo, Djibouti, Egypt, Eritrea, Ethiopia, Kenya, Madagascar, Malawi, Mauritius, Namibia, Rwanda, Seychelles, Sudan, Swaziland, Tanzania, Uganda, Zambia and Zimbabwe. Nine SADC countries are COMESA members: Angola, Democratic Republic of Congo, Malawi, Mauritius, Namibia, Swaziland, Tanzania, Zambia and Zimbabwe.

with Tanzania having announced its intention to do the same. The majority of SADC countries therefore remain members of this organisation, with two of them (Namibia and Swaziland) also belonging to the SACU. If this were to continue, this double or triple membership of regional trade agreements could pose complicated problems in controlling the flow of merchandise.[10]

Prospects for economic integration in southern Africa

The SADC countries signed a trade protocol in 1996, which provided for a free trade area to be put into place at a regional level. The trade negotiations led to the launching of a tariff dismantling process in the year 2000, with complete trade liberalisation coming into effect in the year 2008.

Taking account of the economic and trade imbalance between South Africa and its partners, this project provides for the South African side to open up more rapidly. This opening up is to be spread over five years as from 2000. Half of South Africans imports coming from SADC were already exempt from customs duties; duties on a further 30 per cent of imports were removed, pushing to about 80 per cent the total imports that carry zero duty. For less than 10 per cent of imports, the elimination of duties will take place over five years, which will leave a remainder of a bit more than 10 per cent of imports that are not covered in the framework of the agreement (this relates to agricultural and textile and clothing products, as well as to automobiles). The other participating countries have a delay of eight years at their disposal to proceed with their customs tariffs dismantling, with the time and products concerned varying from country to country.

The direct impact of such an agreement is generally measured by evaluating the scale of "trade creation" linked to a reduction in the cost of imports in relation to domestic products, and "trade diversion" effects caused by a reduction in the relative price of imports coming from the

---

10 To SADC, SACU and COMESA, two agreements in particular can be added: the Cross Border Initiative (CBI), a programme for the dismantling of intra-regional customs duties supported by the Bretton Woods institutions, the African Development Bank and the European Commission; and East African Co-operation (EAC), which groups together Kenya, Uganda and Tanzania.

signatory countries in relation to that of imports coming from third countries. The first type of effect, which translates into an efficiency gain for the productive system, is considered to be positive, as opposed to the second which actually tends to increase participants' specialisation in production in which they would not necessarily be competitive in the absence of the agreement. Considering the already high degree of existing integration, as well as the relative complementarity of the region's economies, this regional agreement seems to hold more interest for southern Africa than this type of project has generally generated in the rest of Africa, where they have all failed until now.

Unlike what has generally been witnessed on the continent, the significant share of intra-regional trade is an asset. Indeed, it is probable that the higher the latter, the more trade creation effects will supersede trade diversion effects and the more significant the resulting static gain.

The percentage of intra-regional trade (more than 20 per cent of total trade) is more than double the average percentage in Africa and more than double the percentage reached during the 1980s between the four Latin American countries (Argentina, Brazil, Paraguay, Uruguay) which today make up Mercosur. Malawi, Mozambique, Zambia and Zimbabwe are the four countries that exchange the highest percentage of their overall trade, both exports and imports, with their regional partners. They are therefore susceptible to be the most affected relative to the size of their economies – all things being equal otherwise – by the establishment of a free trade area, with the impact being either positive or negative according to the economic sector. Conversely, the impact will necessarily be more limited in the case of the SACU countries, for which the share of intra-regional trade is marginal.

This relative degree of integration results in some complementarity of productive supply at the regional level. Graph 12, which displays the results of a bilateral complementarity index calculation, shows that the only existing complementarity is between South African supply and the demand of its partners. On the other hand, the supply structure of the latter is generally rather removed from South African demand. Only two countries in the region are the exception: Zimbabwe, which is endowed with a rather diversified industrial apparatus and a high-performing agricultural sector, produces quite a number of goods adapted to South African demand; Angola, whose exports are mainly made up of crude oil in which South Africa is lacking, also displays some degree of complementarity with this country.[11]

CHAPTER 7 A regional power

Graph 12:
Complementarity index between South Africa and other southern African countries

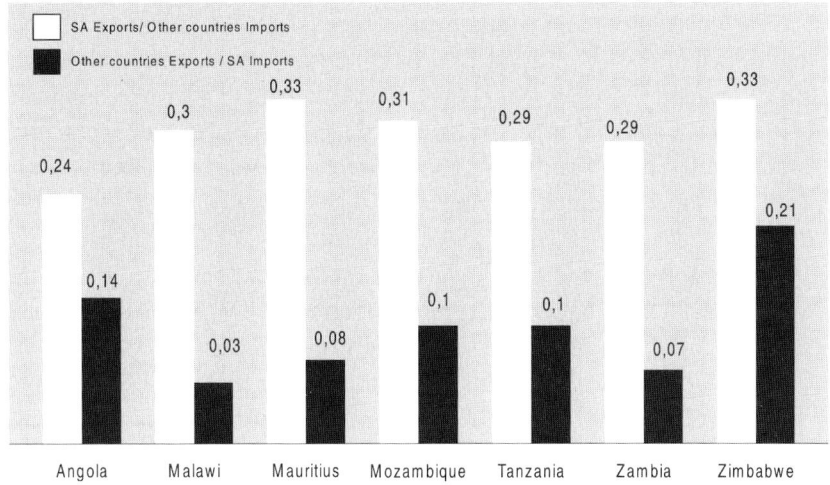

Source: Cling, 1998

Methodological note: This index measures the gap between the export and import structures of two countries. It has a value of 0 when no goods exported by the first country are imported by the second. It is 1 when the structure of the first country's exports corresponds exactly with that of the other's imports.

The fact that the southern African countries' export structure is on average quite removed from that of South Africa's imports does not contradict the assertion that some potential does exist for expanding their exports to this country, despite their low current level. In line with the African Development Bank[12], UNCTAD even believes that this characteristic stems more from historical and cultural reasons than from macroeconomic factors:

The reasons for the low level of SADC exports to the RSA are to be found rather at the microeconomic level: for obvious historical reasons, the business culture in international purchasing and supply management in RSA neglected the northern neighbours. Similarly, exporters in SADC concentrated on the world markets rather than on South Africa.[13]

---

11 Astonishingly, this index does not show up any complementarity between the exports of Mauritius and South African imports. This is explained by the concentration of these exports on textile products, which only represent a small share of this country's imports.
12 African Development Bank, 1993.
13 UNCTAD, 1998.

This potential has been confirmed by studies conducted with the assistance of gravitational models which correlate the level of bilateral trade with the distance between countries and with characteristics linked to the size of their economies.[14]

The existing complementarities between SADC countries, apart from South Africa, are even more limited than they are with South Africa. Trade expansion between these countries is constrained by the predominant share of raw materials in their production structure with little trade potential among themselves: Malawi, whose exports are made up almost entirely of tea and tobacco, and bordering Zambia, exporter of mining products, obviously have little to trade between themselves. These countries have already largely reduced customs duties on their reciprocal trade, in the framework of multilateral agreements (such as COMESA) or bilateral ones. For these two reasons, the impact of this project will probably be concentrated on the trade between South Africa and the other SADC countries (apart from the SACU). This project will not affect intra-SACU trade, which represents more than two-thirds of total intra-regional trade.[15]

The overall effect of establishing a free trade area will be all the more significant for the participating countries as the reduction in customs duties will be large scale. This reduction will firstly result in an increase in intra-regional trade. The countries with the highest initial customs duties are a priori those that will experience the sharpest increase in their imports. Generally, duties on raw materials are very low, whereas those on manufactured products and in particular consumer goods are very high at the regional level. These can be thigher in the most protectionist countries (Mauritius and Zimbabwe) that are trying to protect their domestic industry than in countries that have opened up the most (Mozambique and Tanzania). Average SACU tariff rates are listed among the lowest in the region. Nevertheless, whereas the SACU has the largest proportion of reduced rates (below 10 per cent), it also has the largest proportion of "tariff peaks" which affect in particular products such as textiles where its partners have a competitive supply. Secondly, the lowering of customs duties resulting from this process will force the participating countries to restructure their fiscal revenue. This will be on a large scale for countries such as Zimbabwe, which combines a high percentage of intra-regional imports and a high initial tariff level.

---

14 Cassim and Hartzenburg, 1999.
15 Stahl, 1997.

Considering the inadequacy of the countries' supplies relative to their partners' demands, and in particular to that of South Africa, a new swell in intra-regional trade imbalances can be expected, marked by the "base effect" linked to the massive existing bilateral trade imbalance between South Africa and its partners: this country will markedly improve its trade and payments balance, whereas all the other countries of the zone – apart from Mauritius – will see it deteriorate. This short-term conclusion has to be put in perspective. In all cases it shows the urgent need for corrective mechanisms within the SADC to reduce the massive bilateral trade and financial imbalances between South Africa and its partners. It appears imperative to expand South African investment in the region, whether through direct investments or project financing. The broadening of the financing of the Industrial Development Corporation and the Development Bank of Southern Africa to neighbouring countries is a response to this concern, with the latter already having launched more than R5 billion worth of industrial and infrastructure projects in the SADC between 1994 and 2000.

In line with the dynamic effects generally witnessed in similar cases, establishing a free trade area should eventually lead to a modification in the international specialisation of the different countries in the functioning of each of their comparative advantages. The specialisation of South Africa's partners in labour-intensive activities and raw materials – particularly in the context of subcontracting for South African industry – should increase as a result, whereas the function this country fulfils as a supplier of more complex manufactured products to the region should be reinforced. Following this pattern, an acceleration of the relocation of South African industries to countries of the region would further their development according to the Asian "flight of the wild geese" process, where those countries experienced an economic take-off in successive waves.

This is obviously a hypothetical scenario and some fears to the contrary have evoked the risk of polarisation of investment and productive activities to South Africa's advantage. This risk cannot be completely ignored as such is the extent of the relative attractiveness for investors of the region's most developed country, which is also its main market, where infrastructure quality is highest and the productive fabric more solid.

It has to be noted that this phenomenon does not seem to have affected the SACU countries, a customs union that is to some degree the prototype of the trade agreement project launched by the southern African countries (the regional free trade area agreement, however, can be distinguished from a customs union by the absence of customs tariff harmonisation, which prevents participants from benefiting from transfers such as those existing in the SACU).

On the contrary, belonging to the SACU indisputably has had a rather beneficial impact on the development of the BLNS countries by favouring the creation of a "pole of convergence" around South Africa. Besides, if living standards in South Africa's SACU partners apart from Botswana are much lower than in this country, they are nevertheless higher than in any of the other countries of the region. Similarly, it has to be noted that the SACU countries have recently increased the share of manufactured products in their exports, whereas this share has stagnated in other countries of the region (apart from Mauritius), as in almost all sub-Saharan African countries.

As a result of benefiting from free access to the South African market, the BLNS countries have been able to attract some direct investment through their low wage costs (and during the apartheid era by the possibility of avoiding sanctions imposed on South African products) and thus to build up an embryonic industrial base. These investments originate especially from South Africa, which is the main investor in all these countries. The previous relocation of South African textile factories owned by Chinese thus allowed Lesotho to become the leading textile exporter in all of continental Africa. Close to half its exports are directed to the South African market.

The emphasis put on the removal of customs duties by the SADC countries has given rise to criticisms,[16] considering that the main obstacle to expanding intra-regional trade in fact stems more from non-tariff barriers in the broad sense, which are not taken account of in the agreement, than from tariff levels. The quotas imposed by South Africa on Zimbabwean textile and agricultural exports in the framework of the bilateral agreement signed in 1997, the poor quality of road and railway infrastructure in most of the countries of the region, the protectionist regulations applied to imports, the delays in passing borders, and the taxes levied on road transit are some examples of these numerous barriers. It can be noted in this regard that, at the very least in the short term, planned infrastructure development in the framework of large regional projects will stimulate exports to South Africa from the countries concerned as

---

16 Compare in particular Thomas, 1997a.

CHAPTER 7 A regional power

much as the customs agreement in question. This is particularly the case for water exports from Lesotho in the framework of the Lesotho Highlands Water Project, and for that of energy (electricity and gas) from Mozambique.

Furthermore, it is obvious that the eventual success of the proposed free trade area will depend to a large extent on the way in which the signatory countries manage to harmonise their economic policies. The positive effects described above have been realised in the SACU countries only because they have gradually harmonised their budgetary and monetary policies with those of South Africa. The membership of Lesotho, Namibia and Swaziland of the Common Monetary Area, a fixed exchange rate zone constituted around South Africa, has most likely favoured this convergence. Too significant divergence in its policies, which would result in gaps in inflation and economic growth between the countries of the region and into monetary distortions, would also endanger the sustainability of this process. A harmonisation of national financial systems (to facilitate international payments, the creation of a regional stock exchange, and so on), such as that envisaged in the framework of current discussions within SADC, is equally necessary. Therefore, despite the foreseeable macroeconomic difficulties of pursuing trade co-operation, it remains indispensable.

South Africa's willingness to contribute to the development and industrialisation of the entire region has led to the definition of a "Spatial Development Initiatives" concept. It concerns the development of the most disadvantaged regions in an integrated way, often straddling several countries, with the assistance of partnerships between the public and private sectors. The projects included in the framework of these initiatives cover industrial, agricultural and tourism investments, at the same time as road, railway and port infrastructure in particular. The rehabilitation and development of transport infrastructure is a priority for all the countries of the region. The low regional population density (180 million inhabitants for an area not much smaller than that of China), the landlocked position of many countries,[17] as well as the need to repair destroyed or abandoned infrastructure after two decades of civil war in Angola and Mozambique justify the particular importance this concept has been accorded.

About fifteen Spatial Development Initiatives have already been identified throughout southern Africa. The more ambitious among them

---

17 Botswana, Lesotho, Malawi, Swaziland, Zambia and Zimbabwe.

are situated along the many transport "corridors" built during the colonial period to transport raw material exports bound for developed countries. The six southern African coastal countries (South Africa, Angola, Democratic Republic of Congo, Mozambique, Namibia and Tanzania) constitute the maritime extremities of these corridors, which run across the entire region. Mozambique thus has three "corridors". That of Nacala, the northernmost, links the Mozambican port of the same name to Malawi; that of Beira is the closest maritime outlet for Zimbabwe; finally, that of Maputo links the capital of Mozambique to that of South Africa.

Insofar as Maputo was the outlet for half the external trade of Gauteng province (Johannesburg-Pretoria) before Mozambique's independence, the Maputo corridor can be considered the most important among them. The saturation of Durban's harbour has prompted South Africa to speed up the renovation of Maputo's harbour and its access infrastructure (railway-road), essentially situated on South African territory. Whereas the construction of a new road has already been completed, the remainder of the projects are still at a much less advanced stage, particularly as far as the rehabilitation of the Maputo harbour and the Mozambican part of the railway linking the two countries is concerned. The management of the entire corridor will be entrusted to a private company.

A consortium headed by Bouygues has constructed a highway of nearly 500 kilometres between Witbank (close to Johannesburg) and Maputo, which allows the journey between the South African and Mozambican capitals to be shortened by 100 kilometres. This project's particularity lies in its method of financing, which grants a dominant share to the private sector, with the contribution of government not exceeding 10 per cent of the total investment. The highway was thus constructed in the Build Operate Transfer (BOT) framework, with the consortium paying for the building operations by setting up toll gates. This is a radical departure from the usual method of financing projects in Africa, which generally depend completely on international aid.

Several heavy industry project investments have followed the corridor. The most important is the Mozal project, which consists an aluminium factory in Maputo, whose cost is almost equivalent to the Mozambican gross domestic product. In the South African Mpumalanga province, situated along the corridor, Nkomati Nickel is building a nickel production factory which will benefit from the reduction in the cost of transport brought about by the project, whereas Sasol is examining several petrochemical projects. There are also plans to build an iron and steel factory in Maputo,

CHAPTER 7 A regional power

Map of main corridors – Spatial Development Initiatives in southern Africa

Source: South African Department of Trade and Industry

as well as a new deep-water port south of the capital, which will benefit from being connected to the road network to South Africa. The completion of the South African part of the Windhoek-Pretoria highway allows the Maputo corridor to join the Trans Kalahari Highway to Walvis Bay, situated on the Atlantic coast, through a fast route. The Namibian port of Walvis Bay is linked to Pretoria by a 2 000-kilometre road.

The Spatial Development Initiatives are mostly at the early stages and it is therefore difficult to judge their chances of success. The success of these projects will depend to a large extent on the willingness of the countries of the region to co-operate across borders. The fact that these projects have been launched by South Africa, from where the bulk of the investments originate, moreover risks offending the national sensitivities of the other countries in the region. The role of public financing and incentive measures can also not be ignored (the tax advantages granted to Mozal have undeniably been a determining factor in launching this project). Even if they reach their objective, which is to speed up the development of high-potential under-developed regions, the impact of these initiatives on the overall development of the countries concerned could well remain limited. That will in particular be the case if the initiatives result in increasing the polarisation of activities in coastal areas and in intensifying the dual nature of economies, without large projects having a spillover effect on local economies. The proposal put forward by South Africa to confine the management of these regional projects to the SADC is a double-edged sword: on the one hand, it could make them more acceptable to the countries of the region while also facilitating the raising of finances from donors; conversely, it risks coming up against the operation difficulties of this organisation, which is hardly in any position to manage such ambitious projects.

South Africa's dominance at the regional level is both an asset and a handicap for the development of southern Africa. While acting as a driving force through its companies but also in institutional and project co-operation, this country sometimes experiences difficulties in asserting its natural ambitions and fulfilling its leadership role at the regional level. These difficulties do not prevent the regional integration process implemented within SADC from being the most credible and advanced in Africa. Because of the insufficient size of the regional market, the indispensable corollary of emphasising this process is to pursue a higher degree of integration into world trade. The choice to reinforce South Africa's "anchoring" to the European Union, analysed in the next chapter, is in line with this strategy.

CHAPTER 8

South Africa's "anchoring" to the European Union

South Africa has inadvertently found that the agreement it is forging with the EU has become for the EU a model for future relations with the broader ACP. There is indeed much that is ironic in this; South Africa was excluded from Lomé precisely because it was considered not to be a typical ACP country, only to find the basis of the trade relationship being constructed with it (a FTA) becoming the favoured model for relations with 'typical' ACP countries.
— Rob Davies, chairperson of the Parliamentary Portfolio Committee on Trade and Industry[1]

In the euphoria that followed the democratic transition, South Africa believed that it could become a full member of the Lomé Convention, encouraged in this belief by some European leaders. This membership would have given it non-reciprocal access to the European Union's (EU) markets and financing. It became apparent very quickly, however, that this was an unrealistic scenario.

While accepting South Africa's "qualified" membership, which excludes the trade benefits granted to other signatories to the Lomé Convention, the EU proposed that they sign a reciprocal free trade agreement. This agreement was concluded in 1999, after four years of difficult negotiations. It is the first agreement of its kind concluded with a country that does not form part of the Union's "inner circle" of trading partners, such as the countries of central or eastern Europe, who are likely to join the EU eventually, or the southern Mediterranean countries with whom Europe maintains privileged relations. It is also the first agreement that includes mostly agricultural products.

To begin with, an attempt at evaluating the impact of this agreement on the South African economy is indispensable. It is necessary in this

---

1   Davies, 1998.

regard to distinguish between static trade effects, probably modest in scale, and dynamic effects, by their nature much more difficult to measure. These effects, on which the South African side has based most of its expectations, are in fact linked to the positive impact that improved production specialisation and a more internationally credible economic policy would have on growth in the long term. The EU has undertaken to assist South Africa on this course through the "trade, development and co-operation" agreement. As with everything South Africa does, this agreement will also have an impact on the whole of southern Africa.

A second question that needs to be asked, which flows in part from the first, is about the possibility of generalising this pattern of reciprocal preferences to all the ACP countries. As a matter of fact, the EU presents the agreement with this country as a model in view of the reform of the trade regime of the Cotonou Convention, which replaced the Lomé Convention in 2000. These proposals are in line with the EU's trade policy, which consists of signing an increasing number of reciprocal free trade area agreements with all its trade partners irrespective of their level of development. Can this model be applied to all the ACP countries, even though South Africa has been refused the benefit of this convention's trade regime precisely because of these distinctions?

From "qualified" Lomé membership to a free trade agreement with the European Union

South Africa's "qualified" membership of the Lomé Convention (and now of the Cotonou Convention), which binds the EU to 71 ACP countries, took effect in 1998. Contrary to the country's wishes, the EU refused South Africa full membership, which would have given it access to Community markets without having to reciprocate. This access would have placed it at the top of the "pyramid" of tariff trade preferences granted by the European Union to developing countries. The trade regime established in the framework of this convention is actually more favourable than the one governing relations with non-ACP countries, be they reciprocal free trade agreements signed with the southern Mediterranean countries, the "super" Generalised System of Preferences (GSP) intended for the least developed countries as well as the countries of the Andean

---

2   This tariff system consists of unilaterally granting the reduction or removal of customs duties to developing countries. The European GSP was launched in 1971.

CHAPTER 8 South Africa's "anchoring" to the European Union (EU)

Pact, or the GSP granted to other developing countries.[2] Insofar as all the other SADC countries are signatories to the convention, South Africa's membership has also been considered as a means of speeding up the regional integration process by harmonising the relations maintained between each of the SADC countries and the EU.[3]

From the European point of view, this refusal could be justified for two main reasons. First of all, considering South Africa's level of development, the granting of unilateral preferences would probably have been incompatible with WTO rules which do not allow developed countries to grant preferential treatment more beneficial than that granted in the framework of the GSP, except in the case of a derogation; besides, the European GSP had been granted to South Africa in 1995. Next, the predominance of this country within the group of ACP countries (South African exports to the EU represent close to half of those from these countries) meant that full membership would have risked destabilising the functioning of the convention. Besides, several ACP countries opposed its admission.

Its "qualified" membership excludes South Africa from taking advantage of most of the trade and financial benefits granted to ACP countries. It also does not benefit from the commodity protocols, as part of which the European Union buys fixed quotas of certain ACP export products (sugar, beef, bananas and rum) on the basis of European, and not world prices.[4] "Qualified" membership nevertheless allows South African companies to tender for all the projects financed by the European Investment Bank or in the framework of the European Development Fund in all the ACP countries. The sum total of these projects amounts to Euro 14,6 billion for the period 1995 to 2000, which represents 55 per cent of the total aid granted by the EU. It also allows South African products to be included among those originating in the ACP when determining the local content of products exported to the European market.

Furthermore, South Africa benefits from significant aid from the EU, in the framework of the European Programme for Reconstruction and Development (EPRD). Unlike in other ACP countries, this financing comes directly out of the Community budget and not from the European Development Fund set up under the EU-ACP Convention. It involves donations amounting to around Euro 125 billion a year, which, in addition

---

3   Davies, 1998.
4   Historically, these protocols were established to maintain the trade flows fostered by the European countries with their former colonies for these products.

to the bilateral aid granted by member countries, makes the EU South Africa's leading donor by far. These donations benefit diverse social and infrastructure projects. They are generally granted to the government or public administrations, as well as to non-governmental organisations.

In 1994, following its refusal to give South Africa non-reciprocal duty-free access to the European market, the EU proposed signing a free trade agreement with South Africa. Originally, the plan was to negotiate this agreement parallel to negotiating South Africa's qualified membership of the Lomé Convention in order to prove the clearly complementary nature of these two processes.

This parallel strategy, however, quickly proved unfeasible. The negotiations that were formally opened in Brussels in June 1995 in view of signing a trade, development and co-operation agreement were only concluded nearly four years later. In fact, they went through a long gestation period before suddenly accelerating at the end of 1997 when South Africa presented its detailed tariff offer, followed by that of the EU at the beginning of 1998.

The outcome of the long and difficult negotiations remained uncertain until the last moment. The ambition demonstrated by both the European and South African negotiators regarding the extension of the areas covered by this agreement largely explains the difficulties that were encountered during these negotiations.

South Africa insisted that the EU open its market to South African agricultural exports, which went against the rules of the Common Agricultural Policy and the politically highly sensitive nature of this sector in Europe. The EU, for its part, insisted that there be no limitation to trade in goods, and that services (transport, insurance, financial services, and so on) and issues linked to trade such as public procurement and labels of origin also be included. The results achieved in this area, however, have been meagre because of the reluctance on the part of South Africa, who wanted to retain room for manœuvre in view of future multilateral negotiations, to such an extent that the differences on these issues almost led to the failure of the agreement.

The EU has notably demanded that South Africa agree to renounce the names of "port" and "sherry", included in its domestic market. Respect for labels of origin, beyond these two products, is a major preoccupation of European countries in general, which justifies the importance given to this issue not only vis-à-vis South Africa, but also in all its multilateral negotiations.

CHAPTER 8 South Africa's "anchoring" to the European Union (EU)

In accordance with what are considered WTO rules on regional agreements, this agreement covers about 90 per cent of trade between the two countries[5] and abides by the maximum duration for tariff elimination, set at 10 years for most products and at 12 for sensitive products from the enforcement of the treaty in the year 2000, which means that the free trade area will be fully implemented by 2012. Like the free trade agreement concluded within the SADC, this agreement is asymmetrical both in terms of the degree of liberalisation and the timetable to take account of the inequality in the level of development between the two partners.

The EU therefore undertook to eliminate customs duties on a list of products covering 95 per cent of its imports coming from South Africa over a period of 10 years. This overall percentage covers total liberalisation of industrial products but is limited to 67 per cent of agricultural products. Out of these, 12 per cent are subject to quotas. This is the case particularly for wine, for which a tariff exempt import quota of 32 million litres has been set. Besides the fact that Europe wanted to protect some of its "sensitive" agricultural products, for which it feared competition from South African producers (maize, canned fruits, and so on), this limited percentage can also be explained by the exclusion of fishing products from this agreement. South Africa in fact opposed the granting of fishing rights to EU vessels, which would have been an inevitable compensation for an agreement in this area.

South Africa undertook to do the same for 86 per cent of its imports of European products over a period of 12 years (89 per cent industrial and 81 per cent agricultural products). Private motor vehicles, which form part of the main products exported by the European Union, are excluded from the agreement for the time being, as are chemical products and textiles. This exclusion is in response to the concern to protect either sectors that are dynamic, but still insufficiently competitive at the international level (automobiles, as well as chemical products to a lesser extent), or, sectors undergoing a crisis (textiles) where it is necessary to obtain respite from the prospect of inevitable restructuring.

As its name indicates, the agreement is not limited to trade but also covers issues of co-operation and development aid. The chapter of the agreement dedicated to co-operation between the two partners comprises a list of general declarations of intent concerning co-operation in various economic sectors (industry, information technology, energy, mines, trans-

---

5   The WTO in fact mentions the "bulk" of trade, without laying down a precise figure.

port, tourism, agriculture and services) as well as in the promotion and protection of investments, assistance for trade development, assistance for micro-enterprises and small and medium enterprises, support for the process of economic empowerment of historically disadvantaged groups, and support for efforts to protect and promote the rights of workers and trade unions.

This framework agreement is in fact complemented and clarified by a European Commision regulation, which lays down detailed directives for EU co-operation with South Africa for the period 2000 to 2002 in the framework of the EPRD.[6] The three main pillars for this co-operation are the following: support for the integration of the South African economy into the world economy and world trade; fighting against poverty through improving living conditions and providing basic social services; support for "good governance", which includes democratisation, protection of human rights, sound public management, reinforcing local communities and the participation of civil society in the development process. This financial element of this agreement is essential – even if the EU does not recognise it explicitly, significant aid will need to be given to South Africa to finance the restructuring prompted by the bilateral agreement to supplement the contribution from private sector capital.

Measuring the impact on South Africa and its neighbours: a difficult exercise

The agreement concluded between the EU and South Africa is of great significance to this country of which the European Union is by far the leading trading partner: 39 per cent of South African exports were directed towards the European market and 40 per cent of its imports originated from the EU in 1997.[7]

The sectoral structure of their bilateral trade corresponds to the previously described pattern (Chapter five) of South Africa's international specialisation. As is the case for its exports to all developed countries, South African exports to Europe basically consist of raw materials (Table 1): the five principal products exported, which represent more than half the total, are mining products (gold, coal, metallic and non-metallic minerals)

---

6 European Commission, 1999.
7 This part is based on Cling, 1998.

CHAPTER 8 South Africa's "anchoring" to the European Union (EU)

or agricultural products (fruits and vegetables). However, semi-manufactured (iron-steel, chemical products, and so on) or more value-added products (furniture, automobiles, chemical products, and so on), which are listed globally among the leading export items, lag far behind. Conversely, almost all South Africa's imports consist of manufactured products: mainly transport equipment and capital goods. South Africa's trade challenge is to expand its global exports while at the same time diversifying their composition beyond mining products, without having to see its performing industries disappear under the effect of a rapid expansion of EU product imports.

The short-term impact of customs liberalisation on bilateral trade can be analysed in a manner analogous to that of the free trade area project examined in Chapter 7. It will depend mainly on three effects, assuming that supply can satisfy all additional demand at the same price (in other words, assuming that "supply is infinitely elastic"):

- In the first place, the increase in trade will be all the more significant as current customs duties are high; in fact, customs duties applied to South African products before the signing of this agreement were much lower than those applied to EU products on the South African market, which is mostly because around three-quarters of South African products exported to the European market already benefit from much reduced customs duties in the framework of the GSP; the total elimination of these duties on the bulk of bilateral trade will therefore benefit EU exporters more than South African exporters, everything else being equal.
- In second place, the elimination of customs duties will result in a fall in import prices in relation to domestic prices and therefore into a "trade creation" effect (in the usual definition); South African imports are generally considered not very price elastic; this characteristic reflects the deficiencies in the productive apparatus.
- Finally, the increase in the competitiveness of European products in relation to those of other exporters will a priori lead to an increase in their market share, and the same effect will act in favour of South African products on the European market; the already high share of the EU in South African imports suggests that in this case the "trade diversion" effect could remain limited; by contrast, EU imports from South Africa,

Table 10:
Main products traded between the European Union and South Africa (1997)

Main products exported by South Africa (million euro)

Products	Total	Percentage of total
1. Gold	1942	21,4
2. Coal	958	10,5
3. Fruits and vegetables	708	7,8
4. Non-metallic minerals	625	6,9
5. Metallic minerals	560	6,2
6. Iron-steel	552	6,1
7. Non-ferrous metals	438	4,8
8. Furniture	300	3,3
9. Sundry industrial machinery	227	2,5
10. Fertiliser	205	2,3
Total 10 products	6 515	71,6
TOTAL	9 096	100,0

Main products imported by South Africa (million euro)

Products	Total	Percentage of total
1. Road vehicles	1 008	10,4
2. Diverse industrial machinery	870	8,9
3. Telecommunications equipment	820	8,4
4. Specialised machinery	763	7,8
5. Electrical machinery	588	6,0
6. Office machinery	428	4,4
7. Pharmaceutical products	359	3,7
8. Sundry manufactured products	342	3,5
9. Generators	291	3,0
10. Sundry chemical products	278	2,9
Total 10 products	5 747	59,0
TOTAL	9 736	100,0

Source: Eurostat; Nomenclature: Harmonised System

which are directed towards low value-added products and are therefore quite homogenous, may be more easily substituted with those from other suppliers.

According to an UNCTAD study conducted with the assistance of a partial equilibrium model,[8] the first of these effects would predominate, so much so that the impact of the agreement could be more significant for EU exports than for those of South Africa. Additional South African imports from the EU, affecting most industrial products (apart from automobiles, which will remain sheltered by high-level protection) would comprise between 2 and 12 per cent, with a diversion effect occurring against Japanese and American products.

On the other hand, South African exports to the EU market would increase by only around 1,5 per cent (excluding the diversion effect, which is not calculated by UNCTAD in this direction). Responding to South African expectations in view of the international expansion of these sectors, the direct impact on agricultural and textile products, whose market access has been considerably improved, would be significant, but it would be more limited on other manufactured products. On the whole, according to this study, South African imports would increase from one to four per cent, whereas the effect on exports would be negligible. This would result in an increase of South Africa's deficit registered with the EU and in an overall deterioration of the trade balance.

Considering the limited anticipated impact of this agreement on the expansion of South African exports, confirmed by other similar studies, one has to question the motivations that have urged South African leaders to sign this kind of agreement with the European Union. There are three main motivations. The first concerns fighting the erosion of tariff preferences that have resulted from the signing of free trade agreements by the EU with the eastern European countries in transition and with other developing countries such as the southern Mediterranean countries and Latin America, whether Mexico or maybe even soon Mercosur. Indeed, these countries are often at a similar level of development as South Africa and are therefore direct competitors in quite a number of agricultural and industrial sectors. It is therefore indispensable for South Africa not to find itself in an unfavourable situation in terms of access to the EU market, which absorbs the bulk of its exports.

---

8   Jachia and Teljeur, 1998.

The signing of this agreement also indicates a willingness to give greater importance to relations with the European Union. This decision in return implicitly relegates to the background the expansion of south-south relations, be it with other sub-Saharan African countries (with the exception of those of southern Africa), or with its Latin American or Asian partners. The "butterfly" strategy, advocating that South Africa try to take advantage of its geographical location midway between the southern cone of America and the Asian continent, even though not officially abandoned, has therefore at least been returned to more modest ambitions.

This favouring of a more realistic strategy has been informed by the slow progress in this direction. Similarly, the rapprochement with the European Union has taken place to the detriment of the United States, which continues to court and invest significantly in South Africa but, unlike the EU, without having proposed a real partnership with this country until now (the "A fuca bill" is purely unilateral).

In this context, it is obvious that South Africa can derive significant benefit from "anchoring" itself to the EU as far as the credibility of its economic policy is concerned, especially in the trade arena. Most developing countries are pursuing this objective when they conclude these kinds of agreements with developed countries. It is particularly crucial in the case of South Africa, which has suffered from a lack of international investor confidence in its government since the democratic transition in 1994, with the irreversibility of the reforms it instituted both externally and internally often being cast into doubt. Establishing a contractual trade relationship with a leading global trade power is also a long-term guarantee for the expansion of markets for South African products.

Similarly, some studies believe that the trade interest of a north-south free trade agreement is in fact secondary compared with the direct investment effects.[9] According to these, the preferential access granted to the developed country market will stimulate a flow of direct investment from the developed country to the developing country, with the aim of exporting back to the developed country. This effect should work not only for South Africa, but also for other countries in the region directly or indirectly associated with an agreement between South Africa and the EU. Nevertheless, the hope that this agreement will stimulate a flow of direct investment is rather hypothetical. The examples of agreements between industrialised and developing countries are quite contradictory in

---

9 Winters, 1996.

this regard: the signing of the North American Free Trade Area (NAFTA) on the whole has stimulated considerable investment and employment in the *maquiladoras* in Mexico, with firms in cross-border areas exporting primarily to the United States; this phenomenon seems much less pronounced in the case of the Maghreb, for example, maybe because the EU is surrounded at its periphery by a number of developing countries or countries in transition that offer as many and largely equivalent investment opportunities. As a result of its distance from the EU, South Africa seems rather less well placed in this regard at a global level.

In the second place, the South African government is hoping that the tariff dismantling realised in the framework of this agreement will stimulate the much needed restructuring of South African industry and in the same way support the modernisation strategy implemented since 1994. In this sense, the free trade agreement can eventually widen the outlets available to South African products, on the condition that they are competitive, while also improving the allocation efficiency of domestic resources (trade creation effect). In this logic, the insignificance of the agreement's direct effects on export growth is secondary insofar as its long-term effects are not yet measurable, since they will depend on the success of the restructuring that is under way, itself influenced by trade liberalisation. The conclusions of an assessment of this agreement conducted on behalf of the European Commission are consistent with this approach, which involves minimising the short-term advantages of opening up the EU market in relation to those that would come from restructuring the economy.[10]

The export supply of non-agricultural South African products will be much more affected by the restructuring of the South African economy under way than by the free trade area. If the South African government's strategy succeeds, export supply to the EU is bound to increase substantially, whether or not there is a free trade area. On the other hand, if the latter fails, given the weakness of a large portion of the manufacturing industry, it is rather unlikely that a free trade area will in itself cause a significant increase in the competitive supply of a large range of manufactured products.

The effects of this agreement on South Africa's neighbours, particularly the BLNS countries, who are *de facto* associated to the agreement because of their membership of a customs union with this country (the SACU), also need to be considered.

The largest and most immediate effect is going to be of a fiscal nature.

---

10 Institute for Development Studies *et al.*, 1997.

Moreover, the BLNS countries will in fact suffer a significant decline in customs revenue collected at the SACU borders:[11] about half Lesotho and Swaziland's budget income consists of customs revenues collected mainly by South Africa and redistributed to the member states according to a distribution formula. The elimination of the bulk of customs duties levied on imports of European products is going to result in a decline of close to 20 per cent of these two countries' fiscal revenue, everything else being equal, which involves an external shock that could extend to 10 per cent of GDP in the case of Lesotho. These countries will be driven to restructure their tax systems in order to compensate for the loss in customs revenue. But this restructuring will not be sufficient. This is why the framework programme of co-operation with South Africa foresees giving "particular attention to providing support for the adjustment efforts in the region caused by the establishment of the free trade area in the framework of the trade, development, and co-operation agreement, and especially within the South African Customs Union".[12]

The trade effects will be much more modest. Generally, all the region's countries will be subject to increasing competition from South Africa on the EU market. This effect nevertheless has to be put into relative context by the very limited overlap in the export structures of South Africa and other southern African countries' to the EU. Moreover, all other agreements of this kind concluded between the European Union and other partners (Maghreb, Turkey, and so on) have caused similar effects. For practical reasons, the preferential access granted to European products on the South African market will *de facto* be extended to all the SACU countries. Nevertheless, this constitutes a limited threat to southern African exporters or producers in the BLNS countries, with some exceptions.[13] On the other hand, these countries will benefit from the lower domestic prices resulting from the lowering of customs tariffs.

---

11 Institute of Development Studies and Botswana Institute for Development Policy Analysis, 1998.

12 European Commission, 1999.

13 Only some products such as red meat produced by Botswana and Namibia or refrigerators produced by Swaziland risk being threatened by European products. South Africa has placed the latter product on its exclusion list in the framework of this agreement in order to protect production in this country.

CHAPTER 8 South Africa's "anchoring" to the European Union (EU)

Model for a new EU-ACP trade regime?

The negotiations between the EU and the ACP countries for an agreement that would succeed the Lomé Convention started in 1998 and were concluded in 2000. A new agreement was signed in Cotonou in June 2000 which replaces the old Convention for twenty years. The negotiations concerning a new trade regime between the EU and the ACP countries will start by September 2002. For the EU, the free trade agreement concluded with South Africa constitutes a model of how to apply its proposals, which aim to challenge the current unilateral preferences.

This challenge originates partly from the review highlighting the way in which this mechanism operated over more than two decades. In fact, the *Green Paper on the Relations Between the European Union and the ACP Countries on the Eve of the Twenty-First Century,* developed by the European Commission as a reflection in preparation for these negotiations, observed that the Lomé Convention had been incapable of halting the process of marginalisation of the ACP countries in the global economy.[14] Apart from some exceptions raised in this report (Botswana, Ivory Coast, Mauritius, Jamaica and Zimbabwe), ACP countries have not really taken advantage of this convention to increase their share in the European market. On the contrary, their market share (excluding South Africa) has been halved between the 1976 to 1980 and 1996 to 1998 periods, going down from 6,8 per cent to 3,4 per cent (Table 11).

Table 11:
European market share held by ACP countries, southern Africa and South Africa (1976–1998) (%)

	'76–'80	'81–'85	'86–'90	'91–'95	'96–'98
ACP total	9,9	8,2	7,0	5,1	4,5
(excluding South Africa)	6,8	6,0	4,9	3,5	3,4
Southern Africa total (SADC)	3,8	2,8	2,9	2,2	2,0
(excluding South Africa)	0,7	0,6	0,8	0,6	0,6
South Africa	3,1	2,2	2,1	1,6	1,4

Source: Eurostat

14 European Commission, 1996.

The relative stability of the southern African countries' (excluding South Africa) market share masks a divergence in development between a small number of performing countries (Botswana, Mauritius and Zimbabwe) and the rest of the region, which has suffered a decline comparable to that evident in other ACP countries. The halving of South Africa's share of the European market during this period stems from partly different reasons from those generally witnessed in ACP countries. Not only has this country not benefited from any preferential treatment on the EU market, but it has been subject to the impact of international sanctions implemented during the apartheid period.

Moreover, the establishment of the WTO has made the continuation of the current system of unilateral preferences more difficult: this is not so much because the rules have changed but because they have become more restrictive. In fact, Article 1 of GATT, which includes the so-called "most-favoured-nation" clause, always imposed the extension to all signatory countries of any unilateral advantage granted to a partner. One exception, described as "special and differential treatment", concerns developing countries. The rule, however, stipulates that any unilateral trade benefit granted to one member must be extended to the entire group. Whereas this rule has not always been respected before the establishment of the WTO, with no provision made for any sanction against offenders, the establishment of a dispute settlement body under the WTO lends much greater rigour to the regime, as the condemnation of the EU regarding its banana import regime has shown in particular. In order to conform to the WTO, the EU had to ask the member countries for a waiver to maintain the Lomé Convention's current system of preferences. Since this waiver expired at the beginning of 2000, it was necessary to ask for its renewal without any guarantee of success. In brief, there was no assurance that the convention would endure in its current form.

Unlike the approach retained by the past convention, which did not differentiate between ACP countries, the Cotonou arrangement entails differentiation based on geography and also on the level of development of these countries, noting the increasing heterogeneity of the ACP countries, a fact emphasised by South Africa's membership. To ensure the compatibility of the convention's trade regime with WTO rules, the EU proposed to sign asymmetrical free trade agreements with ACP countries, referred to as "Regional Economic Partnership Agreements" (REPAs). These agreements would link the EU to customs unions consisting of ACP countries. In this arrangement, sub-Saharan Africa

CHAPTER 8 South Africa's "anchoring" to the European Union (EU)

would be carved into four zones: southern, eastern, western and central Africa, with Nigeria remaining apart from this division, as is presently the case.[15]

In the absence of such agreements, the ACP countries would rejoin the European GSP. This alternative would be a priori less favourable in terms of access to the European market and would cause the ACP countries concerned to lose the contractual nature of their relationship with the EU. Moreover, it would risk putting them in a situation of direct competition with other countries benefiting from this system and in particular with the emerging Asian and Latin American countries, except if a special (possibly improved) GSP, based on their lowest level of development, could be reserved for them. The overhaul of the European GSP planned for 2004 could provide the occasion for exploring such a route.[16] In any case, the LDCs that do not participate in REPAs could retain the benefit of the unilateral trade preferences granted by the EU in the framework of the "Everything But Arms" initiative launched in 2000, which also concerns eight non-ACP LDCs.[17]

The REPA arrangement is obviously the one preferred by the EU. It inscribes the ACP countries in the framework of EU's new trade policy, which consists of signing these kinds of free trade agreements with its main trading partners. When all is said and done, would these projects benefit the African countries concerned?

The impact of putting into place free trade agreements can be evaluated by using a method similar to the one used in the case of South Africa.

The studies on this subject, conducted on behalf of the European Commission, led to some general conclusions:

- The importation of EU products would experience a sharp increase, resulting more from a trade creation than a *trade diversion* effect (the elasticity of substitution between imports from the EU and those from the rest of the world being considered modest); insofar as the loss of unilateral preferences would not affect ACP countries' exports, one would witness a deterioration in their trade balance.

---

15 European Commission, 1997.
16 European Council, 1998.
17 Afghanistan, Bangladesh, Bhutan, Cambodia, Laos, Maldives, Nepal, Yemen. Burma (Myanmar) is also a least developed country but it has been removed from the European GSP.

- As in all the usual models, the static gain would result from a fall in prices and an increase in competitiveness linked to the liberalisation of the domestic market (multilateral liberalisation, however, would be preferable in this sense); even if this reservation is not shown by these studies, it is not very likely, however, that this effect would result in an improvement of productive supply considering the supply-side constraints in most ACP countries, which is precisely one of the main reasons why these countries have not been able to benefit fully from the convention's unilateral preferences; the weight of these constraints and the insubstantial diversification of their productive apparatus, with some exceptions (Mauritius in particular), constitute a basic difference that separates them from South Africa.
- The negative impact on fiscal revenue would vary greatly from country to country but could be very significant for some of them, where the share of customs revenue in the budget is still predominant.
- The LDCs would gain little from this type of agreement, since they can retain the benefit of non-reciprocal preferences.

These studies, even though they are official, appear sceptical of the EU proposals. Besides, similar doubts have been raised in the context of a European Parliament Development Commission report:

The European parliament fears that the Commission's proposal to negotiate regional free trade and economic partnership agreements is premature, hardly realistic and that it will translate into an increase in poverty and a reinforcement of social tension in the ACP countries; noting in particular that it will bring about considerable social adjustment costs in non-industrialised countries ...[18]

Despite the uncertainty surrounding the impact of implementing the EU projects and the ACP countries' initial opposition to the questioning of the trade regime established in the framework of the Lomé Convention, a principled agreement was reached to examine the definition of new trade relations with the EU.

---

18 European parliament, 1998.

CHAPTER 8   South Africa's "anchoring" to the European Union (EU)

The first years of the 21st century are going to be given over to negotiations towards this goal. Considering the very long delays that risk being introduced to implement these projects (the economic partnership agreements, as they are officially called in the Cotonou agreement, will only be finalised by 2020), the multilateral tariff dismantling timetable agreed upon in the framework of the WTO risks resembling rather closely that of the new arrangement.

The commitment to free trade announced by the ACP countries and their EU partners is above all a political message intended to win acceptance for implementing the unilateral system of preferences that goes against WTO rules for a few more years. It puts these countries in a position to negotiate an extension of the waiver granted to the Cotonou Convention until the beginning of 2008, which is the time limit set for the extension of the current trade regime.

On the South African side, signing a trade agreement with the EU means that the renegotiation of the trade pillar of Cotonou will not have a direct impact on this country. However, this renegotiation will impact significantly on other southern African countries and therefore indirectly on South Africa on at least three accounts: on the one hand, duty-free access granted to EU products by all or some of the SADC countries in the framework of a REPA will be detrimental to South Africa's market share and will therefore threaten this country's predominance at the regional level (this would also apply to a lesser degree if other African countries sign these types of agreements); on the other hand, such an agreement would influence the regional integration process under way; finally, the economic impact on the development of these countries would necessarily affect South Africa, in one way or another.

Even though the benefit that the ACP countries could draw from it is difficult to prove, several factors cast doubt on the feasibility of the REPA projects, so that the EU-RSA agreement will probably remain largely isolated. Let us therefore not forget that out of 71 ACP countries, 39 are LDCs for which maintaining unilateral preferences present no problem, as shown above. It is therefore difficult to see what interest these countries will have in accepting entry into free trade agreements with the EU, except if they are forced to do so, as was the case with Lesotho, following South Africa's signing of an agreement of this kind involving its SACU partners.

Moreover, the regional groupings identified as possible EU partners for negotiating free trade areas (SADC in the case of southern Africa) are still at the beginning of their trade integration processes. Presently, only the West African Economic Monetary Union (WAEMU), comprising eight countries (Benin, Burkina Faso, Ivory Coast, Guinea Bissau, Mali, Niger, Senegal and Togo) has implemented a customs union in 2000. This will mean a transfer of national trade policy competencies to the regional organisation, which will allow it to negotiate directly with the EU. This is not the case in the remainder of the ACP countries where the process is much less advanced, and where the proposed timetable obviously seems to be rather unrealistic. In the case of the SADC, the implementation of a customs union is not yet on the agenda. Considering the highly unequal progress achieved by these countries in their external liberalisation, such a project, which will present the drawback of being externally imposed, seems very premature.

Finally, as South African leaders have reminded other ACP countries, the EU-RSA agreement has shown how difficult it is to negotiate a free trade agreement with the EU, considering the member states' range of offensive and defensive interests, and also the lack of experience and institutional capacity of the South African negotiators. A fortiori, one may doubt the capacity of the 70 other ACP countries to negotiate this type of agreement with such a powerful partner. In addition, this renegotiation will take place simultaneously to the multilateral trade negotiations that should start around 2002, in which most ACP countries will already experience difficulty in participating fully.

In signing the free trade agreement with the EU, South Africa has demonstrated the same voluntarism it has practised in its multilateral liberalisation since 1994. As shown above, this agreement epitomises a significant gamble: firstly, it assumes successful economic restructuring to be under way and the existence of capacity to manage the adjustment costs satisfactorily; it relies on an influx of direct investments attracted by duty-free access to the EU market under this agreement; finally, it expects that an opening up of the economy will lead to an improvement in international specialisation, notably allowing for a reduction in the share of raw materials in exports, while on the whole favouring a successful integration into the world economy. Only the future will tell if the voluntarism demonstrated in signing this agreement will eventually bear the expected fruits, even if recent history urges some prudence in this area. In any case, the stakes are crucial both for South Africa and the southern Africa region.

Furthermore, by signing this agreement South Africa has contributed to questioning the logic of unilateral preferences favouring the ACP countries, which has prevailed under the Lomé Convention for several decades, and in its wake has even dragged along its customs union partners in southern Africa who have until now benefited from the unilateral preferences granted in the framework of this convention. Coming after its "qualified" membership to the Lomé and then to the Cotonou Convention, this "anchoring" to the EU is paradoxically bringing this country closer to its ACP partners and contributing to regional integration in southern Africa. The analysis in this chapter has shown, however, that it is unlikely that the EU's wish to generalise this system to all the ACP countries would succeed, which would probably otherwise not be desirable owing to their lower level of development.

This debate leads one to question the rationality and coherence of the EU's trade policy and its linking it with development aid strategy. A common point between the EU approaches to South Africa and other ACP countries is actually the intention to combine aid and trade, which historically has been a fundamental merit of the Lomé Convention.[19] Such an approach is specific to the EU co-operation policy, which distinguishes it fundamentally from American positions, symbolised by the much vaunted "trade not aid". The EU's respecting of its international trade commitments or the new modalities of its trade policy advocating "open" regionalism should not relegate to the background what should remain the principle objective of such a policy, either with South Africa or with other countries of the continent: the objective remains the reinforcement of these countries' supply capacity and the improvement of their economic and social development prospects.

---

19 Bocquet, 1998.

Conclusion

South Africa has two different futures which can possibly be realised. It can be transformed into a democratic society with a successful and thriving economy, or it can become a disaster area. South Africans will not have the luxury of simply muddling through. Either we are going to get things right, and then there will be a great future for all of us. Or we are going to make the same mistakes so many countries have made, and then, because of the explosive mix of political forces, we are going to destroy ourselves ... One day we will either be a Sweden, or we will be a Lebanon.
— Pieter le Roux, Director: Institute for Social Development
University of the Western Cape

The South African economy has been undergoing a rapid transformation since the end of apartheid. A number of forces that were contained and suppressed for a long time suddenly erupted. The negative view of this country abroad was succeeded by a more benevolent attitude, albeit often also fraught with anxiety. The same phenomenon occurred inside the country where a great many new analyses and economic policy advisors have emerged.

As is to be expected under similar circumstances, such rapid transformation cannot take place without generating highly contradictory developments. The resumption of growth has therefore not interrupted the rapid increase in unemployment. At the same time, the expansion of black business is an indicator of the energy and dynamism of new black entrepreneurs, eager to make up for decades of oppression. The emergence of a new black middle class has to some extent increased the inequalities within this population category. State restructuring and the reduction of the budget deficit have led to the deterioration in the quality of some public services. The opening up of the economy and increasing competition have caused the closing down of some factories and the loss of industrial jobs. The end of the country's isolation aggravated economic and trade antagonism at the regional level, but has not prevented a rapid new expansion of regional co-operation.

It is therefore normal that diagnoses of these developments sometimes differ. This is even more so as analyses may often be distorted by a "Eurocentric" prism, which could lead to an assessment of this country based on Eurocentric criteria, without taking into account its environment, history and specific situation. To apply developed country criteria to South Africa, for the simple reason that some of its infrastructure, its juridical environment or its financial system are worthy of the "first world", would obviously be an error of perspective. Without posing any limitations, it is essential to assess properly the immense difficulties that this country still has to overcome after some years of democracy. Because of the considerable inequalities that continue to prevail, a balanced diagnosis also has to take into account the situation of different ethnic groups, and in the first place, quite obviously of the black group making up three-quarters of the population. As the South African writer and Nobel laureate for literature, Nadine Gordimer, observed in this regard, referring to the way in which Europeans view her country:

Being white, they only identify with whites, be it consciously or unconsciously.[1]

This attitude has obviously led to a distortion of many observers' judgement, insofar as each ethnic group reacts differently to the changes that have occurred since 1994, based on the way in which the latter affect them. This results in highly contrasting assessments of the country's future. Whites, who have lost not only political power but also part of their privileges, notably the right to employment, are logically the most pessimistic, whereas blacks consider their situation to have improved and therefore are much more optimistic about the future. An opinion survey conducted on the eve of the June 1999 general elections on a representative sample of the population was proof of this fracturing.[2] It showed that 62 per cent of blacks maintained that they were confident about the future of their country under the presidency of Thabo Mbeki, whereas only 13 per cent of whites felt the same, the general feeling of the other ethnic groups being rather close to the latter. The wish for national reconciliation, the improvement of relations between the races and the reduction of

---

1 Interview with the daily newspaper *Libération*, 27/3/1999.
2 Reality Check survey, *The Star*, 28 April 1999.

inequalities also seem to be much stronger among blacks and coloureds than in the other groups. Whites thus appear to be the most conservative and the least open with regard to a multiracial society offering equal opportunities to all, which in fact is hardly surprising if one considers that the majority of whites voted for the National Party during its half a century of government rule.

The titles of some recent books looking to the future are suggestive of their authors' anxieties. *Die my beloved country*, by analogy with the famous novel by Alan Paton, who described what he considered to be this country's long-standing agony[3]. Furthermore, *When Mandela goes* ... was foreseeing a total disintegration of society and economic collapse following Nelson Mandela's departure to retirement.[4] In similar vein, some political scientists believe that should the current regime of moderate growth continue, one would probably see an increasingly sharp questioning of the neo-liberal economic policy followed by the government, which would make the country ungovernable and increase the temptation to implement undisciplined populist policies. Others point to the rise in criminality, which is threatening the rule of law and is casting doubt on the normal functioning of society. It is difficult, however, to assess the consequences of this criminality, and it cannot be ruled out that South Africa might have to accept it for lack of sufficient means to fight it and especially for lack of being able to eradicate the social roots of this ill. As Stephen Ellis writes, this, however, does not mean that the country is heading towards catastrophe:

> *The examples of Mexico, Italy or Colombia, to name only three, can throw light on what is happening in South Africa by showing how a highly developed system of crime syndicates, with connections in political parties and the security forces, can coexist with a high growth rate and significant legal economic activity.*[5]

Rejecting the temptation to turn everything into a disaster in favour of a more reasoned approach inevitably leads one to outline some of the elements that should be included in a prospective analysis of South Africa. Despite the difficulty of the exercise and the risks involved (the main one being without doubt that it could make this book obsolete much faster!), let us therefore ask the question: where is South Africa heading?

---

3   Peron, 1994.
4   Venter, 1998.
5   Ellis, 1997.

CONCLUSION

It would be tempting to imagine, as South Africans sometimes dream, a scenario where South Africa, like Malaysia, would become a new tiger (or a lion to go back to an African animal) pursuing a path of growth and development. This corresponds to the rainbow nation dream, where social inequalities would become partially obliterated thanks to high economic growth and a voluntarist policy to increase the weight of blacks in the economy and in the workplace. The policy implemented since independence by the Malaysian government with regard to the bumiputras – to the detriment of the Chinese community who controlled the commanding heights of the national economy – has been used as an example from this perspective. This policy has allowed those of Malay origin, historically completely powerless, to control a substantial part of the economy and occupy a significant number of decision-making positions within firms and the civil service today.

A number of factors differentiating the two countries lead one to question the credibility of an Asian growth scenario over the next years. Besides, no estimation relating to the first years of the 21st century would venture to predict a South African GDP growth higher than 3 per cent a year. In fact, to reach this rate, which would hardly suffice to stabilise the overall unemployment rate in the country and absorb new entrants into labour market, would already constitute a second South African "miracle". A first difference is South Africa's regional environment. Following the example of other Asian countries, Malaysia has been able to benefit from an extremely buoyant regional environment since its independence, owing to the growth of all its neighbouring markets and the diffusion effects of direct Japanese investments, followed by those coming from the four dragons once they also started relocating their labour-intensive manufacturing. In fact, the flow of direct investments not only served to stimulate growth but also offered the opportunity, by imposing partnerships with local firms, of redistributing much sought-after economic power. This is not the case for South Africa, which is the dominant power from a regional point of view in relation to countries experiencing difficulties even more serious than its own, and which is required to take on the role as the regional engine of growth, a role which it does not have all the means to fulfil. Moreover, insufficient direct investments are constraining the realisation of black empowerment, especially in already existing firms, and this empowerment is also turning out to be much more time consuming and complex to implement.

From a domestic point of view, the factors underlying rapid growth have also not yet been mustered. In the absence of sufficient direct investment, the lack of savings is, as seen above, a constraint which is limiting growth. Without a resolve to base its economic growth on that of its domestic market, this country also does not seem to have laid the foundations for an international specialisation likely to ensure a gradual enlargement of its markets. South Africa suffers in this regard from being neither a low wage country nor a country with competitive high-technology supply at the global level. Over the next few years, the inadequacy of human capital will probably represent a bottleneck holding up improvement in the quality and competitiveness of this supply. This inadequacy is being aggravated by the brain drain of a white minority anxious about its future.

Finally, Malaysia's recent difficulties bring to the fore a number of structural weaknesses of the Malaysian "model" that have long been unrecognised, which urges one to avoid idealising the functioning of this economy and the policies followed since independence. The latter relate in particular to the inefficiency of some public investments and the non-optimal allocation of resources which have resulted from the government's policy of subsidising domestic capital. It also needs to be underlined that the establishment of a bumiputra bourgeoisie has led to an increase in inequality within this community, of which the majority had been overexploited and subject to a very strict wage policy. This trend is one of the main risks confronting black empowerment and affirmative action policies.

At the other extreme, a number of observers reckon that South Africa is bound to experience a widespread crisis of the kind Zimbabwe is experiencing or, at least, that its recent history will provide more lessons for the future of this country than the usual comparisons with the emerging Asian or Latin American countries.[6] According to these observers, only if these lessons are heeded, will South Africa be able to avoid following the Zimbabwean route of economic disaster.

In fact, the two bordering countries have experienced a fairly similar history throughout the 20th century. Both acquired their *de facto* independence from Britain very early on, the first in 1910 and the second in 1923 in the framework of a self-government system. Both were then governed by a white minority, which only ceded power to the black majority after long struggles and after the imposition of international sanctions, which had as much a political as an economic impact. However, in both cases, the transfer of political power to the majority was not accompanied

---

6 Stoneman, 1998.

by an equivalent transfer of economic power, in particular because of international pressures, anxious to avoid the wilful destruction of the interests of developed countries' multinationals that were firmly established in these countries. This aspect is central to understanding the problems of social distribution:

> *Herein lies the relevance of Zimbabwe's experience, because the survival of white economic power meant the dashing of the hopes of the black majority, and the imposition of a range of constraints against redistribution, causing disillusion with the new government and making it even more repressive.*[7]

Without disputing the validity of this argument, one can however not attribute all Zimbabwe's current problems to the constraints imposed by the Lancaster House agreements signed with Great Britain in 1979.[8] This country actually did not know how to escape the hardships affecting almost all African countries. After some years of euphoria sustained by the benevolence of donors and the international community, it was necessary to face the facts: like other countries on the continent, Zimbabwe has experienced an economic decline, dictatorship and an increasing impoverishment of its population since independence. Categorised as a medium-income country for several decades, Zimbabwe has reversed and is considered only a low-income and unstable country, like most African countries.

This "return to the ranks" of the ex-treasured child of the Bretton Woods institutions still searching for a model that is nowhere to be found on the continent, was accompanied and provoked by the gradual deterioration of the political system. Added to widespread corruption at the highest level has been the drift by President Mugabe, is one of the leaders that has been in power the longest on the continent, towards totalitarianism. The way in which black empowerment is being managed in South Africa demonstrates the risks of this type of policy if it is implemented without minimum transparency. In fact, nepotism and clientilism have prevailed, causing a number of financial scandals and

---

7   *Ibid.*
8   The Lancaster House agreements were signed in 1979 on the occasion of the transfer of power to the black majority, entering into force in 1980. While asserting their preoccupation to ensure the country's stability during the first years of independence, they were also concerned with protecting the interests of the white minority. They therefore closely protected the properties of this minority for a period of 10 years, preventing the government from practising a bold redistribution policy.

resounding bankruptcies. Finally, the exponential advance of AIDS in the two countries is an additional handicap: in Zimbabwe it is estimated that life expectancy has already been reduced by 10 years, wiping out all progress made since 1980, with this downward movement bound to continue. All indications are that South Africa, where the rate of AIDS prevalence among the sexually active population is already estimated to be around 25 per cent, is following the same route with some years' delay. This will have particularly serious implications for the functioning of the health and education systems.

Zimbabwe's history should undoubtedly serve as a warning to South African policy makers. One should avoid, however, exaggerating the importance of the commonalities brought to the fore above, or substituting reasoning for the dogma of the inevitability of African decline, which seems to confirm this country's development like so many others since independence. Nevertheless, one should not forget what differentiates these countries from one another. In the first place, Zimbabwe attained independence in an extremely unfavourable regional environment, characterised by the frontline states' struggle against the country of apartheid. Unlike what one is witnessing in South Africa, there was a drift towards totalitarianism from very early on. In 1984, or four years after its independence, the prime minister removed the president so that he could hold both functions, while also announcing his willingness to establish a single party regime. In the same year, the massacres perpetrated against the Ndebele minority, which have still not been officially recognised, caused several tens of thousands of deaths in the span of a few months, or as many as the civil war of the 1970s. None of these developments can be perceived in the case of South Africa. Even if black empowerment operations have given rise to some criticism, this policy nevertheless seems relatively balanced. Similarly, the government's overall competence is largely recognised. Finally, the assessment of the first years of the transition as portrayed in this book provides evidence of serious economic restructuring, rather than the beginning of decline.

If one separates the two extreme scenarios discussed above, one may consider the possibility of South Africa following a scenario of moderate growth, accompanied by the maintenance of high inequalities and serious social tensions, without the latter however degenerating into a situation of civil war or a total loss of the state's legitimacy. Such a scenario is close to the development of a country such as Brazil during the 1990s, and close to what seems to await it over the next years.

CONCLUSION

These two countries have several structural characteristics in common.[9] First, their average per capita income is very similar. According to the usual indicators, they are the most unequal countries in the world, with considerable differences in income and standards of living between the whites and the other categories of the population (mostly blacks in the case of South Africa and coloureds in that of Brazil) in each case: it is therefore noteworthy that a third of black South African women and an equivalent proportion of coloured and black Brazilian women are employed as domestic workers. It is without doubt no coincidence that high inequalities and endemic poverty in both countries go hand in hand with very low savings rates, both the lowest among emerging countries. These two countries are also both quite urbanised, as a consequence of which the rural areas of both have been partly emptied from their destitute populations without employment have proliferated in large urban agglomerations. As a result of social inequalities, urban violence is a scourge in both cases. Additional commonalities include import substitution industrialisation economic policies followed until recently (probably with a higher success rate in the Brazilian case, thanks to a substantially more developed domestic market), as well as state interventionism and the traditional predominance of public enterprises within the productive apparatus. Finally, both countries, which are regional powers, are involved in projects promoting integration within their respective subcontinents.

Here again, a number of differences divide these countries, be it in terms of size (the Brazilian economy is five times larger than that of South Africa), ethnic composition (that of the Brazilian population is much more varied), geographical location or history, and economic policies: there is no equivalent in South Africa to the debt crises suffered by Brazil in 1982 and 1998.

Nevertheless, the Brazilian experience probably has some lessons for South Africa. It shows, just as in the two preceding comparisons, the difficulties that most countries encounter in embarking on a development path and the pitfalls they need to avoid. It also confirms the fact that, judged by the Brazilian experience, the absence of radical transformation in South Africa would not necessarily be synonymous with a social explosion, which, after all, does not mean that one has to give up "improving lives".

Finally, and perhaps the main conclusion of this attempt at comparison, extreme scenarios that are generally the only ones taken into account by

---

9   Friedman and De Villiers, 1996.

most authors of this type of exercise, are not necessarily the most credible ones. To reduce the future to two or three scenarios leads to the confining of reality to patterns that are much too clear-cut. The logic according to which South Africa will have either a very prosperous economy or become a disaster-stricken country, but which rules out any middle road, has until now been contradicted by the facts. South Africa's future will in all likelihood continue without economic miracle or disaster, but with the complexity of a country subject to multiple struggles and to the internal contradictions that are the driving force behind its development.

BIBLIOGRAPHY

Adam, H., Slabbert, F., & Moodley, K. 1997. *Comrades in business: Post-liberation politics in South Africa.* Tafelberg: Cape Town.

African Development Bank. 1993. *Economic integration in southern Africa.*

African National Congress. 1955. *Freedom Charter.*

African National Congress. 1994. *Reconstruction and Development Programme: A policy framework.* Umanyo: Johannesburg.

Anglo American Corporation of South Africa Limited. 1996–1999. *Annual Report.*

Anglo American Corporation of South Africa Limited. 1996–1998. *Chairman's Statement.*

Anglo American Corporation of South Africa Limited. 1997. *Submission to the Truth and Reconciliation Commission.*

Bach, D. & Cahen, M. 1993. Afrique australe: un défi polymorphe, l'intégration. In Darbon, D. (ed.) *La République Sud-Africaine; Etat des lieux.* Karthala: Paris.

Bayart, J.F., Ellis, S., & Hibou, B. 1997. *La criminalisation de l'Etat en Afrique.* CERI-Editions Complexe: Paris.

Bell, T. 1997. Trade Policy. In Michie, J. & Padayachee, V. (ed.) *The political economy of South Africa's transition: Policy perspectives in the late 1990s.* The Dryden Press: London.

Bell, T., Farrell, G., & Cassim, R. 1998. *International trade and competitiveness in a mineral rich economy: The case of South Africa.* Trade and Industrial Policy Secretariat, Technical workshop on trade, competitiveness and finance: Johannesburg.

Bethlehem, R.W. 1988. *Economics in a revolutionary society: sanctions and the transformation of South Africa.* AD. Donker: Craighall.

Bertelsmann, T. 1998. *The European union and South Africa: Reaching agreement?.* The South African Institute of International Affairs.

Berthélemy, J.C. & Söderling, L. 1999. *The role of capital accumulation, adjustment and structural change for economic take-off: Empirical evidence from Africa growth episodes.* CEPII working paper No. 99–07, April.

Bhorat, H. 1997. Trends and shares in South African manufactured exports. *Trade and Industry Monitor.* Vol. 3, September.

Bhorat, H., Hodge, J., & Dieden, S. 1998. The impact of structural change and production method changes on employment growth of occupational groups in South Africa. *Trade and Industry Monitor,* Volume 6, July.

Biggs, T., Miller, M., Otto, C., & Tyler, G. 1996. *Africa can compete: Export opportunities and challenges for garments and home products in the European market.* World Bank Discussion Papers.

Black, A. & Kahn, B. 1998. The performance of South Africa's non-traditional exports since 1980. *Trade and Industry Monitor,* Vol. 7, October.

Bocquet, D. 1998. *Quelle efficacité économique pour Lomé? Redonner du sens au partenariat entre l'Union européenne et les pays d'Afrique, des Caraïbes et du Pacifique.* Rapport au ministre de l'Economie, des Finances et de l'Industrie. La Documentation Française: Paris.

Bomsel, O. Paris. 1998. Redéploiement de l'industrie minière sud-africaine; Opportunités pour les entreprises françaises. Centre d'Economie Industrielle, Ecole des Mines, April.

Bosworth, B., Collins, S.M. & Chen, Y. 1995. *Accounting for differences in economic growth.* Paper presented at the seminar organised by the Institute for Development Economics in Tokyo on Structural Adjustment Policies in the 1990's: Experience and Prospects, October.

Business Map. 1999. *Empowerment 1999: a moving experience.* March.

Cassim, R. & Hartzenburg, T. 1999. *Trade related aspects of regional integration in southern Africa.* Mimeo.

CEPII. 1998. Compétitivité des Nations. *Economica.* Paris.

Chipeta, C. 1993. *Regional relations and post-apartheid co-operation.* Southern Africa Development Community.

Clark, N.L. 1994. *Manufacturing apartheid: State corporations in South Africa.* Yale University Press: New Haven and London.

Cling, J.P. 1998. Afrique australe: Intégration régionale et ancrage à l'Union européenne. *Economie Internationale,* la revue du CEPII, No. 74, Second Trimester.

Cling, J.P. 1999. La politique économique sud-africaine face à la mondialisation. *Politique Africaine,* No. 73, March.

European Commission. 1996. *Green Paper on relations between the European Union and ACP countries on the eve of the 21st century.* Brussels.

Bibliography

European Commission. 1997. *Negotiating directives for a new co-operation agreement with the ACP countries.* Communication of the Commission to the European Council and Parliament, DE96, Brussels, December.

European Commission. 1999. *Proposition de Règlement du Conseil relatif à la coopération au développement avec l'Afrique du Sud.* Brussels, March.

Commission of Enquiry on Aparthied in South Africa. 1998. La France et l'apartheid: Documents de la commission d'enquête sur l'apartheid en Afrique du Sud. *Editions l'Harmattan et Droits et Liberté,* Paris, 1978.

European Council. 1998. *Negotiating directives for a development partnership agreement with the ACP countries.* Brussels, June.

Coussy, J. 1995. Cheminements institutionnels et dynamique capitaliste dans l'intégration de l'Afrique australe. Les Etudes du CERI, No. 10, December.

Coussy, J. 1999a. L'Afrique du Sud à l'épreuve de la crise asiatique: la vulnérabilité d'une petite nation confrontée aux aléas de la globalisation, Les Etudes du CERI, No. 54, July.

Coussy, J. 1999b. La réinsertion de l'Afrique du Sud dans l'économie internationale. *Tiers-Monde,* Volume VL, No. 159.

Coussy, J. 1999c. Régionalisation ou atomisation de la Convention? dans GEMDEV (sous la direction de J.J. Gabas), L'Union européenne et les pays ACP, Un espace de coopération à construire. Karthala: Paris.

Darbon, D. (sous la direction de) 1993. *La République Sud-Africaine; Etat des lieux.* Karthala: Paris.

Darbon, D. 1999. Afrique du Sud: la difficile naissance d'un dragon africain. In Institut Français des Relations Internationales (1998), Rapport Ramsès.

Davenport, T.R.H. 1991. *South Africa, a modern history.* MacMillan: London, fourth edition.

Davies, R. 1998. South Africa's Trade Negotiations with the European Union: Implications and lessons for African, Caribbean and Pacific Countries. *Development Perspectives for Africa towards the 21st Century.* Institute of West-Asian and African Studies, Chinese Academy of Social Sciences, Beijing, People's Republic of China, October.

Department of Finance. 1996. *Growth, Employment and Redistribution: A macro-economic strategy.*

Department for International Development (DFID). 1998. *Poverty and inequality in South Africa.*

Department of Public Service and Administration. 1998. *White Paper on Affirmative Action in the Public Service.* Pretoria, April.

Disraeli, B. 1981. *Sybil or the two nations.* Oxford University Press: Oxford.

ECDPM. 1999. *The EC's impact studies on regional economic partnership agreements.* Lomé Negotiating Brief No. 5, Maastricht, February.

Erwin, A. 1998a. Parliamentary speech. Department of Trade and Industry Budget Vote, May.

Erwin, A. 1998b. In Mills, G., Heine, J. *et al. Looking sideways: The specifics of south-south co-operation.* South African Institute of International Affairs, May.

Erwin, A. 1999. No quick fixes for unemployment. *Business Day,* 26 May.

Fallon, P. & Lucas, R. 1998. *South Africa labour markets: Adjustments and inequalities.* Informal Discussion Paper on South Africa, Southern Africa Department, World Bank.

Fallon, P. & Pereira da Silva, A. 1994. *South Africa, economic performance and policies.* Informal discussion papers on aspects of the economy of South Africa, No. 7, World Bank, Southern Africa Department.

Fine, B. & Rustomjee, Z. 1996. *The political economy of South Africa, from minerals-energy complex to industrialisation.* Witwatersrand University Press: Johannesburg.

Fischer, S., Hernandez-Cata, E., & Khan, M.S. 1998. *Africa, is this the turning point?* IMF paper on policy analysis and assessment, International Monetary Fund, May.

Friedman, S. & de Villiers, R. (ed.) 1996. *Comparing Brazil and South Africa; two transitional states in political and economic perspective.* Centre for Policy Studies and Foundation for Global Dialogue, Johannesburg.

Friedman, S. 1997. New attitudes needed for Africa's rebirth. *Business Day,* 23 June.

Fukuyama, F. 1991. L'Afrique du Sud demain. *Commentaire,* No. 55, July.

Gelb, S. (ed.) 1991. *South Africa's economic crisis.* David Philip: Cape Town.

Gervais-Lambony, P. 1997. *L'Afrique du Sud et les Etats Voisins.* Armand Colin: Paris.

Government's report to the Nation. 1998. *The building has begun.*

South African Government. 1994. *White Paper on Reconstruction and Development.* Pretoria, September.

Hawkins, T. 1997. *Economic policy and performance in Africa: what can South Africa learn?* AIPI/Francolin Publishers: Cape Town.

Bibliography

Hofmeyr, J. 1996. The South African labour market. In Maasdorp, G. (ed.) *Can South and Southern Africa become globally competitive economies?* MacMillan: London.

Houghton, D.H. 1964. *The South African economy.* Oxford University Press: London.

Imani Development. 1998. *Study on the impact of introducing reciprocity into the trade relations between the European Union and the SADC Region.* Report prepared for the European Commission, September.

Industrial Development Corporation. 1997. *The impact on the South African economy of accelerated trade liberalisation in the context of currency depreciation.* May.

Innes, D. 1984. *Anglo American and the rise of modern South Africa.* Heinemann Educational Books: London.

Institute of Development Studies (University of Sussex) *et al.* 1997. *Economic assessment of the proposed free trade area between the European union and South Africa.* March.

Institute of Development Studies and Botswana Institute for Development Policy Analysis. 1998. Study to assess the economic impact of the proposed EU-SA Free Trade Agreement on Botswana, Lesotho, Namibia and Swaziland. Sussex, UK and Gaborone, Botswana, December.

Jachia, L. & Teljeur, E. 1998. Free trade with Europe – the winners and losers: The results of the SMART simulation. TIPS Working paper No. 11, July.

James, W.G. 1992. Our precious metal, African labour in South Africa's gold industry, 1970–1990. David Philip: Cape Town; James Currey: London and Indiana University, Bloomington.

Jeffery, A. 1998. *The Employment Equity Bill of 1997: A briefing to business.* South African Institute of Race Relations, February.

Kanfer, S. 1993. *The last empire: De Beers, diamonds, and the world.* The Noonday Press, Farrar Strauss Giroux: New York.

Kornegay, F.A. & Landsberg, C. 1998. *Mayivuke iAfrika! Can South Africa lead an African renaissance?* Centre for Policy Studies, International Relations Series, Vol. 11, No. 1, January.

Krugman, P. 1995. *Dutch tulips and emerging markets.* Foreign Affairs, July/August.

Lipton, M. 1985. *Capitalism and apartheid.* Gower: Aldershot.

Lundahl, M. & Moritz, L. 1994. The Quest for Equity in South Africa-Redistribution and Growth. In Odén, B., Ohlson, T., Davidson, A., Strand, P., Lundahl, M., & Moritz, L., *The South African Tripod.* The Scandinavian Institute of African Studies: Uppsala.

Maasdorp, G. (ed.) 1996. *Can South and southern Africa become globally competitive economies?* MacMillan: London.

Macroeconomic Research Group. 1993. *Making democracy work: a framework for macroeconomic policy in South Africa.* Centre for Development Studies, South Africa.

Maïer, K. 1998. *Into the house of the ancestors: Inside the new Africa.* John Wiley & Sachs: New York.

Mandela, N. 1994. *Long walk to Freedom: the autobiography of Nelson Mandela.* Little, Brown and Company: London.

Mandela, N. 1999. *Parliamentary Opening Speech.*

Marais, H. 1998. *South Africa, limits to change: The political economy of transformation.* UCT Press: Rondebosch and Zed Books: London.

Marcus, T. 1989. *Modernising super-exploitation, restructuring South African agriculture.* Zed Books Ltd.: London.

Mbeki, T. 1998. *Africa, the time has come.* Tafelberg: Cape Town; Mafube: Johannesburg.

Michie, J. & Padayachee, V. (ed.) 1997. *The political economy of South Africa's transition: Policy perspectives in the late 1990s.* The Dryden Press: London.

Mills, G. 1998. South Africa, the United States and Africa. *South African Journal of International Affairs.* Volume 6, No. 1, Summer.

Natrass, N. 1998. *Growth, employment and economic policy in South Africa: A critical review.* The Centre for Development and Enterprise, September.

O'Meara, D. 1996. *Forty lost years: The apartheid state and the politics of the National Party.* Ohio University Press: Athens; Ravan Press: Randburg.

United Nations, General Assembly, Security Council. 1998. *Causes of conflict and the promotion of sustainable peace and development.* Report of the UN Secretary General, April.

Pallister, D., Stewart, S, & Lepper, I.. 1987. *South Africa Inc., the Oppenheimer Empire.* Media House Publications & Lowry Publishers: Sandton.

European Parliament, Development Co-operation Commission. 1998. Rapport sur la communication de la Commission sur les orientations en vue de la négociation de nouveaux accords de coopération avec les pays d'Afrique, des Caraïbes et du Pacifique (ACP), Rapporteur: Michel Rocard, March.

Parsons, N. 1982. *A new history of southern Africa.* The College Press: Harare.

Peron, J. 1999. *Die the beloved country.* Amagi Books: Johannesburg; Lilburne Press: London.

Bibliography

Pérouse de Montclos, M.A. 1997. Les nouveaux enjeux de l'immigration en Afrique du Sud. *Afrique Contemporaine,* No. 184, October–December.

Petersson, L. 1998. *Post apartheid southern Africa: Economic challenge and policies for the future.* Routledge Studies in Development Economics: London and New York.

Pillay, P. 1996. The South African economy: issues and options. In: Friedman, S. & de Villiers, R. (eds). *Comparing Brazil and South Africa: two transitional states in political and economic perspective.* Centre for Policy Studies and Foundation for Global Dialogue: Johannesburg.

Reader, J. 1997. *Africa: a biography of the continent.* Hamish Hamilton: London.

Rodrik, D. 1999. *The new global economy and developing countries: Making openness work.* Overseas Development Council: Washington.

Le Roux, P. 1992. The social democratic imperative. In: Howe, G. & Le Roux, P. (ed.) *Transforming the economy; policy options for South Africa,* Universities of Natal and Western Cape: Durban.

Ruffin, J.C. 1991. L'Empire et les Nouveaux Barbares, Rupture Nord-Sud Collection Pluriel, Jean-Claude Lattès, Paris.

Saunders, C. 1988. *The making of the South African past: Major historians on race and class.* David Philip: Cape Town.

Schreiner, O. 1987. *The story of an African farm.* Century Hutchinson: London. First edition in 1883.

Sidiripoulos, E. 1997. Maths and science remain at the bottom of our national priorities list. *Fast Facts.* South Africa Institute of Race Relations, December.

Simon, D. (ed.) 1998. South Africa in southern Africa: Reconfiguring the region. J. Currey: Oxford; Ohio University Press: Athens; David Philip; Cape Town.

Sisulu, M., Mkosi, M., Setai, B., & Thomas, R.H. 1994. Reconstruction and democratising the Southern African Customs Union. National Institute of Economy Policy. Report of a workshop held in Botswana, March.

South Africa Foundation. 1996. *Growth for all.* Johannesburg.

South Africa Foundation. 1997. *Perspectives of business leaders.* Autumn.

Sparks, A. 1996. *Tomorrow is another country.* Heinemann: London.

SRI International. 1998. *Benchmarking South Africa for labour-intensive development.* January.

Stahl, M. 1997. *Hard-core tariffs on intra-SADC trade and their elimination in the context of the implementation of the SADC trade protocol.* Trade and Industry Policy Secretariat, December.

Stoneman, C. 1998. Lesson unlearned: South Africa's one-way relationship with Zimbabwe. In Simon, D. (ed.) *South Africa in southern Africa: Reconfiguring the region.* J. Currey: Oxford; Ohio University Press: Athens; David Philip: Cape Town.

Thomas, R.H. 1997a. A South African view of the SADC trade and development protocol. In: Schwersensky, S. *The Maseru Protocol on Trade.* Friedrich Ebert Stiftung: Johannesburg.

Thomas, R.H. 1997b. *The WTO and trade co-operation between the ACP and the EU: Assessing the options.* ECDPM Working Paper No. 16, Maastricht, March.

Tsikata, Y. 1998. *Liberalization and trade performance in South Africa.* World Bank, mimeo.

United Nations Conference for Trade and Development. 1998. *Trade in the Southern African Development Community: What is the potential for increasing exports to the Republic of South Africa?* International Trade Centre, May.

Vale, P. & Maseko, S. 1998. South Africa and the African Renaissance. *International Affairs,* 74–2.

Venter, G. 1998. *When Mandela goes.* Doubleday: Johannesburg.

Wheartcroft, G. 1993. The Randlords, the men who made South Africa. Weidenfeld: London.

Wilson, F. & Ramphela, R. 1991. *Uprooting poverty: The South African challenge.* David Philip: Cape Town & Johannesburg: James Currey: London.

Winters, L.A. 1996. *Regionalism versus multilateralism.* Discussion Paper Series, No. 1525, London, Centre for Economic Policy Research.

World Bank. 1994a. *South African agriculture: Structure, performance and options for the future.* Discussion Paper No. 6, World Bank, Southern Africa Department, Washington DC.

World Bank. 1994b. *Reducing poverty in South Africa: Options for equitable and sustainable growth.*

World Economic Forum. 1998. *The Africa Competitiveness Report.* Geneva.

Yeats, A., Amjadi, A., Reincke, U. & Ng F. 1997. *Did domestic policies marginalize Africa in international trade?* World Bank, Directions in Development, Washington.

STATISTICAL SOURCES

Anglo American Corporation of South Africa Limited. 1999. *Prospectus.*

Central Statistical Service. 1997. *Earning and spending in South Africa.* Selected findings of the 1995 income and expenditure survey.

Central Statistical Service. 1998. *Employment and unemployment in South Africa; October Household Survey 1994–1997.* Statistical Release P0317.10, August.

Commissioner for South African Revenue Service. 1990–1998. *Monthly Abstract of Trade Statistics.*

Financial Times. 1999. Global 500: World's top companies. 28 January.

South African Reserve Bank. 1999. *South Africa's national accounts 1946–1998.* Supplement to the June Quarterly Bulletin.

South African Reserve Bank. 1994. Labour, price and other selected economic indicators of South Africa 1923–1993. Supplement to the September Quarterly Bulletin.

South African Reserve Bank. 1999. *Quarterly Bulletin.* June.

South Africa. 1997. *Yearbook 1998.* Government Communication and Information System: Pretoria.

South African Institute of Race Relations. 1998. *South Africa Survey 1997/1998.* Johannesburg.

Statistics South Africa. 1998. *The people of South Africa; Population Census, 1996.*

UNAIDS. 1999. *Aids epidemic update.* December.

United Nations Conference on Trade and Development. 1999. *World Investment Report 1999: Foreign direct investment and the challenge of development.* United Nations: New York and Geneva.

World Bank. 1999. *World Development Indicators.*

INDEX

ABC shoe shop 24
ABSA 54, 145
ACP countries 161–163, 173–179
Affirmative action 56, 68–72, 76, 83, 184
Africa 28–30, 35, 48, 56, 62, 81, 103, 105, 107–108, 110–111, 114, 118–140, 152, 174–175, 185–186
African Development Bank 153
African Explosives and Chemical Industries (AECI) 24, 27
African Global Mining 74–75
African investments 72–73
African Life 73
African Mining Group 73
African National Congress (ANC) 11, 36, 65, 73, 75, 78–82, 84, 86, 104, 123, 134
African Renaissance 14, 122–123, 130, 132, 134–136
Afrikaner 54, 73, 86, 130
Agricultural products 25, 51, 106, 109, 125, 156, 161, 164–165, 167, 169
Agriculture, agricultural 25, 27–28, 34, 46, 48, 50–51, 59, 66, 68, 91, 105, 108, 136, 147, 151–152, 157, 166
AIDS 128, 186
Albania 57
Alexandria 133
Aluminium 25, 38, 114, 145, 158
Amalgamated Banks of South Africa, *see* ABSA
America 29, 31–32, 34, 50, 58, 107–108, 115, 169–170, 179
Amin, Samir 34
Andean Pact 163
Anglo American 14, 16, 17, 23, 27–32, 53, 73, 75, 78, 80, 82, 119, 144–145
Anglo Base Metals 33
Anglo-Boer War 35, 136
Anglo Coal 33
Anglo Forest Products 33
Anglo Ferrous Metals 33
Anglo Industrial Minerals 33

Anglo Industries 33
Anglo Platinum 32–33
AngloGold 32–33
Anglovaal 53
Angola 48, 125, 128, 140, 148, 152–153, 157–159
Apartheid 11–14, 16, 25, 28–30, 35, 38–39, 45, 47–48, 54, 56, 58, 62, 68–69, 71, 79, 81, 87, 93, 103–105, 124, 130, 133–134, 136–138, 141, 143, 147, 149, 156, 180, 186
Apprenticeship Act (1922) 58
Argentina 31, 137, 152
Argyle mine 22
Asia 19, 29, 35, 40, 45, 76, 91, 93, 107–108, 110, 112–115, 118, 127–128, 132, 155, 170, 175, 183
Atlantic Ocean 159
Australia 22, 23, 27, 29, 34, 119
Austria 31
Automobile 25, 105–106, 108–109, 111, 113, 115–116, 135, 151, 165, 167, 169
Aventura 88
Avmin 27

Balance of payments 32, 41, 49
Bantu Education Act (1953) 58
Bantu Homelands Citizenship Act (1970) 58
Bantustan, *see* homeland
Barclays Bank 26
Barnato, Barney 74
Basic Conditions of Employment Act 97
Basutoland 136
Bechuanaland 136
Beira 158–159
Belgium 31, 137
Benin 178
Bermuda Islands 30
Bevcon 25, 27
Bibault, Hendrik 130
Billiton 114, 119, 145
Black business 72–76, 180

Index

Black empowerment 56, 72–76, 183, 185–186
BLNS countries 143, 149–150, 156, 171–172
Blue Ribbon bakery chain 24
BMW 115
Boart Longyear 25
Boers 35, 136
Bolivia 57
Boschendal 23
Botha, PW 49
Botswana 20, 29, 123, 128, 136, 141, 143–144, 146–147, 149–150, 156, 159, 173–174
Bouygues 158
Brazil 19, 29, 31, 51, 107, 110, 114, 152, 186–187
Bretton Woods 84, 127, 134, 185
Britain, *see* Great Britain
British American Tobacco (BAT) 119
British Petroleum (BP) 139
British South Africa (Chartered) Company 136
Brussels 164
Budget deficit 49, 82, 85–89, 93, 180
Budget policy
Built Operate Transfer (BOT) 158
Burkina Faso 178
Burundi 139

Cahora Bassa 145
Cairo 140
California 34
Cameroon 139
Canada 18, 22, 27, 29–30, 34
Cape 34, 58, 63, 136, 140
Capital goods 39–40, 109, 111, 142, 144, 167
Capital productivity 45–46
Capitalisation 17, 26, 30, 33, 53, 72
Cargill, Jenny 133
Carmel pickles 24
Carthage 133
Central Selling Organisation (CSO) 16, 19–22
Centre d'Etudes Prospectives et d'Informations Internationales (CEPII) 109–110

CFA franc zone 127
Chamber of Mines 18
Charter Consolidated 30
Chase Manhattan Bank 49, 52
Chemicals, chemical 38, 45, 106, 108, 111, 113, 142, 144, 165, 167–168
Chile 29, 31
China 112, 114, 118, 156–157, 183
Chrome 52–53, 75
Ciskei 64
CMI 75
Coal 27, 29, 31, 33, 38, 50, 75, 106, 109, 166
Cobalt 30
Coca Cola 116
Collahuasi mine 31
Colombia 31, 182
Columbus plant 25, 114
Commission for Conciliation, Mediation & Arbitration (CCMA) 97
Common Agricultural Policy 164
Common Market of Eastern and Southern Africa (COMESA) 150, 154
Common Monetary Area (CMA) 157
Commonwealth 50
Communist Party, *see* South African Communist Party
Comparative advantage 103, 112
Comparative disadvantage 111
Competition 98
Competition Act 98
Competitiveness 98
Compound 62
Congress of South African Trade Unions (COSATU) 11
Conglomerates 27, 53, 73, 80, 104, 144
Constitution 11, 13, 58, 85, 87, 97, 130, 136, 146
Consumer goods 37, 104, 112–113, 115, 154
Co-operation 134, 136, 141–142, 147–148, 157, 160, 165–166, 172, 179, 181
Copper 29–31, 140, 144–145
Core business 27, 29

199

Corobrick 25
Corridors 158–159
Cotonou Convention 162, 173–174, 177, 179
Criminality 182
Crony capitalism 76
Current account balance 87
Current account deficit 88
Customs duties 37, 85, 104–105, 113, 115, 127, 143, 149, 151, 154, 156, 165, 167, 172
Customs union 108, 138, 143–144, 149–150, 152, 154–157, 171–172, 174, 177, 178

Dar-es-Salaam 33, 140
Davies, Rob 161
De Beers (Consolidated Mines) 18–22, 24–25, 29, 32–33
Debswana diamond company 20
Debt 37, 43, 49–50, 74, 87, 92, 94, 128, 131, 187
Deflation 88
Delta conglomerate 144
Democratic Republic of Congo (DRC) (formerly Zaire) 22, 30, 125, 139, 145–146, 148, 158–159
Denmark 56
Denny mushrooms & asparagus 24
Department for International Development (DFID) 63, 57
Developing countries 12, 14, 43, 48, 63, 102, 118, 123, 128, 131–132, 134, 163, 169, 170–171, 174
Development Bank of Southern Africa 115, 155
Diamond Trading Company (DTC) 22–23
Diamonds 16, 18, 19–22, 25, 27, 29, 34, 74, 144
Direct Investments 118, 138, 142, 144, 155, 178, 183
Discussion Document on Economic Policy 80
Disraeli, Benjamin 55
Diversification 17, 18, 23–25, 103, 106–107, 128, 129, 148, 155
Durban 158

Dutch Disease phenomenon 42

Eagle insurance, *see* SA Eagle
East Rand 17
Eastern Cape 64, 68
Eastern Europe 31, 81, 161
Economic policy 35, 48, 51–52, 78–84, 92, 98, 103, 134, 162, 170, 180, 182
Edgars 23
Education 39–40, 45, 48, 55–56, 66–69, 76, 87, 136, 186
Egypt 133
El Salvador 117
Ellis, Stephen 182
Embargo 38, 50, 107, 143
Emerging markets 92–93, 116
Employment 13, 37, 39, 45, 48, 51, 56, 60–63, 69, 70, 72, 83–84, 86, 91, 95, 97–98, 104, 113, 131–132, 147, 171, 181, 187
Employment Equity Act (1998) 70–71, 97
Empresas Sudamericanas Consolidadas 31
Energy 25, 37–38, 46, 88, 109, 114–115, 139, 145, 148, 157, 165, 180
Engelhard 27, 31
Engen 139
England 55
Erwin, Alec 95, 141
Eskom 38, 140
Europe 28–29, 31, 34, 81, 107–108, 111, 118, 120, 123, 130, 161, 165–166
European Commission 27, 166, 171, 173, 175
European Development Fund 163
European Investment Bank 163
European Parliament Development Commission 176
European Programme for Reconstruction and Development (EPRD) 163, 166
European Union (EU) 14, 31, 107, 118, 121, 160–167, 169–170, 173–175
Exchange rate 49, 85, 91, 102, 105, 108, 127, 157
Export rate 108

Export-oriented growth 53, 102
External constraint 40, 88, 94
External trade 107, 158

Fanta 23
Farm Fare eggs & chickens 24
Ferro-alloys 25, 29
Ferrochrome 52–53
Ferrous metals 33
Fez 133
Finance, financier 33, 40, 48–49, 54, 66, 72–73, 76, 83, 93–94, 119, 134, 148, 166
First National Bank (FNB) 26, 54
First Rand 26–27, 33
Flexibility 85, 95–96, 98, 146
Food processing 72, 120, 144
Ford 23
Foreign direct investment (FDI) 120
Foreign investment 27, 29–30, 80, 103–104, 116–117, 119, 131, 138
Forest Products 25, 27, 33
France 31, 50, 137
Free State 18, 36, 136
Free trade agreement (FTA) 151–152, 161–162, 165, 169, 173, 175, 177
Free trade area 39, 142, 150–152, 154–157, 162, 164–165, 167, 171–172
Free trade zone *see* free trade agreement
Freedom Charter 65, 80
Friedman, Steven 135
Frontline states 147, 186
Fukuyama, Francis 81–82
Furniture 24, 106, 108–110, 113–114, 167–168

Gabon 140
Gaborone 147
Gauteng 63–64, 146, 158
Gencor 119
General Agreement on Tariffs and Trade (GATT) 37, 104–105, 114, 116, 174
General Export Incentive Scheme (GEIS) 105, 109
General Mining 73
General Motors 24

General system of Preferences (GSP) 162–163, 167, 175
Germany 31, 56, 81, 137
Gold Rush 34
Gold, gold-bearing 16–19, 23, 25–26, 29–34, 36–39–41, 46–47, 51, 53, 59, 74–75, 91–92, 106, 110–111, 145–146, 166, 168
Gordimer, Nadine 181
Government of National Unity 13, 84
Great Britain 27, 29, 31, 34–35, 50, 120, 137, 184–185
Greece 12
Gross Domestic Product (GDP) 35–40, 42, 44, 48–53, 56, 63, 69, 84, 86–88, 90, 92–94, 96, 98, 108, 123, 125–126, 129–132, 135, 141, 146, 150, 158, 172, 183
"Growth for All" 96
Growth model 12, 35, 40, 102–103, 127
Growth, Employment and Redistribution Programme (GEAR) 79, 84–88, 93–98, 134
Guinea Bissau 178

Haggie 25
Hawkers 61
Health 27, 48, 65–67, 87, 139–140, 186
High Road scenario 82
Highveld Steel & Vanadium Corporation 25
Highly Indebted Poor Countries (HIPC) 128
Hillside aluminium plant 114
HIV 128
Homelands 13, 47–48, 56, 58, 62–64, 86, 130
Hosken Consolidated Investments 73
Human Sciences Research Council (HSRC) 69
Hungary 31
Hush Puppy shoes 24

IBM 116
Illovo 139, 145
Imperial Chemical Industries (ICI) 24

201

Import rate 108
Import substitution 12, 35–40, 52, 83, 102, 108
India 19, 114
Indian Ocean 114
Indonesia 110, 112
Industrial Development Corporation (IDC) 37, 48, 74, 114–115, 155
Industrial policy 95, 113
Industrial products, *see* manufactured products
Inflation 84–85, 88–89, 92–93, 96, 157
Inga Dam 146
Interest rate 49, 74, 86, 92–94
Intermediary goods 39, 103, 109, 112, 142
International Labour Organisation (ILO) 61
International Monetary Fund (IMF) 84, 91, 96, 124, 129
Investment inward stock 119–120
Investment rate 35, 42–43, 86, 94, 127, 131
Investments abroad 119
Ireland 50
Iron 25, 45, 52, 106, 108–109, 111, 113, 133, 144–145, 158
Italy 31, 56, 114, 182
Ivory Coast 123, 173, 178

Jamaica 173
Japan 20–21, 23, 114–115, 118, 169, 183
Jenny Wren fabrics 24
Johannesburg 17, 23, 31, 63, 140, 145, 158
Johannesburg Consolidated Investment (JCI) 73–75
Johannesburg Consolidated Mines (JCM) 73
Johannesburg Stock Exchange (JSE) 26, 31–33, 53–54, 72–73, 92
Johnnic 73, 75
Johnson Mathey 31

Kagiso Trust Investments 73
Kampala 140

Karoo 51
Katanga 30, 145
Kaunda, Kenneth 29
Kenya 143
Khatse Dam 146
Khula institution 74
Khumalo, Musi 74
Kimberley 18–19, 34
Kinshasa 146
Kombis 61
Konkola Deep 29
Kopano ke Matla 73

Labour 12, 35–38, 40, 43, 45–47, 55–56, 59–60, 64, 68–72, 84–85, 95–98, 102, 112–115, 118, 141, 146, 183
Labour Court 97
Labour productivity 45–47, 98
Labour Relations Act 97
Lancaster House 185
Latin America 82, 119, 127, 132, 152, 169–170, 175, 184
Latin-American scenario 82
Le Roux, Pieter 180
League of Nations 137
Least developed countries (LDC) 129, 134, 141, 163, 175–177
Lebanon 180
Lesotho 136, 143, 146, 148–150, 156–157, 159, 172, 177
Lesotho Highlands Water Project 146, 157
Liberalisation 79, 102, 105, 116, 131, 151, 165, 167, 171, 176, 178
Liberia 125
Liberty Life 53
Limpopo 141
Lisheen Irish zinc & lead mine 31
Lobito 159
Lomé Convention 161–163, 173–174, 176, 179
London 19, 26, 30–32, 119
Lonhro 27, 75, 139, 145
LTA 25
Luxembourg 30

Madagascar 148, 159

Maghreb 130, 171–172
Maïer, Karl 133
Maize 46, 165
Malange 159
Malawi 139, 143, 145–146, 152, 154, 158–159
Malaysia 110, 116, 128, 132, 134, 183–184
Mali 25, 30, 178
Mandela, Nelson 11, 13, 67, 73, 79, 122, 132, 182
Manganese 29, 52–53
Manuel, Trevor 93
Manufactured products 28, 37, 41, 52, 102–103, 105, 108, 111, 115, 118, 129, 142, 155–156, 165, 167–169, 171
Maputo 145, 158–159
Maquiladoras 118, 171
Marais, Hein 118
Market share 108–109, 111, 124, 143, 167, 173–174, 177
Mauritius 123, 129, 143, 148, 154–156, 159, 173–174, 176
Mbeki, Thabo 13, 55, 80, 130, 133, 181
McCarthy 23, 25
McGregor 53
Mediterranean countries 161–162, 169
Mepanda Uncua Dam 146
Mercedes 116
Mercosur 152, 169
Meridien-BIAO bank 139
Metropolitan Life 26, 73
Mexico 107, 110, 118, 169, 171, 182
Mineral and Resources Corporation (Minorco) 30, 32
Minerals 16–17, 46, 52, 109, 125, 142, 144, 167
Mines, mining 14, 16–23, 27–30, 32, 34–38, 46, 51–53, 57, 59, 61, 64, 74, 91–92, 106, 108, 138, 145, 154, 165–167
Mines and Workforce Amendment Act (1956) 58
Mineworkers Investment 73
Minhas Gerais 19, 30–31
Mobutu 125

Momentum Life 26
Mondi 25
Monetary policy 85, 88, 92–93
Monopoly 19–20, 22, 25, 46, 80, 98, 104
Monroe (doctrine) 140
Mont Fleur scenario 82
Morro Velho 31
Motlana, Dr 73
Motor Industry Development Programme (MIDP) 115–116
Mozal project 158–159
Mozambique 124, 143, 145–146, 148, 150, 152–154, 157–158
Mpumalanga 158
MTN 139
Mugabe, Robert 185
Multinationals, multinational corporations 23, 27, 53, 116, 134, 138, 185

Nacala 158–159
Namibe 159
Namibia 29, 48, 128, 133, 137, 143, 149, 151, 157–159
Natal 136
National Company of Belgian Railways (Société Nationale des Chemins de Fer Belges) (SNCB) 145
National Economic Consortium 73
National Party 13, 49, 62, 84, 104, 122, 131, 182
Natives Land Act (1913) 58
Natives Laws Amendment Act 58
Natives (Urban Areas) Act (1923) 58
Navachab 29
Nedcor 54
Net Open Forward Position (NOFP) 92
Netherlands 31, 50
Netcare 140
Network 65–68, 115, 139–140, 146, 159
New African Investments (NAIL) 73, 75
New York 49
New Zealand 34, 88

203

Newmont 18
Nickel 27, 29, 31, 144, 158
Niger 178
Nigeria 125, 128–129, 139, 175
Nkomati Nickel 158
Nkrumah, Kwame 122
Non-ferrous metals 106, 108–109, 111, 113 168
North America 28, 30, 107
North American Free Trade Area (NAFTA) 171
Northern Province 64, 68
Northern Rhodesia (Zambia) 145
Ntsika institution 74
Nyerere, Julius 122

OECD 132
Ogilvie Thompson, Julian 78
OK supermarkets 24
Old Mutual 53, 119, 144
Olé sunflower oil 24
Oligopoly 118
OPEC 38, 41
Oppenheimer, Ernest 17
Oppenheimer, Harry 16, 22, 40
Oppenheimer, Nicky 22, 31, 86
Orange Free State, *see* Free State
Orapa 20

Palladium 52
Pan Africanist Congress (PAC) 36
Paraguay 152
Parent company 24–25, 30, 32
Parliament 48, 67
Pass laws 58, 63
Paton, Alan 182
Per capita income 12, 35, 43, 45, 57, 59, 124, 187
Peru 31
Petrofina 139
Platinum 18, 25, 27, 32–33, 52–53
Poland 31
Polarisation 155, 160
Population census 14, 63, 147
Population Registration Act (1950) 58
Port 164
Post Office 88
Potassium 31

Poverty 57, 62–64, 77, 123–124, 132–133, 141, 146, 166, 176, 187
Pretoria 63, 158–159
Primary products 109, 119
Privatisation 74–75, 85, 87, 116, 138
Prohibition of Mixed Marriages Act (1949) 58
Protea hotels 88
Protectionism, protectionist 53, 104, 125

Rainbow nation 13, 183
Ramaphosa, Cyril 75
Rand Merchant Bank 26
Raw materials 17, 24, 26, 40–41, 46–47, 52, 91, 102, 105, 109, 111–112, 115, 125–126, 128, 141, 145–146, 154–155, 166, 178
Real Africa Holdings (RAH) 73
Recession 50, 86–88, 124, 126–127
Reconciliation 13, 78, 181
Reconstruction and Development Programme (RDP) 56, 65–68, 76, 82–85
Redistribution 56, 66–67, 79–80, 82, 86, 149–150, 185
Regional Economic Partnership Agreements (REPAs) 174–175, 177
Regional Investment Development Programme 48
Rembrandt 53–54, 119
Renamo 124
Report on Poverty and Inequality in South Africa 57
Reserve Bank 85, 92–93, 119
Restructuring 24, 27, 32, 50, 75, 79–80, 83, 86–87, 171–172, 178, 180, 186
Reynders Commission 40
Rhodes, Cecil John 18–19, 74, 136, 140, 142
Rhodesia 137, 125–146
Richards Bay 114
Richemont 119
Rockefeller 16
Rodrik, D. 102
Rothschild 16
"Rubicon speech" 49

Russia 22–23, 31
Rwanda 122, 139–140

SA Eagle 23, 26
Sadiola gold mine 25, 30
Safcol 87–88
Saldanha Steel 25, 114
Samcor 25
Sanctions 26, 49–50, 79, 88, 102, 104–105, 109, 111, 119, 137, 149, 156, 174, 184
Sanlam 53, 73
Sappi 119
Sasol 38, 158
Savings rate 42–43, 86, 93–94, 127, 187
Scaw Metals 25
Scenario 82, 84, 112, 155, 161, 183, 186
Scott's clothing store 24
Scramble for Africa 35, 138
Semi knocked down vehicle (SKD) 37
Semi-manufactured products 105, 109, 112, 114, 167
Semi-transformed products 41, 91
Senegal 178
Services 13, 67–68, 120, 138, 145, 164, 166, 188
Seychelles 27, 54, 56, 64, 143, 148, 159
Shacks 62–63
Sharpeville 23, 38
Shebeens 61
Sherry 164
Sierra Leone 125
Skills Development Act 97
Smuts, Jan Christiaan 136–137
Société Nationale des Chemins de Fer Belges (SNCB) (National Company of Belgian Railways) 145
Solly Kramer's 23
Somalia 125
South African Airports Company 87
South African Airways 87, 116
South African Breweries (SAB) 23, 25, 119, 139, 144–145
South African Communist Party (SACP) 11, 36

South African Institute of Race Relations (SAIRR) 57, 71
South America 28, 31, 107
South Korea 112, 114, 123
South West Africa (Namibia) 137
Southern Africa 14, 119, 128–129, 138, 140–160, 173–174
Southern African Customs Union (SACU) 108, 138, 143–144, 149–152, 154–157, 162, 171–172, 175, 177, 179
Southern African Development and Co-operation Conference (SADCC) 147
Southern African Development Bank 48
Southern African Development Community (SADC) 116, 142, 147–148, 150–151, 153–157, 160, 163–165, 173, 177–178
Southern African Power Pool (SAPP) 146
Southern Bell Company (SBC) 116
Southern Life 26
Southern Rhodesia (Zimbabwe) 137, 145
Soviet Union 81
Soweto 42, 69
Soyinka, Wole 122
Spain 31
Spatial Development Initiatives 157, 159–160
Spazas 61
Specialisation 102–103, 109–113, 124, 152, 155, 162, 166, 178, 184
Spoornet 139, 145
Standard Bank 54, 139
Statistics South Africa (SSA) Institute 61
Steel 24, 38, 45, 52, 106, 108–109, 111–114, 145, 158, 167–168
Structural adjustment programme (SAP) 49, 84, 127
Subsidiary 19, 24–26, 29–30, 73, 119, 144
Sudan 125
Sunset clauses 87
SWAPO 48

Swaziland 57, 136, 139–140, 143, 145–146, 149, 151, 157, 172
Sweden 180
Swissair 87, 116
Switzerland 119

Tanzam line 140, 159
Tanzania 30, 81, 140, 143, 145, 148, 151, 153–154, 158–159
Tazara 159
Telecommunications 38, 66, 68, 72, 109, 113, 120, 139, 148, 168
Telkom 74, 87, 116
Telkom Malaysia 116
Terra Industries 27
Textiles 114, 125, 142, 151, 154, 156, 165, 169
Thailand 51, 57, 114
Thatcher, Margaret 50
Thebe Investment 73
Third World 77
Third World Forum 34
Thompson, Julian Ogilvie 78
Timbuktu 133
Titanium 53
Togo 178
Tongaat-Hulett 144–145
Total factor productivity (TFP) 43–46, 131
Tourism 98, 157, 166
Townships 56, 62
Trade balance 88, 169, 175
Trade deficit 110
Trade policy 37, 103, 115, 150, 162, 175, 179
Trade unions 11, 46, 59, 71, 87, 96, 166
Trans Kalahari Highway 159
Transnet 98
Transition 13–15, 35, 78, 86, 88, 122, 132–133, 147, 149, 161, 169–170, 186
Transkei 64
Transport 45, 65, 106, 108–109, 139–140, 142, 148, 157–158, 164–165, 167
Transport equipment 109–112, 142, 167–168

Transvaal 136
Tungsten 25
Turkey 172
Tutsis 122

Uganda 128, 139–140
Unbundling 27, 81, 116
Unemployment 12, 55, 60–63, 77, 79, 91, 93, 96, 103, 146–147, 180, 183
United Kingdom (UK) 57
United Nations (UN) 38, 56, 129
United Nations Conference on Trade and Development (UNCTAD) 153, 169
United States (US) 21, 24, 29–30, 32, 50, 58, 71–72, 107, 118, 120, 140, 170–171
Uranium 18, 23
Uruguay 152

Vaal Reefs 18
Vaal River 146
Vanadium 25, 52–53
Venda 65
Venezuela 31
Vermiculite 52–53
Verwoerd, Hendrik 68
Victoria Falls 145
Vietnam 117

Wage costs 37, 156
Walvis Bay 159
Washington Consensus 79
Water 64, 66–67, 128, 146, 148, 157
West African Economic Monetary Union (WAEMU) 178
West Coast 25
Western Cape 63–64
Western Deep Levels 18
Western Reefs 18
Windhoek 159
Witbank 158
Witwatersrand 34, 145
World Bank 51, 57, 62, 84, 92, 150
World Economic Forum 117, 127
World Trade Organisation (WTO) 163, 165, 174, 177

Yum Yum peanut butter 24

Zaire, *see* Democratic Republic of
    Congo
Zaire River 146
Zambezi 145
Zambia 29–30, 81, 136, 140, 143–145,
    152–154, 159
Zimbabwe 29, 64, 128–129, 133, 136,
    140, 143–146, 152, 154, 156, 158,
    173–174, 184–186
Zinc 30–31, 144
Zirconium 53

THE FRENCH INSTITUTE OF SOUTH AFRICA (IFAS)

The French Institute of South Africa, established in Johannesburg in 1995, is responsible for maintaining a French cultural presence in South Africa. It is also a body of research in the social and human sciences. It is dependent on the French Ministry of Foreign Affairs and its aim is both to stimulate and support French scientific and academic work on South and southern Africa.

Under the authority of its scientific council, the French Institute of South Africa plays a part in developing and supervising research programmes in partnership with academic institutions or other research bodies in the various disciplines of the social and human sciences. The French Institute also gives its support to researchers doing work on the region by granting research bursaries and subsidies and encourages scientific exchange with its South African partners. It runs a specialised library, assists with the publication of research results and the organisation of symposiums and conferences.

The French Institute publishes a quarterly magazine, the *Newtown Zebra*, which includes a research supplement and a series of occasional papers titled *Les cahiers de l'IFAS*.

INSTITUT FRANÇAIS D'AFRIQUE DU SUD
66, Wolhuter Street
PO Box 542 Newtown, 2113
Johannesburg
Afrique du Sud

Tel: + 27 11 836 05 61
Fax: + 27 11 836 58 60
ifasrech@ifas.org.za
www.ifas.org.za